D1541771

AN ARMY
IN SKIRTS

Frances DeBra Brown

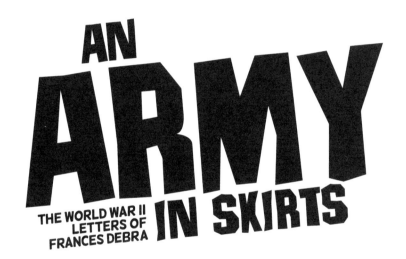

AN ARMY IN SKIRTS

THE WORLD WAR II LETTERS OF FRANCES DEBRA

FRANCES DeBRA BROWN

Indiana Historical Society Press
Indianapolis 2008

© 2008 Indiana Historical Society Press

The illustrations are copyrighted in the name of the author.

Printed in the United States of America

This book is a publication of the
Indiana Historical Society Press
Eugene and Marilyn Glick Indiana History Center
450 West Ohio Street
Indianapolis, Indiana 46202-3269 USA
www.indianahistory.org
Telephone orders 1-800-447-1830
Fax orders 1-317-234-0562
Online orders @ shop.indianahistory.org

The paper in this publication meets the minimum requirements
of American National Standard for Information Sciences—Permanence of Paper for Printed Library Materials,
ANSI Z39. 48–1984

Library of Congress Cataloging-in-Publication Data

Brown, Frances DeBra.
  An army in skirts : the World War II letters of Frances DeBra / Frances DeBra Brown.
    p. cm.
  Includes index.
  ISBN 978-0-87195-264-6 (cloth : alk. paper)
  1. Brown, Frances DeBra—Correspondence. 2. United States. Army.
Women's Army Auxiliary Corps—Biography. 3. World War,
1939-1945—Participation, Female. 4. World War, 1939-1945—Personal
narratives, American. 5. Soldiers—United States—Correspondence. 6.
Women soldiers—United States—Correspondence. I. Title.
  D769.39.B76 2008
  940.54'1273092–dc22
  [B]
                                                    2007050358

A publication from the Eli Lilly Indiana History Book Fund

No part of this publication may be reproduced, stored in or introduced into a retrieval system, or transmitted, in any form or by any means (electronic, photocopying, recording, or otherwise) without the prior written permission of the copyright owner.

To Halton Martin Brown, my husband and the light of my life, and to my parents, Rupert S. DeBra, who was a lifelong influence on my life, and Iva DeBra, who was the underlying force for our family.

To Emma DeBra Walton, my sister, and my brother-in-law, John Walton, who was serving his country on the other side of the world and didn't know his future wife was waiting for him.

To my daughters, Debby Brown Pearson and Suzy Brown Wheeler, for their support throughout the years.

To Betty Weesner and her family, whose lives were intertwined with mine. To so many who have helped me and given me great encouragement, especially Margaret "Peggy" Nightingale and Ann Slack.

To all the women who served in the Women's Army Auxiliary Corps and the Women's Army Corps. We were raised as ladies and we acted as ladies, hence the name of my book *An Army in Skirts*.

TABLE OF CONTENTS

PREFACE

In the summer of 1942, as U.S. Marines struggled to take over an island named Guadalcanal in the Solomon Islands from Japanese forces and German troops battered British forces in North Africa, four hundred white and forty black women gathered at an old cavalry barracks at Fort Des Moines in Iowa. These women had been carefully selected from more than thirty thousand applicants to begin six weeks of basic training as officer candidates for a force that had been ridiculed by some newspaper critics as a "Petticoat Army"—the Women's Auxiliary Army Corps (WAAC), an organization created by legislation signed that May by President Franklin D. Roosevelt after a long and contentious debate in Congress.

Oveta Culp Hobby, former chief of the women's interest section in the public relations bureau at the War Department, had worked hard to ensure the passage of the WAAC bill. For her efforts, Hobby, the editor of a Houston newspaper and the wife of former Texas governor William P. Hobby, had been selected by Secretary of War Henry L. Stimson as the first director of the WAAC. Oveta Hobby believed that women trained for noncombatant military jobs in such areas as clerical and administration, supply, and transport would enable thousands of men to be freed for combat roles to help speed the United States to victory. "WAACs will do the same type of work which women do in civilian life," Hobby said in her numerous speeches. "They will bear the same relation to men of the Army that they bear to the men of the civilian organizations in which they work." Addressing the corps' first officer recruits in Iowa, she warned them that they were making the change from peacetime activities to wartime tasks. "You have taken off silk and put on khaki," said Hobby. "All for essentially the same reason—you have a debt and a date. A debt to democracy, a date with destiny."

Those who had signed up for training had been warned that their work would "be no picnic for glamour girls." With an average age of twenty-five years old, and required to be at least five feet tall and weigh a hundred pounds or more, the volunteers had, more often than not, been successful civilians, with nine out of ten graduating from college and many leaving good jobs as office administrators, teachers, and secretaries to join the WAACs. Some had a personal stake in the war, as they were the siblings of men in the service and widows of soldiers, sailors, and marines killed at Pearl Harbor and Bataan. They tackled their training with enthusiasm, prompting one grizzled sergeant to declare that the women recruits learned "more in a day than my squads of men used to learn in a week."

As the WAAC officer candidates were being trained in Iowa, army recruiting centers across the country were taking applications from women who wished to serve as enlisted personnel. One of the women who answered the call to serve her country was Edna Frances DeBra, who had been born and raised in Danville, Indiana, located just twenty miles west of the capital city of Indianapolis. Frances's father, Rupert, worked at the *Danville Republican* newspaper, where he wrote a column about life in Hendricks County, while her mother, Iva, served as a court reporter for the county.

After graduating from high school, Frances, who desired to pursue an art career, moved to Chicago, where she attended the American Academy of Commercial Art and worked as a commercial artist for an advertising agency. With America's involvement in World War II, she quit her job and worked as a radio tester at a Western Electric plant until she could enlist as a WAAC. She enlisted on April 29, 1943, at Fort Benjamin Harrison in Indianapolis, swearing to "support and defend the Constitution from all enemies, foreign and domestic." Frances received basic training at Fort Oglethorpe, Georgia. On July 3, 1943, Congress approved converting the WAAC into the regular army as the Women's Army Corps—a change that gave women full military status, including insurance and pensions. Given a choice at returning to civilian life or becoming a WAC, Frances reenlisted and served at Marianna Army Air Field in Marianna, Florida.

It was in Florida where Frances received her orders for overseas service in England. She survived an extreme bout of seasickness on her crossing of the Atlantic Ocean on the *Queen Mary* and made it safely to London. While in England, she lived and worked through attacks by such advanced German weapons as the V-1 and V-2 missiles and slept in the London subway system at night. During her time in England, Frances frequently saw Admiral Harold R. Stark, the commander of U.S. naval forces in Europe.

Most of the women who served as WACs held a limited range of job assignments: 35 percent worked as stenographers and typists, 26 percent were clerks, and 22 percent were in communications work. Only 8 percent were assigned jobs considered unusual for women: mechanics, draftsmen, interpreters, and weather observers. Frances became a three-stripe sergeant and worked as a draftsman, lettering detailed information on planning maps for the projected landing and advancements and the location of troops ten and twenty days after the initial D-Day landings on June 6, 1944—information classified as top secret. Transferred to Paris, France, two weeks after it was liberated, she worked in G-3, the headquarters for special troops in the European theater of operations.

At the Paris headquarters she saw General James Gavin of the Eighty-second Airborne Division and General Benjamin Davis, America's first African American general. During her off-duty time, Frances attended classes at the École des Beaux-Arts, sketched the war-weary Parisians, and one day, while strolling along the banks of the Seine River, met famous author Gertrude Stein. It was also in Paris where she met and fell in love with a young combat veteran from the Mississippi Delta, Halton Brown, who proposed marriage to her several times, once on an observation deck of the Eiffel Tower. Frances returned to the United States in November 1945 and received her honorable discharge from the WACs at Fort Dix, New Jersey, on November 11. She made it back home to Danville on November 16.

Frances, one of the approximately 150,000 American women to serve in the army during World War II, married Brown and the couple made their home in Cleveland, Mississippi, raising two daughters. In Cleveland she did commissioned spot drawings for stationery and letterheads. In 1960 her family moved to Lexington, Mississippi, where Frances gave private art lessons and began miniature painting. In 1966 she and her family moved to Yazoo City, Mississippi. There she continued to teach, paint miniatures and egg tempera miniatures, and began a career in art conservation. Her miniature art was accepted in London by the Royal Society of Miniature Painters, Sculptors, and Gravers for its art show at The Mall Galleries, The Mall, London, England. Frances's miniatures have also been accepted by the Washington, D.C., New Jersey, and Florida Miniature Art Societies Exhibits. Her art has won prizes and awards for portraits and still lifes approximately the size of a half-dollar. She is a member of the American Institute for Conservation and the International Institute for Conservation. Frances has cleaned and repaired hundreds of paintings and has done conservation work for the Mississippi State Capitol, the Hall of Governors, and the Old Capitol of Mississippi Museum.

1

ACTIVE SERVICE AND BASIC TRAINING

For the past year I had been working as a radio tester at Western Electric, a defense plant in Chicago, which made radios for naval planes. I was scheduled to move over to the radar project soon, and at this time radar was a scientific marvel—very high tech. But I felt that I did not want to miss the tremendous experience of the war, which would affect so many people.

I took the train (the James Whitcomb Riley—a diesel coach train also a very advanced mode of transportation at that time) from Chicago home to Danville, Indiana, and went into Indianapolis to enlist. The officer in charge of requirement was a mathematician, a first indication of the diversity in experience of the women who made up the Women's Auxiliary Army Corps (WAAC).

We had intelligence (IQ) tests and physicals at Fort Benjamin Harrison, which was inside the city limits of Indianapolis. This was April 29, 1943, that I enlisted in the WAAC. We were sworn in, and I still remember promising to "support and defend the Constitution from all enemies, foreign and domestic."

I returned to Chicago to wait the call to active duty. The order to report to Fort Oglethorpe, Georgia, on May 24, 1943 (my father's birthday), soon came. Leaving my job at Western Electric, which took two days to fill out all the forms and complete all of the procedures, I packed my belongings and went home to Danville, for a couple of days before reporting for duty.

✖   ✖   ✖

Iva and Rupert DeBra. Rupert wrote a weekly column for the Danville Republican, *and Iva was a court reporter for the same paper through her eighties.*

Fort Oglethorpe, Georgia
May 31, 1943

Dear Dad and Mother,

I know you have been wondering about me but the Army keeps you very busy, and I think they informed you that I arrived safely. We received our mailing address Friday noon, so I waited until I could give it to you. Now I'll try to give you some idea of the things that happened.

While waiting in Indianapolis for the Cincinnati train, I recognized a girl in the station who was sworn in with me. Since we were wearing large buttons that proclaimed we were WAAC ENROLLEES, we were hard to miss. I had company on the train. We arrived in Chattanooga at 4:15 PM as per schedule and joggled to camp in the back of an Army truck. Was my suitcase heavy! I regretted that I had it, yet I've used practically everything in it.

You should have seen me rinsing my hair the other evening with lemon. There was no place to do it except in the shower. So I cut the lemon in two and squeezed it on my scalp and tried to rub it in. It seemed to work alright—at least I look about the same. The Sayman's soap lathers beautifully in hard water. I'll let you know when I need more.

To get back to Monday, we were taken to a part of the Post called the Reception Center—given a brief physical Tuesday morning and spent some time drilling. The "about faces," and "right flanks" are complicated but I like it. We march everywhere.

Tuesday afternoon—we were fitted for our uniforms, shoes and etc. My shoes fit pretty well, just a little stiff. But the uniform, all three skirts had to be taken up and one shirt needed the sleeves shortened. So here I am, on Sunday still waiting for my Army clothing. The girls that were fitted have been wearing their uniforms for several days. I am giving thanks for bringing several dresses, because some came with only one and wearing one dress for a week in Georgia is really bad.

✖　　✖　　✖

I marched in ranks wearing a blue-and-white flowered dress and cotton lisle stockings with service oxfords, quite a contrast.

We wore the heavy cotton stockings all thru basic training, then we were able to wear rayon hose. Not since my childhood had I worn cotton stockings. To get them washed and dried took two nights and a day. They were washed and hung up to dry the first night, the next morning they were rolled in a towel and placed in my closed footlocker. The second night

I hung them out again, and happily by the second morning they were dry enough to wear or put away. Georgia in the summer was <u>very</u> hot and humid, <u>no</u> air-conditioning and very few fans.

✖   ✖   ✖

Wednesday morning we went to the Classification Center, and took more tests, mechanical and etc, then we were interviewed for our past work history. I don't suppose we will hear anymore about that until we finish Basic Training. Finally Friday noon we received our orders to move to the South Post and into our own Company. The Reception Center is a separate part of the Post. The barracks here in Company 14 are very nice.

✖   ✖   ✖

The barracks, two stories, contained our bunk beds, upper and lower, in a large open room. There was one enclosed room with a door for the cadre member in charge. There was a footlocker at the end of the bed and hanging space with a shelf on the wall to the rear.

We went outside to a separate building for washing, showers, and toilet facilities known in the army as the latrine.

The showers, which I never did care for, were usually ice-cold water. The army could never keep enough hot water for the WAAC. So I was glad at the time in one way that the weather was hot because an icy shower is a shock to the nervous system.

The latrine also had a laundry room where we could hang clothes at night (not during the day), iron our shirts, and press our skirts.

The cadre instructed us in the proper way to make a bed. The blanket had to be tight enough to bounce a coin dropped on it. That entailed getting under the bed and pulling the blanket through the springs until everything was tight. The upper sheet was turned down over the blanket exactly six inches measured with a GI toothbrush. It was an art!

We came to know what GI meant. Shoes, blankets, garbage cans, food—we were "Government Issue."

✖   ✖   ✖

Saturday morning is the time for Formal Inspection. They were a little less strict yesterday since we had just moved in, but still everything had to be just so. Shoes laced and under the bed in a precise fashion, bed with no wrinkles and clothes hung and buttoned in a certain way. It is a good thing I brought clothes hangers, because most of the girls arrived without any and they are having trouble. I loaned three of mine so I have to double up, but it is not bad. Even our footlockers have a special place for everything. Saturday morning they are open but the rest of the week they remain closed.

Also the barracks are swept and mopped and your bunk and all surrounding surface dusted. The inspecting officer wore white gloves and she usually found a few places to dirty them. Believe me it is a job to get everything spotless and tucked away just right. I'm trying to do the best I can, but the time is short.

For instance, tomorrow we roll out at 6 AM, fall in for Reveille at 6:30 (takes about 15 minutes), go to breakfast at 6:45 and march to class at 7:45. In that time you dress, wash, make your bed, sweep the barracks, dust and leave everything ready for inspection that morning. It takes hustle.

Yesterday afternoon we had a smallpox vaccination and tetanus shot in the left arm, typhoid shot in the right. Everything was fine until about three hours later, and then the arm with the typhoid shot began to swell. So now I have one arm that feels like lead. Everyone else is in the same shape and I expect it will be fine by tomorrow.

I know I like the Army, sometimes it does shake me to realize how little I can call my soul my own, but it is something that must be finished, so I'll make a good job of it.

Now "Mess Call" will be soon and this afternoon I have to mark my clothes. I know what "Fall Out" and "On the Double" means and soon I'll be in such a state that when I hear a loud noise I'll "snap to attention."

Also, I'll be so neat, quick and polite when the Army finishes that no one will be able to live with me.

Lots of love,
Frances

✖ ✖ ✖

EQUIPMENT IN BASIC TRAINING

The summer uniforms were suntans. We were issued a jacket with plastic buttons and three skirts. Our insignia was the Pallas Athena that we wore on our collar. A special eagle, which was sometimes called the "Buzzard," was on the plastic buttons of our suntan jackets, the overcoat, the ODs (olive drabs), and the metal insignia of our hats. This was the famed "Hobby Hat" (named for Colonel Oveta Culp Hobby, director of the WAACs) that was very fragile and needed to be treated with great care. It could not take the squashed look of the rakish flight cap of the air corps.

I had three rayon slips, khaki colored of course, two pairs of lace-up service oxfords, and a utility coat that had a removable lining and a button-on hood. This coat was the backbone of our wardrobe except in overcoat weather. We were also issued a dark green raincoat with an attached hood made of some mysterious substance and along the same style as the one the men wore. They certainly shed rain but left you feeling like something the cat drug in.

We had three cotton shirts and a washable tie, also khaki colored. The tie was a complication for me. I had no idea at all how to tie it. For two or three days one of my friends fixed the knot in mine, then after a good deal of coached practice I finally managed to tie my own necktie.

The issued shirts were styled with a convertible collar without the standing collar band that the men's had. The shirts never did fit neatly around the neck with a necktie, which we almost always wore. The sleeve length could be anything, so early on I started shortening the sleeves by hand. Perma Press was a much later process, so the cotton shirts were washed by hand with a bar of soap, starched, dried, sprinkled, and ironed. The spun rayon shirts, which I finally got from home, could be lightly pressed and look presentable.

There were two pairs of blue-striped seersucker pajamas, a green-striped seersucker fatigue dress, a washable sweater, and a cotton fatigue hat. The last three items were used for KP or Kitchen Police. At that time only the girls in the motor pool were issued coveralls. We had white towels, olive-drab blankets, and a barracks bag with a drawstring.

Our handbag was a pebble-grained leather envelope, styled by KORET, and in the general shape of a half circle. It had an adjustable shoulder strap. We would have preferred to wear it on one shoulder, but regulations demanded that we wear it across the body. They were made of seal skin, goat skin, or water buffalo, none of these leathers were crucial to the war effort. Mine was surely water buffalo. We also had two pairs of beautiful brown kidskin dress gloves.

✖ ✖ ✖

Frances in uniform wearing the "Hobby Hat" and kidskin gloves and carrying the pebble-grained purse.

Fort Oglethorpe, Georgia
June 7, 1943

Dear Dad and Mother,

It seems that Sunday will be my day to write letters. At least our time is our own today and we need it. We have mail call on Sunday, so I got both of your letters today.

The first of the week was pretty tough because you have no idea what is expected of you. But by now we are beginning to know about where and when we are suppose to be. That helps a lot. A letter came from Peggy. This is her address.

M. Allison SK 3C USNR
A&R Office Personnel
USNAS Corpus Christi, Texas

✖   ✖   ✖

Peggy Allison from Louisville, Kentucky, and I had shared an apartment in Chicago. She joined the WAVES in the summer of 1942, about the same time I left the commercial art studio and went to work for Western Electric.

She was engaged to William Nightingale from Vincennes, Indiana, and he was in the army at Fort Knox, Kentucky. He was in the First Armored Division and was wounded in the North African Campaign.

✖   ✖   ✖

It certainly is hot here and I do mean hot. By the time we finish marching to "Mess" and to the classrooms, finish drilling and parading, we probably walk at least eight miles a day, maybe more, and all of this in the hot sun. I'm very lucky because my shoes have been fine. A little stiff but that is all. They gave me a 7A. But some of the poor kids are in an awful fix. They have blisters on the top of their toes, on the heels and goodness knows where else.

Yesterday we had our second typhoid shot, and WAACs keeled over to the left and to the right all evening. Every now and then they would come across someone stretched out cold. My arms are a little sore but that is all. We really are kept on the move all the time, from one minute to the next. They say this is the toughest training center and I can well believe it. Maybe they're trying to weed out anyone who isn't strong. At least I am fine and my morale has picked up considerable. There are a lot of things about the Army that I can't say that I like and I hope they move me out of Georgia, but taken all in all, I'm glad I am in and I've certainly learned a good many new things.

For instance, I ironed my first shirt today! I can't say I did very well but after 5 or 6 weeks in a couple of months I should be a whiz. I also washed my towels yesterday. GI towels are lovely, big thick white things, very fine for taking a shower, but gosh awful to wash.

I soaked mine for half an hour in bleach and they are still drying. I hope they dry by tonight because when we have inspection tomorrow there aren't many places to hide wet laundry.

So far I've only received one "gig." That is the term used for a demerit. A "gig" sheet is posted after every inspection. Last Monday after one of our breaks on KP, I lay down on my bed and forgot to straighten it and they ran two inspections on us that day.

I mailed my watch to you yesterday. It is mailed in a Sucret box in which I kept my bobbie pins so try and send it back. It is insured so I hope it arrives all right. Please have Mr. Pearson fix it and let me know how much it costs. I think it is the main spring but at least send it back as soon as you can.

They are sending my suitcase home on the 18th. I hope it arrives in fairly decent condition. It is certainly being ruined here. That is about all. The food is okay but I know what Peg means about the pleasure of eating from a plate instead of a tin tray.

I certainly have a lovely family.

Love,
Big Sis

Fort Oglethorpe, Georgia
Sunday June 1943

Dear Family,

Here I am again, almost a wreck, but not quite. Things have been happening. To begin with last Tuesday while we were having physical training, the First Sergeant called me along with four others out into the road and started drilling us before everyone including the officers. Then we returned to the barracks without anyone giving a reason for it. About 15 minutes later, the Corporal came in and told Helen Coon and me that we were wanted in the Orderly Room. I went in to see Lieutenant Holm first.

She said she had been told to pick out two girls from the company for Cadre members. They are non-commissioned officers that stay with the training companies and help train the other new girls. We have three sergeants and a corporal in our company.

She said she wanted to recommend me for Cadre work, that it was the fastest way to OCS School if I wanted to consider Officers Training.

We talked about it and I explained my ideas about radio work. She said that even with radio training, they send very few trained technicians to Officers School. I know that but I told her I thought I would stay with the radio. So there it stands, the other girl accepted. Out of 75 girls I was one chosen to go into that type of work so it was a compliment (but very small understand) and Auxiliary in this Army is pretty low.

The middle of the week we received our "dog-tags," identification tags to you. There are two of them and they hang jiggling around our necks. That really made me feel as though I were in the Army.

I am beginning to believe, they're simply trying to see how much we can take. Friday afternoon we were taken on a tour of the Post, which meant a steady march from 1 p.m. to 3:15. By the time we returned my fingers were so swollen from hanging down that I couldn't

remove my ring and usually it slips off easily.

Since the Generals were visiting Saturday the lawn had to be taken care of. That meant the country side had to be swept with a broom and then the lawn was clipped by hand.

After supper we cleaned our barracks, you should see me on my knees scrubbing the floor with a scrub brush. I have housemaid knees already.

Yesterday morning, I was sent with five other girls to take a radio test. This was a mechanics test, so I had very little trouble with it. The others had no experience, so of course they couldn't answer the questions. At eleven

Emma DeBra, Frances's sister.
Emma filled her sister's requests for
suitcases, shirts, and other items.

o'clock we were standing around with our shoes shining and everything in apple pie order, when in came the Corporal to take six of us to KP at the Officers Mess. The girls they had there were swamped. So I had KP until after 8 o'clock yesterday evening.

KP is really something! I started out scrubbing garbage cans and ended up washing dishes and mopping floors. I keep telling myself that I am being improved in some way when I scrub a garbage can. But they are half as tall as I am—they come up to my waist. So the only way to get to the bottom is to hang upside down inside them. They should have tested us for the strength of our stomachs before we joined the WAAC. However I am a swell garbage can scrubber and after I had cleaned several of the smelly things, we were lined up for the officers to pass by us as they went out through the kitchen. I hope they didn't get too much of a whiff, for I felt that I had an aroma that extended at least three feet.

It is alright as long as I can laugh about it. And I really am glad I joined the Army because otherwise the War would still have been something in the newspapers.

I hear that we will have our gas drill next week, which should be interesting. We're going to Lookout Mountain at 11 o'clock today. It will be our first time out of confinement.

Lots of love,
Big Sis

Fort Oglethorpe, Georgia
June 1943

Dear Emma,

I was surprised but pleased to get your letter. I'll try to keep you informed on the WAAC activities. For instance I had KP Saturday at the Officers Mess. The Generals and Colonel [Oveta Culp] Hobby went out through the kitchen inspecting the WAAC Mess Hall. I had silver stars within a foot of me.

The Generals finally left and things returned to normal. Sunday we went on a picnic up on Lookout Mountain. The incline railway up the mountain is supposed to be the steepest in the world and I believe it. We saw all the monuments on the top of the mountain. In fact, the whole country side is dotted with cannon and statues—the Battle of Chattanooga was very important.

Sunday was our first day off the Post. Chattanooga doesn't offer much in the way of amusement, so we came back and had supper at the Service Club and saw the movie with Judy Garland.

Yesterday morning I had another code test. I hope they squeeze me into radio school. It seems my mechanical scores are quite high and my code aptitude is quite low, so it hangs in the balance. We had our third typhoid shot yesterday afternoon. (By the way, I am finishing this letter on Tuesday because "Lights Out" caught me.)

Oh yes, please send my small suitcase to me. I think by Parcel Post. If I am sent out of here after my Basic, I'll need something to carry my iron and shirts in. Thanks loads.

Love,
Big Sis

Fort Oglethorpe, Georgia
June 21, 1943

Dear Family,

The watch arrived Friday night and seems to work fine. Now I almost forgot to put it on but it is a comfort to have. I hope the suitcase is under way. I'm getting excited because Company 13, the one next door (we use the same mess hall) finished their basic training yesterday, so all yesterday afternoon and today—their orders have been coming in and the girls leave one by one.

When the orders are received, you may be told to pack and move in a couple of hours. So that is the reason I need the suitcase. Next week will be a long week because I am wondering where I'll go and what I'll do. I just hope they move me out of Georgia.

Yesterday afternoon, a couple of friends and I walked over to the North Post to have some shoe heels repaired. I know I'll have to wear these a long long time so I'm trying to take good care of them.

I think about your strawberry jam. As soon as I hit your territory I'll want some with biscuits, but goodness knows when that will be. I understand we get two and half days furlough a month. They allow you to accumulate 10 days before you can go on leave, so I'll see you sometime.

A card came from Aunt Minnie today along with your letter. I washed clothes last night and went to Church on the Post this morning and then ironed shirts. I should be mighty good at it soon. The biggest trouble is the starch. It never comes out the same way twice, so my shirts are always a surprise.

I think we are having supper at the Service Club tonight and then we'll go to the Post movie. Quite a spree.

This is Father's Day so lots and lots of love.

Big Sis

Fort Oglethorpe, Georgia
June 23, 1943

Dear Mother and Dad,

This stationary was a present from Meggs. Nice, isn't it? At least it fits in my notebook, so I can write in between classes.

We had our trip to the gas chamber yesterday. It was only tear gas. The first time we went in and out with out masks on, then the second time we went in with our gas masks on, removed them and walked out. It burns your skin and causes your eyes to smart, but I do know how to wear a gas mask. If we go overseas we will be issued them.

The suitcase came Monday evening. Thanks a lot, now I feel better. Since I have it, they will probably keep me indefinitely. Still I might be on my way sometime during the weekend or next week and the suspense will be over. If I shouldn't get radio school, I wouldn't be surprised if I were put in Cadre work. Well, time will tell. The next three days should pass quickly.

Army food is beginning to pall on me, the way restaurant food did. If I go to a new Post it will change I hope. It is not bad just monotonous.

Thanks for sending the suitcase.

Love,
Frances

Fort Oglethorpe, Georgia
Late June 1943

Dear Dad and Mother,

Mother's letter came in the noon mail. You will be agreeably surprised at all of the letters I have been writing. The money I am enclosing should take care of the watch, stationary and incidental postage. Thanks for taking care of it for me.

Saturday, we were all ready and waiting for formal inspection, the whistle blew and we all fell out for parade. We marched over to the Parade Ground at 9 a.m. and got back to our mess hall at 2:15 p.m. All that time we marched, paraded and saluted for the movie cameras, in the hot sun. Today we were photographed in the open air theater and the temperature must have been 110 degrees. I am grateful that the nights are nice and cool.

Saturday was our official Graduation Day but so far we haven't had our orders. It is a little unusual, ordinarily they come in the day Basic Training is finished but our First Sergeant says we'll all be gone by Saturday.

Last Saturday I went into town with a couple of friends and had dinner. It was a nice piece of trout but I do miss vegetables. I attended Church on the Post and the rest of Sunday I spent getting my clothes in order.

Our company picture was taken. It is a pretty good one; you can at least see my head. I'll send it home as soon as I can find some packing for it.

That is about all. Be sure and save some strawberry jam for me. I'll probably get a furlough in about 4 months.

> Lots of love,
> Big Sis

Fort Oglethorpe, Georgia
June 28, 1943

Dear Mother and Dad,

The package came this noon, now I can return the hangers I borrowed, thanks ever so much.

Yesterday I was the Barracks Police—that means I guard the barracks all day from the time I wake the KPs until I make bed check (be sure everyone is in bed at the proper time). Barbara Bayless and I went into town to have dinner. Another girl took my place on BP until I returned. We went to the Hotel and had a steak dinner and apple pie. It was good and such a treat to eat from a plate.

We were paid yesterday. It came as a surprise. I was getting ready to cash in one of my traveler's checks, but I was rescued. For some strange reason we were paid only $25, although next Monday I will have been here five weeks. Sometimes it doesn't seem that long and then again it seems forever.

Tonight we scrub, because formal inspection will be tomorrow. I usually hear Kate Smith on the radio as I'm crawling around over the floor. Probably tomorrow some of the girls will receive their orders and the company will begin breaking up.

We paraded this morning and had a great many movies taken. Colonel [Hobart B.] Brown, the Commandant of the Post, gave us a talk. It concerned the rumors that have been spread about the WAAC. Most of them have been traced to Axis Propaganda but they certainly are hampering enlistments. But we'll show them.

Love,
Frances

WAAC basic training graduation class, Fort Oglethorpe, Georgia, 1943. Frances is in the fourth row, third from the left.

2

FORT MEADE, SOUTH DAKOTA

[Moved from Fort Oglethorpe, Georgia, to Fort Meade, South Dakota
July 9, 1943]

Dear Dad and Mother,

I am on the move so I had better keep you posted. The writing is legible because the train is sitting in the station at Terre Haute but just wait until we start up, then it will be a scrawl.

They moved me out quickly! We waited and waited, and then I was put on KP and about 9 a.m. yesterday morning the girls who came over to Staging with me received their orders to be ready to leave for Texas at 8:30 a.m. this morning. (The train just started so from now on my writing may be hard to read.)

I was ready to wave goodbye to them but at 2:30 p.m. I was told to pack my barracks bag and have it in the Orderly Room in <u>10 minutes</u>.

We were told, we would be leaving for Fort Meade, South Dakota at 8:30 that evening. So that is where I am going. You could have knocked me over with a feather. That possibility hadn't entered my mind. I hear it is in the Black Hills and a very nice place, so I'm sure I will like it.

I won't be able to mail this letter until I arrive so it is alright for me to tell you about this.

We left the Post in a group, rode in Army trucks to the Station in Chattanooga and boarded the train. The accommodations are excellent. We have an entire car to ourselves and it is made into Pullman compartments. The compartments were a new experience for me and the others. I'm sharing one with two other WAACs, one girl is from Texas and the other from New York. We got along fine, but there are three from my old company that I shall miss. As soon as we boarded the train we went to bed.

Frances (far right) and companions at Mount Rushmore State Park, 1943. Frances's first assignment following basic training was at Fort Meade, South Dakota.

This morning we came through Evansville, Vincennes and this evening we should be in Chicago. [As a Hoosier I did know this part of the country.]

I am hoping we will have a few hours in Chicago and I can see Pete and Park [Edna Peterson and Helen Parker, two girlfriends from Chicago]. Tonight we start west for the Dakotas. I am eager to see the Bad Lands; we go through them on our way. We should arrive some time Thursday night.

Did you ever imagine I'd be stationed in South Dakota? I certainly didn't.

Thursday

This is in the afternoon and I think the train is trying to make up time, so the writing maybe uneven.

We're in South Dakota now, right in the middle of the Prairie. Talk about flat country! You can count the trees on the fingers of one hand.

Last night we did stop in Chicago, but instead of arriving at the schedule time of 2:30 p.m. we came in at 6 p.m. and needed to change trains. So bag and baggage were hustled out of our car and we ran for our new train. There was no time for a phone call even though it did feel peculiar being back in Chicago for a few minutes. I can write to Pete and Park and tell them I passed through.

The train went northwest and entered Wisconsin before dark. I am sorry I couldn't see more of it in the daylight.

We spent the night in the sleeper and woke up in the middle of Iowa. Since we had to leave the Dining Car at the state line we stopped at a little town named Mitchell for lunch. They held the train while we ate! The Army does see that you are fed. We were the first WAACs to stop there and the people did stare.

We just crossed the Missouri River and the country is getting hilly. I like the landscape. We're supposed to stop for supper along the route and arrive at Rapid City about 4:30 p.m. We will take a bus to Fort Meade.

Friday

We've arrived and it is wonderful. I know this is a very disjointed letter but I am trying to get everything in. We crossed the Bad Lands just before dark yesterday evening and arrived at Rapid City about midnight. We were hustled into Army trucks and on out to the Fort. We simply fell into bed because we were so tired.

Revile was at 6:30 and Mess directly after. Our barracks are too nice for words. They are made of new lumber, and the floors are even being sanded and waxed for us. We have two barracks, a mess hall of our own, a Day room, an Orderly and Supply Room. They are painted white and surrounded with grass. There is a lovely view of the hills.

And the Laundry Room even had a sleeve board—the ultimate in luxury. They have thought of almost everything to make us comfortable. Our captain said they've waited three months for us and the first WAAC arrived about three weeks ago.

I am to have an interview with the captain in a few minutes. Gosh, this was quite a letter.

Love,
Big Sis

Aux France DeBra
A-514210
WAAC Detachment
Fort Mead, South Dakota

✳   ✳   ✳

FORT MEADE

Fort Meade at the edge of the Black Hills was an old cavalry post. The brick buildings—headquarters, hospital and quarters—were located around the parade ground and were probably from the last quarter of the 1800s. The elevation was a mile high and the air was wonderful. It was the first time I had been at that altitude.

The Eleventh Cavalry had been stationed there before the war and there were a number of horses still on the post. Two of the men in the Signal Corps with whom I worked had been with the Eleventh. They were married and lived off the post. They taught me to shine my shoes properly.

At night, the bugler blew taps. It was the only place in the army where I heard it. The Eighty-Eighth Glider Troops were stationed there but I saw very little of them. We were in the Seventh Service Command and wore a blue and white patch.

✖   ✖   ✖

[FROM PEGGY ALLISON]
US NAVAL STATION

Corpus Christi, Texas
July 13, 1943

Dear Fran,

Was glad to get your letter and know where you would be from now on and it does seem that they couldn't have put us further apart. Anyway I may see you sooner than you think because when you take your next leave I may be near enough to see you. I didn't take your advice and so Bill [Nightingale] came down to fetch me as it were and we were married a week ago today in San Antonio with Sonny [her brother an air force cadet] as best man and really Fran I didn't know anybody could be as happy as we are. Bill got a 28 day leave and so we really have made the most of it. . . . He has till the 23rd here with me and then he goes back to the hospital until they decide whether he will be sent to Fort Knox as an instructor or get a medical discharge. . . . We hope they keep him on as he is well enough to do light duty the rest of his life . . . but he'll not be able to go into combat ever again. Mom didn't like the idea at first but she is OK now that she sees it was the best for me. . . . Really, Fran, I feel like there is something worth while all of a sudden. I worry about the man a bit yet, but

Peggy Allison in her WAVE uniform.
Peggy worked with Frances in Chicago.
Peggy resigned from the WAVEs after she
married Bill Nightingale. She and Frances
were lifelong friends.

the change since he got here is really something . . . he was pale and worn out the first day . . . but now we have Texas sun on him and rest and it is doing him a world of good. He has to go to West Virginia again and then I'll put in for my leave. When we see where he is transferred, I'll see what I can do about being transferred, too. I didn't have time to let anyone know but the family. San Antonio was fun and Sonny is tickled to death with his job.

What kind of work will you do if you don't get the radio stuff? I warned you about that if you remember . . . said you should get it in writing but then I guess they know what is best.

Sonny and Bill had a grand time Tuesday afternoon while I was dressing . . . they went swimming and Bill nearly drowned himself. First time he had been swimming since he left the Country . . . so I was almost a widow before I was a bride . . . only thing he would never have gotten back from North Africa if it was suppose to be that way. . . . You should see the scar he has on that left side . . . looks like they decided to build a shelf on his side and whittled him out for it . . . but it is going to get patched up with plastic surgery and then he'll be as right as a new dime. . . . So this is all for now and I hope the news isn't too much of a shock. . . . I am still M. Allison to the Navy till my change in name comes through, so address it either way. Lots of luck at your new place, when you get all squared away write and tell me all about it. . . . I hear it is lovely country too.

Bye,
Peggy

[IN THE HOSPITAL]

Fort Meade, South Dakota
July 20, 1943

Dear Dad and Mother,

I debated telling you about this but I'm in the hospital. I knew my luck was too good to last. It is a strep throat infection. Following Mother's example I decided it was a sore throat and tried to "let it wear off" Tuesday, Wednesday and Thursday but Thursday evening it got the better of me.

My fever was 101.8 degrees so they started feeding me sulfur pills. I am so full of them that I rattle and there is nothing left for me to do but get well. I felt pretty rocky yesterday but woke this morning feeling much better. I'll be in rest in bed for a few days yet.

The girls have been fine to me. They bring me ice cream in the evenings. Besides Mae [Singer] and Sandy [Ruth Sanderson], there is a little girl named Jane [Baranowski] who works here in the hospital. She runs up to see me ever so often. She is a registered Pharmacist. [Jane had just arrived on the Post. She was barely 5 feet tall, one of the few WAACs I could look down on.]

The hospital is an old brick building, part of the original Post. It has tall, tall ceilings and windows. There was one other WAAC in the ward when I came in but she was released this morning. So I have the place to myself.

I write a letter or read awhile and then sleep. That is the complete history. So, if I hear any worrying out of either of you, I'll never mention such a subject again.

We were asked last week, if we wanted to enlist in the WAC AUS (Women's Army Corp—Army United States) or if we wanted a discharge. I said yes, of course. Actually we can change our mind right up to the time we take the oath. Several of the WAACs are asking for a discharge. There are a good many things about the Army that I do not like, but when I start something I always try to finish it. And it hasn't been much different from the

Janie Baranowski. Frances met Janie at Fort Meade. The two WACs corresponded throughout the war, and Janie often sent vitamins to Frances.

way I expected. I have met some marvelous people. Women, I am proud to call my friends. The biggest drawback is the way we are shifted around. You lose touch.

Did I tell you about Peg? She and Bill were married about two weeks ago, I think. He had a 28 day furlough, and doesn't know whether he'll be discharged or kept on as an instructor. She seems happy.

I'll finish and let the "sulfa" fight the bugs awhile. I'm a regular battle field. I can't imagine a lovelier place to be laid up in, I can look out the window and see the hills and the sky.

Bushels of love,
Big Sis

[OUT OF THE HOSPITAL]

Fort Meade, South Dakota
July 1943 (Tuesday)

Dear Mother and Dad,

I know you are anxious, so here is a note to set your minds at ease. I was released from the hospital yesterday afternoon. The Doctor examined me and said I was all right. Aside from a slight dizziness, I feel fine, so I am going back to work this afternoon. However I imagine the place ran very well without me.

Your talk of fried chicken is breaking my heart. Now that I am well, the three of us are going into town and try to rustle some up. So far we have done very well with homemade pie, although the WAAC cooks are really good.

Peg's birthday is the second of August but shopping out here is very different from Chicago and I have a wedding present to consider. It is a good thing I am supposed to be paid at the end of the week.

Lots of love,
Frances

[REENLISTMENT]

Fort Meade, South Dakota
August 9, 1943

Dear Dad and Mother,

I am really in the Army now. We took the oath last Thursday evening [August 5, 1943]. So now I am a Private in the Army. Some ratings were given out last week. Sandy and Jane made PFC. After seeing how some of the people in the Army get their stripes, I'd just as soon have a bare sleeve for the duration. [Sandy and Jane deserved theirs.]

Friday and Saturday we marched in the Parade at Deadwood. It was quite a celebration. Friday we came back to the Post in the afternoon, but yesterday after drilling we stayed and saw the Rodeo. After eating Mess we did the town. Incidentally our cooks worked on field kitchens both days and we ate from mess kits. You simply can't beat those WAC cooks.

Saturday night we made the rounds, rode the Merry-go-round, Ferris Wheel, Octopus and Tilt-a-whirl. I think of them all, we loved the Merry-go-round the best, also Popsicles and ice cream cones. We came back to the Fort about 12 o'clock and left the town to everyone else. They were probably going strong this morning.

We received our Class A Passes yesterday. This gives us permission to be absent from the Post until 12 p.m. when we are off duty. I think Mae will be leaving tomorrow. We want to go to Rapid City and see her off.

We are going into Sturgis tonight and have supper. The way we eat I don't believe Mrs. Wheeler thinks we are fed at all.

✖　　✖　　✖

Sturgis, South Dakota, a very small town, was about one and a half miles from the post. There was a very pleasant walkway between the two places, and we went into town often. We always needed small items and found a small café that was owned by Mrs. Wheeler. She did the cooking and it was so very good. Our mess was all right but it still was army food and this was just like home. I think she enjoyed feeding us and we certainly appreciated it.

✖　　✖　　✖

Signal Office, Fort Meade. Left to right: Lieutenant Hudson, Frances, Sergeant Cook, Sergeant Blender, Pat Rinker, Bud Lassom, and Corporals Harview and Belche.

I went over to the Hospital with Jane this morning. She works a few hours on Sunday to fill prescriptions that may come in. She really knows her business and I ask questions continually.

My code is coming along very well. The men here at the Signal Corp tell me that after I pick up speed and get some experience I can get Lieutenant Hudson (my boss) to transfer me to an Air Base as an operator. So I won't mind spending a few months here.

The $43.00 check from Western Electric and the War Bond is one I bought last month with my allotment. Put it away with the others. I'm writing to Chicago for a pair of sun glasses ground to my prescription. [The high altitude caused a powerful glare and they were really needed.]

Lots of love,
Frances

Fort Meade, South Dakota
August 29, 1943

Dear Dad and Mother,

The birthday is over and a very nice one it was. Pete and Park sent me a dog-tag chain, sterling silver and very handsome. Peg sent rouge and lipstick so I shouldn't run out of cosmetics.

It is quite a bit cooler here now. The nights are cold and the mornings chilly—then when the sun comes up it is warmer and quite comfortable. Jane and I took our ODs to the tailor Wednesday morning for alterations. The Post Rule to wear ODs will probably come through between the first and the thirteenth of September. Some of the girls wear theirs now in the evenings because they feel that they look better.

✖ ✖ ✖

At every station the details of the proper uniform were posted—there were no exceptions. When we were traveling, in camp, and at various workstations, the details of our uniforms were spelled out explicitly.

At first there was some indecision about WACs and head covering. It was decided that we were to follow the normal rules of society instead of the usual practice of the army men. Therefore, we kept our hats on in circumstances such as church, movies, restaurants and any social gatherings. At work, we followed the male practice of an uncovered head.

✖ ✖ ✖

We had one section of the Post here called the 620 Engineers. They are men in the Army who are held "in suspicion." They are not considered dangerous and are allowed into town and etc. but an eye is kept on them. They have a tailor shop and that is where we took our clothes. There are some unusual men here, a Chef from the Waldorf Astoria, a concert pianist, artists, college professors and many others. So the tailor shop is probably good also. The grounds around the barracks are beautifully kept. The section is simply a little distance from the rest of the Post.

Tonight is house cleaning time in our barracks. The Saturday inspection is at 7:15 a.m. and there isn't much time in the morning. We scrub and dust like mad. Tuesday Lieutenant Hudson came in and said he would offer my name for photography school if I wished. It is a three months course in photograph, developing and etc. I would go to Long Beach, New York. That is pretty attractive because no experience is required just an artistic background. I considered it for a couple of minutes and then turned it down. I don't think I'll throw away the radio just yet. Because if I keep plugging away I'll eventually be a radio operator and be transferred that way. So here I sit, turning down offers right and left.

I am finishing this letter on Saturday morning. We've just had our morning inspection and everything was fine. No gigs. But did we work. My morning detail is to clean the showers. I was standing in one scrubbing away before breakfast, my elbow struck the faucet and WOW! Half of my head soaking wet, I was mad! But everything straightened out eventually.

Tonight we plan to go into the "big" town of Sturgis and shop, important stuff like toothpaste and starch. We'll probably wind up at Mrs. Wheelers for a piece of pie and ice cream. She is nice. We talk to her while she dries the dishes—almost like home.

I got a letter from Meggs and I do try to keep writing to her. She says she can be a WAC second hand.

> Lots and lots of love,
> Frances

[MADE PFC]

Fort Meade, South Dakota
September 2, 1943

Dear Dad and Mother,

I hope you had a happy Anniversary. Everything is about the same here except the weather changes, one day it is very cold and the next day very hot. We're getting a little taste of winter, the nights are really cold and two blankets are fine.

We were paid Tuesday as usual. I was overpaid last month and after the war bond was taken out it left me with $6.25. The officer laughed as he handed it to me. So don't be surprised if I give you a hurry up call for a postal money order.

Yesterday, on the first of the month the new ratings came out. Jane and Sandy got their T5 (Technical Fifth Grade). I was given a PFC (Private First Class).

Did I remember to tell you I ordered a pair of sunglasses from Chicago? They're ground to my prescription and were $13.50. That is the reason I'm a little short this month. They are necessary here because the land is flat and in the morning and evening you walk directly into the sun. They tell me the glare on the snow is even worse.

Lt. Hudson, at the Signal Corp, will be taking 15 days leave next week. He is very nice to work for. He is a good ball player also. Last night the officers played the enlisted men from the Hospital. It was quite a game. Jane loves baseball and knew all of the players. I was there, not knowing much about it but asking lots of questions.

I have asked for a 15 day furlough beginning December 1st but I am not counting on it at all. Only 15% are allowed away at a time and it seems that most everyone wants a furlough. We will just have to wait and see.

I would like to go to Chicago and try the next FCC examination. I should be ready by then.

Love,
Big Sis

PFC Frances DeBra
A-514210
WAC Det
Ft Meade, South Dakota

Fort Meade, South Dakota
September 6, 1943

Dear Mother and Dad,

This is a short letter but a very important one, for the first time I am broke. So you had better send me a postal money order. The $6.25 I was paid seemed to melt away.

The sunglasses I ordered came yesterday. One of the screws is a little loose but we intend to go into Rapid City Saturday and I can have it fixed. Sandy needs her glasses fixed and Jane needs a pair of shoes.

Last night Janie and I got the last of our ODs (Olive Drab Winter Uniform) and that took the rest of my $6.25 but I am fixed for the winter. Helen Miller leaves on her furlough tonight. She comes from Mississippi and she has been a-twitter for days.

Could you look at my watercolor brushes and send me a #2, #3, and #5 if I have them. The black or blue handled ones pointed and made by Windsor & Newton. I think I'll make a Christmas Card or two in my spare time. I can get some paper in Rapid City but I'd like to have my own brushes.

I heard from Peg. She said Bill was in a hospital just outside Chicago. Her leave was cancelled so now she is trying for a discharge.

Lots of love,
Big Sis

[TRANSFER TO FLORIDA]

Fort Meade, South Dakota
October 4, 1943

Dear Mother and Dad,

This is another bit of news. I hope you haven't sent my robe or earmuffs yet because I won't need them for awhile.

It is unofficial but I've heard from Lt. Hudson that I am to be transferred out of Fort Meade. The rest of the information comes from the girls in Personnel and Finance. They say I leave here Saturday and am to go to Florida. Glory be, if there is one place in the world, except Georgia where I wouldn't care to go—that is it! But you have no choice in the Army. Until I've been notified by the Company Commander, I can't tell you any more. If I do come through Indianapolis I'll try and let you know, so keep your fingers crossed. The rumor is that I'm being sent to school there, but sounds a little funny to me. All I can tell you is that I hate to leave Janie.

We have been issued brass buttons now that we are in the Army. Lots of brass!

Love,
Frances

✖ ✖ ✖

I left Fort Meade on October 16. My travel orders sent me through Saint Louis and I waited for the train to Indianapolis in the huge Union Station. A good part of the time for anyone in the service was spent in train stations. They gave me a few days leave to stop and see my family in Danville, Indiana. Then back to the train. As I remember, I went through Nashville, Tennessee, and Mobile, Alabama, then across to the Florida panhandle and Marianna on October 24, 1943.

✖ ✖ ✖

3

MARIANNA ARMY AIR FIELD, FLORIDA

[MARIANNA ARMY AIR FIELD]

Marianna Army Air Base, Florida
October 24, 1943

Dear Dad and Mother,

I am writing this before I go to work at 8:30 a.m. I'm back in the "white collar" class. The train in Indianapolis which was scheduled to leave at 11:59, left at 11:25. Fortunately I arrived at the Station early, wandered on the train and two minutes after I was seated the train started. It was my lucky day. I had several hours in St. Louis, and then boarded the train for Nashville at 9:20 a.m. Saw a movie and had lunch in Nashville and left there at 3:55 p.m. It was a steamliner and I made the right connections.

I arrived in Marianna and waited at the station until they picked me up. This Air Base is nothing at all like the Post I left. The buildings are all temporary and spread over a large area but I am gradually getting my bearings. My barracks bag was there waiting so I unpacked this afternoon. The other WACs have all been fine to me. In fact they have gone out of their way to be nice, but it is very confusing to come into an entirely new Company. Slowly I am remembering part of their names.

We "fall out" at 5:45 in the morning and then go to breakfast. Last night we stood formal retreat in our "sun-tans" but the rest of the time I've worn my ODs and been comfortable. I think we will be in them officially by the middle of next month. Since it is damp here, the cold is very penetrating and I maybe glad of my overcoat after all.

I had a letter from Phil [a fellow commercial artist]. He said Peg [Allison Nightingale] was in Chicago last Wednesday. I could gnash my teeth because if they had routed me through there I would have been able to see her.

At least half of this Company has been to radio school, part of them are operators and part of them repair. Some are being used in radio work and others have another type of job. [A good number of the WACs operated the LINK TRAINERS that taught the Air Cadets how to fly on instruments.]

They told me yesterday in Classification that there were no job openings in radio at the moment so would I help on "The Beam," the Post Weekly. They need someone to help with the layout and the makeup of the paper. I said I'd be glad to. So I am starting to work this morning. They use a Multi-Lith press and can print plain colors and reproduce photos. I think I'll enjoy it.

One of the WACs invited me to the Post Movie last night, we saw "Sweet Rosie O'Grady." We also went in the PX for ink and soap. They had no starch so I'll have to go into town.

> More later, love
> Frances

Marianna Army Air Field
October 28, 1943

Dear Dad and Mother,

A little of the indigo blue is wearing off and all of the girls aren't entirely strangers but it still is a little lonesome. I went to the Post Library the other evening and now I have a book for my spare moments.

The WEATHER—Sunday it was quite warm and Monday the ODs were comfortable but since then we've been freezing. The barracks are like paper and the wind whips in and out sometimes we have heat and sometimes not. There is a rumor going around that we'll have to fire our own furnace for the barracks and I am sure we can do a better job than the man who is trying to do it now. I am looking toward my overcoat with longing eyes and it is only a matter of time before I'll be wearing it.

Yesterday, we had gas mask drill. We went into a chamber filled with tear gas then into one of chlorine. After that we were sent back into the chlorine gas without our masks and told to put them on while we were still in the gas! You have no idea how long you can hold your breath until it is necessary. Everything went off without a hitch and I didn't get a whiff of gas. Today we wear the masks over our shoulders from 8 to 12 and wear them over our faces from 8:00 to 8:45. That will be an amusing sight.

I changed my shoulder patch last night from the 7th Service Command to the Air Corp. The 1st Sgt reminded me of it, so I decided it was probably a good idea.

Talk about food in the <u>Army</u>. Fort Meade had really wonderful meals but here the food is the worst I've had since I've been in the Army. I should lose weight now because it settles on your stomach like lead. But that is just a part of the Army too.

I haven't changed all of my buttons yet from plastic to brass but I'll have to soon. I think they are a little short of them in the Supply Room so I haven't pressed the matter.

You can send the corduroy robe to me. I asked the Supply Room if I'd be issued a robe and they said no. Since the barracks are so cold in the evening, I'll need it to keep me warm. Evidently this part of Florida doesn't belong to the rest of the state. At least I'm not picking oranges and basking in the sun—just shivering.

Love,
Frances

Marianna, Florida
Fall 1943

Dear Dad and Mother,

The pictures we took in Fort Meade arrived in fine condition. I think they are good ones. You'd better send me the negatives because I have promised several pictures. Mary [Umholtz], the girl who sleeps to my left, is a photographer down at the Post lab. She will probably print them for me.

We have cool mornings and nights, and then during the day it is as hot as all gee whiz.

The wooden buildings are no protection from the sun so we just sit and steam. I have put in my application for a furlough the last two weeks in January. The holidays are completely filled in this Company.

Our new Service Club will be opening tomorrow. As yet they are short a good deal of furniture but it should be in soon. The Club

Mary Umholtz, a photographer at Marianna Army Air Field, 1943. Mary eventually was stationed in the Philippines.

is next door to "The Beam" office so Dot Horowitz the other WAC here and I have been running over there to give them advice on the arrangement of the furniture. One of the artists is on furlough so now I have more to do. But even then I'm putting as much time on my Christmas Cards as anything else. It doesn't matter as long as I keep myself occupied.

Tonight we scrub for inspection tomorrow. But since I have KP in the morning I won't have to stand for inspection just my footlocker and bed. We have KP only half a day so Saturday afternoon I'll be off. I think I'll go into Marianna, a pair of shoes need heels.

I am beginning to feel a little more at home on the Air Field. I can find my way around now, at first all the buildings looked exactly alike.

I don't believe I'll be able to get any pictures here because Army personnel are not allowed to take them but the Civilians can! One more example of Army thinking—what the difference is I can't see.

Right now, I am sitting in the office burning up. At 8:30 a.m. when we come in, it is cold enough that a fire is needed then too much of the heat lingers on into the hot part of the day and we suffer.

Love,
Frances

Marianna AAFD, Florida
October 31, 1943

Dear Dad and Mother,

Last night was Halloween and the ones who stayed in the barracks decided to alter the beds of the others. They used Grapenuts and brooms, put dummies in the beds and hung sheets from the rafters. When the late ones came back, you should have heard the screams. I got very little sleep.

Today was payday for everyone except me but so far I am holding up financially. Daddy will be happy to know that I bought myself an OD overseas cap. If I ever do get home again I'll be all set.

Do you know Peg was in Chicago for 10 days? Pete [Edna Peterson] wrote and told me they were all ready to come to the train and meet me but I was sent another route. It is a shame, goodness know when we will get together again.

Helen Parker is engaged to Webb Larsen. He is a Lt in the Air Corp and was in the advertising business in Chicago. When he was there on furlough, Phil and I use to talk shop with him. I think they will be happy, that leaves Pete and me. I wonder how long she will hold out. At least I'd better get to go to this wedding.

Did I tell you the Air Field is located in the middle of a pecan plantation? You can see people from the Colonel on down strolling around with their heads bent down looking for the nuts. It is quite a pastime.

Forgive my shaky handwriting but I am just off KP and I have mopped a good acre and a half of floor. I have Jane's [Baranowski] gloves knitted and have started on the scarf. I want to get it done in time to do her some good. We hope to finish KP in time to see "Girl Crazy" tonight at the Post Movie. It will be good.

Time to go back to the Mess Hall. Did Emma get the "patch"?

> Love,
> Frances

[ARMISTICE DAY PARADE]

Marianna Army Air Field
November 13, 1943

Dear Dad and Mother,

Our weather is still baffling. Here I sit at 3 p.m. simply steaming I am so hot while this morning at Formal Inspection my hands were so cold I could hardly move them. We have both extremes in temperatures every day.

We marched in the Armistice Day Parade in Marianna. Since we weren't able to work in the morning, we were allowed to sleep until 6:30 instead of 5:30. We felt pampered.

Peg is back in Texas now hoping for her discharge to go through. Bill [Nightingale] is better but he'll be in the hospital for awhile yet.

I didn't mail you a "Beam" this week because in my opinion it "stinks." I think the next one will be better.

Did I remember to tell you how much we enjoyed the cheese? It disappeared in a flash. We get all the sweets we like but I do get hungry for something like cheese and we have very little of it in the mess hall. [Cheese was rationed and it was necessary to have "points" to buy it. We didn't have ration books because we were in the army.]

The pecans I am sending to you I picked myself. The trees are all over the place with Spanish Moss hanging down from the branches. It is weird, I feel as though we are down in the swamps. You stumble over the nuts when walking down the paths and everyone is out picking them up. I wish they had planted a couple of almond or English Walnut trees too.

Jane's scarf is finished. They've had snow there for the last two weeks!

Love,
Frances

Marianna Army Air Force Base
Sunday November 1943

Dear Dad and Mother,

We went to breakfast at the Civilian Mess this morning [fancy name for a restaurant on the air field]. In our mess hall they serve breakfast at 7 a.m. on Sunday so we wait and go to the restaurant at 8:30. Roberta [Harrison] and I are going to the Chapel on the Field at 11 a.m.

The packages arrived and thanks for sending them. I dashed into town for some Ritz crackers. The cheese will be delicious. Thanks for sending the radio books, now I'll do some studying.

The candy was very good. When I opened the package, lo and behold, the ants had gotten there first but Roberta said they wouldn't hurt it so we carefully brushed them off and ate it anyway. I passed it around and it was certainly appreciated. After this, put a paper around the box and seal it with glue or paper tape. The box sat in the Post Office just long enough for the ants to take over. This is Florida you know! However we enjoyed it just the same.

It will be necessary to put a hem in my robe. It sweeps the floor but it is the exact color [purple] of the ones that were issued. When it is folded on the hanger, you can't tell the difference.

My application for a furlough the last two weeks in January is in. I hope I get it. In some ways it is tough to move around in the Army.

Love,
Frances

Left to right: Mary Umholtz, Roberta Harrison, and Frances, Florida, 1943. Frances stayed in touch with Mary and Roberta throughout the war.

Marianna AAFB, Florida
November 27, 1943

Dear Dad and Mother,

A very Happy Thanksgiving to you. The cake arrived—it is so rich I cut it in small squares and passed it up and down the barracks. They did enjoy it. So now I've had my applesauce cake, the addition of the cherries made it a great success.

Did you say, they may need an artist? Don't be foolish, by now I am practically running the paper. I've just finished with this week's issue and it should be printed by Monday. I'll circle the things I have done. I am supposed to be handling the layout and makeup of the paper. They certainly need someone. They have about two dozen type faces and they only use about four or five. I have that to experiment with then I can also do some lettering and spot drawings. I have really been busy the past week. I am disappointed about not working in Radio but I do think I'll be in it eventually and in the meantime I intend to make "The Beam" the best Army paper in this section of the country. Just think if I hadn't transferred, I'd be coming home on furlough next week.

We had a marvelous Thanksgiving dinner, white table cloths, turkey, pumpkin pie (not quite as good as Mom's) and all of the trimmings. We sat and stuffed ourselves. I also had a letter from Jane, so it was a very nice Thanksgiving.

Guess what she has sent me now—Vitamins, a box of 60. She says I should take one after breakfast every day. I told her ages ago that I didn't believe in vitamins but she does so here I am taking them faithfully.

I am scheduled to go to the Hospital tomorrow for an overseas physical. It is a general thing in the Air Corp. They will probably give me some extra shots then tomorrow I have KP. Golly that does roll around often.

Sunday, I should fix the hem in my overcoat. It is cold enough to wear it part of the time. This is all, it is nearly ten and time for "lights out."

Love and goodnite,
Frances

Marianna AAFB, Florida
December 5, 1943

Dear Dad and Mother,

The package of art materials arrived today. Thank you. Now it won't be necessary for me to borrow a ruling pen from Kuhn. He is the artist who drew "Marianna" and the front cover this week.

Mary Umholtz, the girl who sleeps on my left side, made her Christmas Card last night. She works in the Photo Lab. I made a form for her with the usual lettering and she pasted her picture on it, photographed it and then toned the picture with sepia. It came out fine and she is very proud of it. She is pure Pennsylvania Dutch, big blue eyes and blond hair. When I told her I was a little Penn Dutch, she said she knew there was some good in me the first time she saw me and she guessed that was it. She said to tell Daddy that I was in "good company."

I asked for a three day pass today for the 13, 14 and 15 of December. The 1st Sgt said I'll have to get permission from my office. I got that this afternoon so now if Lt Sayre [WAC Commander] will o'kay it, I'll be all set. I want to go to Tampa and try to pass the 2nd Class FCC exam. Now that the time draws near, I'm convinced that I'll fail it but I have to try. I've been studying the past week and I'll continue until the exam but I do feel pretty shaky about it.

For some reason the Army has issued us mess kits, canteens, and stuff. Why no one seems to know. Just something extra to take care of, I suppose.

The new Service Club opened officially last night. It is next door to "The Beam" office and quite a nice place. But on the outside all of the buildings are unpainted wooden shacks.

I can't decide whether it is camouflage or what. In this pecan grove they aren't very visible.

Service Club, Marianna Army Air Field, Florida. Frances is sitting on the couch.

The girls are really nice here. Not that the other Company wasn't and Janie keeps me very envious with all the news but if there is one thing I have enjoyed in the WAC it is meeting and living with so many different people I never would have known under normal circumstances.

I mailed you another "Beam" today. All of the new stuff is mine but I'm still disappointed in it.

Lot of love,
Frances

Marianna AAFB, Florida
December 12, 1943

Dear Dad and Mother,

I went to Dothan, Alabama yesterday for a little Christmas shopping. Dot [Horowitz], the other WAC at the "Beam," Ceil [Gould] and I left the Field at 1 p.m. The bus ride took an hour and 15 minutes. We went in and out of stores all afternoon and got back to the barracks about 9:30.

There was a WAC wedding last night; one of the girls married an Aviation Cadet. A reception was held in our Day Room after the wedding with cake and punch. It was a festive affair. We got back just in time for the cake.

Yesterday morning we had inspection as usual. We fall out in line at 6:20 a.m. then marched to the Flight Line. The mist rising from the ground and the Spanish Moss hanging from the pecan trees, gave an eerie feeling. It was 8 a.m. before we got back. I was at attention so long; I wasn't absolutely certain whether or not I could sit down. I had yesterday afternoon off to make up for KP last Saturday.

After breakfast I went to work. We are supposed to have a "Beam" out tomorrow and another one finished next Saturday. Then the paper should come out on each Saturday, as a regular thing. But we will never do it with this Editor.

I had several things to finish so I worked through lunch and came back to the barracks about 2:30. I didn't mind the work except I didn't get my laundry done. Usually I wash items like towels and flannel pajamas on Sunday so they will be sure and dry. However I have KP next Tuesday morning and will have the afternoon off.

I did get my photograph taken in Marianna and it will be my Christmas present to you. Mary said her favorite cake is Angel Food so of course I told her about yours. She says to be sure and save her a piece when I get one. She will be going on furlough the 20th so she will be home for Christmas. She is walking on air. I will be the same way in January.

Janie says the 88th Glider Troops (stationed at Fort Meade) have moved out for good. So I imagine it is a pretty dead Post. I hope Janie is transferred soon.

> Love,
> Frances

Hotel Floridian
Tampa, Florida
December 14, 1943

Dear Dad and Mother,

This is my first 3 day pass in the Army. I left Marianna at 8 a.m. Monday morning and arrived in Tampa at 8 p.m. The USO phoned hotels trying to find me a room. I have visions of myself curled up on a street corner, but they finally located a hotel room for me here.

I went to see the FCC Inspector at 9 a.m. this morning. He was very nice and seemed to like the WACs. I started the exam and after a little time out for lunch I finished about 2 p.m. I passed, I really did!

Now I possess a 2nd Class Radio-Telephone License #7T-169. It is twice as large as the 3rd Class one and much more impressive. I am really happy about it but I believe I'll wait a couple of weeks before starting to work on the 1st Class one.

I shouldn't take trips like this right before Christmas and my furlough but then again I might not be this way again so I'll enjoy it. The only way I can foresee getting out of my financial difficulties is to become some kind of Sgt but as long as I buy a saving bond a month, that is saving a little.

I may get a 3 day pass right before my furlough. So far they have been giving them to the WACs that will give me extra time at home.

The package arrived with the cookies before I left and they were delicious. All the girls think Mother is a wonderful cook. I saved the other package and the big one that says "Do not open until Christmas." I only wish I had lots of money to get presents. Everyone has been so wonderful to me.

I should finish. I understand they plan a blackout here in Tampa at 8:45 p.m. and it is nearly that now.

> Good Night,
> Frances

ABOVE: Front cover of an issue of The Beam, *the newsletter that Frances worked on while stationed in Florida.*
RIGHT: The inside front cover of The Beam, *listing Frances with the staff.*

BEAM

PILOT SCHOOL
ed Single Engine
NA ARMY AIR FIELD
ianna, Florida

NO. 7
mber 16, 1943

John W. Persons
anding officer

John F. Gorman
Service officer

R.B. Joyce
Relations officer

• • •

THE STAFF
Supervisor
Lt. A.T. Radka

Editor
Sgt. C.A. Long

Sports Editor
Pvt. Harold Goldie

Circulation Manager
S/Sgt. E.G. Deckner

Artists
Sgt. C.E. Lowrie
Pvt. Howard Kuhn

Make Up
Pfc. Frances De Bra

Compositor
T/5 Dorothy Horwitz

Vari-typist
Miss Sarah Bondurant

Cooperation of
Reproduction

Photographic

OUR COVER — A typical young American Cadet is shown climbing into his ship, ready to take off and soar through the clouds, doing his part in helping uncle Sam build the mightiest air force in the world.

AVIATION AND THE YOUTH OF AMERICA

We are in the midst of the most momentous and most far-reaching war of modern times, a war which has proven, beyond any doubt, the vital importance of air-power as both offensive and defensive mechanisms; a war which we must win. The United States is now engaged in the greatest aircraft production program as only as strong as the manpower which our training program produces to keep our planes flying.

The source of this manpower is in the youth of the country. In youth alone are found the physical fitness, the mental alertness, the personal courage to meet the daring challenge cast down by the needs of our Air Forces.

It is to the boys of 18-26, both civilian and military personnel that this drive is directed. It is to acquaint them with the vast need of men for cadet training. Already the previous large back-log of qualified alplicants is exhausted, and the delay in assignment due to this backlog has been eliminated. It is to open to them the vistas of aviation, the shining future of post-war aeronautical progress which will be the future of the world. It is to give them wings.

THE BEAM is published, edited and written by and for the enlisted personnel and officers of the AAF Pilot School (Advanced Single Engine) MARIANNA ARMY AIR FIELD, Marianna, Florida. Offices in building 116 at Hospital Road and Chapel Street. Phone 350. THE BEAM receives material supplied by Camp Newspaper Service, W.D., 205 E. 42nd St. New York City. Credited material may not be republished without permission from CNS.

Marianna AAFB, Florida
December 21, 1943

Dear Mother and Dad,

We are putting out a special Christmas edition of the paper and that has me putting well tied this week. I have to go back about 7 tonight but I don't mind at all as long as I have something to do.

I finished wrapping my packages yesterday and mailed them this morning. I hope they arrive on time. I have so many nice Christmas Cards from various people.

Don't worry about colds, so far I've felt fine. For instance, we have calisthenics at 6:45 every morning outside. It is about 60 degrees and we wear only a sweater for warmth. I should be really rugged if I survive this Army. I hope the rest of you will miss the flu epidemic too.

✄ ✄ ✄

The WAC who led us in calisthenics was a physical education major. Lyles was her last name and she was from Alabama. I had been aware of a difference between the North and South but I had never bothered my head about it. I went to art school in Indianapolis and Chicago with a number of southerners because they had very few regular art schools in the South at that time. But it had never crossed my mind that there could be a real depth of feeling between the two sections. However, a remark that I heard Lyles make one day opened my eyes to the intensity of it. With utmost seriousness I heard her say, "Since I've been to college and in the Army, I'd just as soon have a YANKEE for a friend as anybody!"

✄ ✄ ✄

The cold weather of last week is about gone. When I got back from Tampa it was bitterly cold, there was snow in the air. You could see it in the street lights. Unusual weather for this place. I even wore my overcoat for the first time but now we are back to the usual half cold, half warm days.

I went to Church with Roberta Sunday. We have a new Chaplin. Now I'd better leave for work. I mailed you a "Beam" today. The issue is pretty good. It is beginning to look more like a professional job.

Love,
Frances

4

CHRISTMAS AT MARIANNA ARMY AIR FIELD, FLORIDA

[CHRISTMAS IN THE ARMY]

Marianna AAFB, Florida
December 26, 1943

Dear Mother and Dad,

It was an unusual Christmas this year but quite nice never the less. In Florida we had rain for Christmas and a cold rain too.

We put the paper together Friday afternoon, a much larger issue and we were proud of it. Everyone else seems to agree. It was a lot of work but we were glad to do it.

At six o'clock Roberta [Harrison] and I went into town and did a little shopping. We came back with crackers, apples and cheese (the clerk sold it to us without points—Christmas Spirit no doubt) and a tiny artificial tree.

Back at the barracks, the girls were sitting around talking in a gloomy fashion but the word cheese <u>electrified</u> them. So with a couple of foot lockers piled up to form a table, we soon had a lovely party spread laid out. Jelly, olives, fruitcake and candy materialized and someone else went for Cokes. Everyone ate until they could hold no more and then we decided it would be fun to open our presents. We went from one bed to another enjoying them, much more fun than opening them alone.

Now, thank you, the shirts, ties and hose are beautiful, I'll be so well dressed I'll hardly know myself. And of course, Daddy knows I will look forward to TIME magazine.

Pete [Edna Peterson] and Park [Helen Parker] sent a bath set of cologne, soap and dusting powder and Peg [Allison Nightingale] sent a picture of herself and Bill [Nightingale] taken in Corpus Christi. She is dressed in her white summer uniform and he has on all of his ribbons. Peg certainly looks happy. She writes that Bill is down there in time for Christmas and I believe they have found an apartment in town.

After opening the presents we went to Midnight Mass at the Post Chapel. It was lovely and after all that I came back and fell into bed.

It rained all Saturday morning, Christmas Day, so we got out of bed late. We went to Church and had a turkey dinner in the Mess Hall with all of the trimmings. All I missed was being in the kitchen at home with all the heavenly odors.

The mail has been tied up for days, so I haven't received any cookies but Mother's Money Order came yesterday. Thank you, I'll be able to use it on furlough, I know. The License was worth it, but I did spend money on the Tampa trip that I have saved for my furlough.

Ceil [Gould] wrote and got me a train schedule for the trains from Marianna to Chicago. Do you know, I can leave Dothan [Alabama] at 4:30 a.m. and get to Indianapolis at 7 p.m.! It will be only 14 hours, I can hardly believe it. I've been sitting looking at the time table all morning, grinning like a Cheshire cat. Now if my furlough goes through for the 20th I'll be all set.

I hope you had a very Merry Christmas and I miss being there so much. However, the War will be over one day.

Love,
Frances

P.S. The shirts are beautiful!

Marianna AAFB, Florida
January 5, 1944

Dear Dad and Mother,

This month seems to be moving right along. Now as planned I'll have a furlough beginning the 20th and a three day pass for the 17th, 18th and 19th. I should be leaving here a week from next Monday but don't plan on it. You can never tell about the Army, anything can happen. Just expect me when you see me.

Janie [Baranowski] has been transferred, she phoned last night. Her orders finally came through and she is going to upstate New York. Sandy [Ruth Sanderson] was transferred to Maryland, so I really think they are about to close the Post at Fort Meade. At least, they are shipping the WACs out.

With the holidays over, things are getting back to normal. Mary [Umholtz] is back and we missed her. Roberta and I were rattling around by ourselves.

The "Beam" is coming out with a short staff this week. Two of the men are on "Bivouac." Dot [Horowitz] is on furlough and [Harold] Goldie is in and out. So that narrows it down to Mrs. Huff, "Deke" our editor, Chuck Lowrie and me. At least we have a lot of peace.

Yesterday morning, Mrs. Huff brought me three cold biscuits and a chicken drumstick. She said she couldn't actually believe that any one liked cold biscuits even as she watched me eat.

Roberta and I went over to the Cadets Code Room at 1 p.m. to practice code. We are allowed there from 1 until 2. I could take about 6 words per minute. I was surprised; it has been about three months since I'd heard any of it at all. I wasn't sure if I could even remember the alphabet, but I did. Maybe I'll be able to go every once in awhile. "Deke" is very nice about letting me off. I can usually take off when I want to because we always work at night when there is rush work to be done. It evens out pretty well.

Gas mask drill is tomorrow. You should see me in one of those. It is certainly a weird sight and I am always most unhappy. They are a nuisance to wear but of course in a gas attack I would feel differently.

The Army finally gave me a pair of woolen gloves. I needed them. I'll have a furlough eventually so keep your fingers crossed.

Lots of love,
Frances

Frances asleep in The Beam *office. Staff shortages and long hours sometimes led to exhaustion.*

Marianna AAFB, Florida
January 12, 1944

Dear Mother and Dad,

I have actually seen my signed furlough! The Major had it. So it begins the 20th with a 3 day pass just before. I'll be leaving Monday morning or Sunday night, so you can expect me sometime Tuesday. It all depends on the schedule and the possibility of delays.

I am honestly so excited I can hardly add 2 and 2, with the pass that will mean 18 days on furlough. Not bad, but after waiting this long I appreciate it.

I haven't been able to find anyone to take up the hem in my overcoat, so I'll have to do it myself when I get there. Don't be surprised at the way I look. I have too much overcoat.

I had KP Sunday afternoon and I am just beginning to recover. For some reason there were only two KPs instead of three and it was rough. However I think I can hold out for another week.

You realize my excitement.

Love,
Frances

[AFTER FURLOUGH]
Marianna AAFB, Florida
February 5, 1944

Dear Mother and Dad,

I arrived safe and sound on the Field about 8 a.m. Friday morning. The train was on time in Louisville and Bill and Peg met me at the train. He looks a good deal like his pictures and I think Peg was right in marrying him.

We talked and talked. They are going to Chicago sometime next month. After he reports to the hospital for a check-up, he will start on a two year electrical engineering course. It is part of the Army's rehabilitation program. Peggy at the thought of going back to Chicago is like an old fire horse at the smell of smoke. She is excited.

Tell Emma I heard lots of Jazz records. Peg even had a jar of cheese she'd bought for me in Texas. I think Bill sometimes feels that she'll drive him crazy but he will get use to it.

I left there about 10:45 a.m. and Bill took me to the train station. The train wasn't too crowded and the time passed uneventfully. I think I read a Ladies Home Journal from cover to cover. We arrived in Montgomery [Alabama] on schedule and since there were no available rooms in town, I went on to the Field on a 12:45 a.m. bus. I slept a good deal on the bus.

After breakfast I started to put my clothes in order. My bed had been moved to the other side of the barracks but it is still opposite Mary and Roberta. They all seemed glad to have me back. Since I had to move my foot locker, wall locker and unpack my suitcase I did a good job of it.

We are to have an "Inspection General" visit us next week and apparently the whole Field has been going crazy for the last two weeks. I am glad I missed it. For instance the girls have had two hours of Chemical Warfare each night for a week and a lot of other work details to do.

I'll be back in the swing of it soon. I think about Mother not wanting me to run outside without a coat—because this morning we were outside on the Line [Flight Line] for inspection from 6:20 to 8:15. No gloves or overcoat, just jackets and it was cold enough to see your breath!

Love,
Frances

Bill Nightingale and Peggy Allison Nightingale.

[PEGGY NIGHTINGALE TO MY SISTER]
February 9, 1944

Dear Emma,

Hi there—I know I am a stranger and all that—but Frances gave me permission to write you. It seems I can't buy Kleenex here (Louisville) for love or money and she said you had plenty in Danville (stacked she said) so I wondered if you'd send me two or three of the large boxes. Grandma has a terrific cold and I've been sneezing all winter and we really are destitute. If you can't just say Poor Peggy and forget it. I'll send you the money right back. Say "How Do" to your family. Frances looked fine when she was here and I enjoyed seeing her a lot. Hope she gets another leave soon because we will be in Chicago then and she won't have to split up her visit except between Chi and you all.

Well, this is all for now. Thank you if you can get us some and don't worry if you can't. Grandma is using DELSY right now but a roll is kinda funny to carry around.

> Bye and say Hello and Love to
> Your Mother and Dad,
> Peggy

Marianna AAFB, Florida
February 14, 1944

Dear Mother,

This is just a note to tell you I'm sending a blue package addressed to you. It is just some letters and clippings I want to keep. Tuck it away somewhere.

The cake came this morning and it looks beautiful, thank you. We will eat it immediately after Lunch. I read your letter to Mary yesterday saying the second piece was for her. You should have seen her eyes. Then Roberta said, "What about me?" So I told her the third piece was for her.

The shoulder patch is for Emma. It is from the 88th Glider Infantry, which was stationed at Fort Meade.

> Thanks ever so much, love
> Frances

P.S. It has been raining since 5 a.m. and we have a flood outside. I'll probably drown the moment I poke my nose out the door. It must be that "Florida Spring" I've heard so much about.

5

WORK ON THE FLIGHT LINE

The work was in shifts, eight hours, the usual—7 a.m.–3 p.m., 3 p.m.–11 p.m., 11 p.m.–7 a.m.—and they changed weekly. This was the first work I had done out of an office.

The flight line was about a mile from our barracks and the rest of the camp—such as the PX, civilian mess, The Beam *office, library, and administration.*

I wore coveralls that I borrowed from Mary Umholtz because the army hadn't issued me a pair. They were not required for office work and the army only gave you what you needed. This was February so I had a regular flight jacket (known as a bomber jacket now). It was made of leather, had a wool fleece lining, and was very warm. All this was topped by my fatigue hat.

The planes at the field were AT-6s, Advance Trainers, and they were in the air twenty-four hours a day. It was very strange at first to hear them overhead constantly but after a time you ceased to notice it.

The radios, the transmitters, and the receivers were all checked at a certain number of hours, just like the planes. This was important because a cadet in the air without radio contact was a danger to himself and others. So we were careful about the condition of the sets.

I climbed upon the wing of the plane, got into the cockpit, removed the transmitter and receiver, and with one under each arm I jumped from the wing to the ground. They probably weighed about fifteen pounds a piece, so it was a good load for me.

Then I took them into the hangar to the test bench, placed them on the test rack and checked the output, power, frequencies, and all the rest. I wrote out the checklist and signed it, then returned the instruments to the plane, ready to go again.

This was my eight-hour shift. Of course some days there was more work and sometimes less. I remember the nights at the hangar under the bright lights most vividly.

Since I had worked on these same radios at Western Electric before I enlisted, they were familiar to me. In Chicago I tested the transmitters as they came off the assembly line.

It was work that I was accustomed to, although I never did get use to the shift changes. I worked there for a month before I was shipped overseas.

✖   ✖   ✖

Marianna AAFB, Florida
February 16, 1944

Dear Dad and Mother,

I am a working girl at last. We have finished the ships up to now and we will have to wait for awhile. As I told you I am on the 11 p.m. to 7 a.m. shift this week. Next week it will be the 7 a.m. to 3 p.m. shift. We change weekly.

This is the second night and I think I will like it. You see the planes are checked at 50 hours, 100 hours, and etc. As they are sent through the Maintenance Hanger we give the radios a check too, not hard work, and pretty simple really.

The thing I love is being around the planes. Tell Emma, a P40 is in tonight but they always have their own crews and we never touch them. I can already tell the difference between the air and liquid cooled engines, just by sight.

I slept this morning and then went back to the Library and "The Beam" for a little while this afternoon. I can only sleep so long and then I have to do something with my spare time. I tell the people at the paper I'll probably wind up with two jobs. Maybe that would keep me busy enough. I don't like sitting around in the Army.

I have KP Saturday morning, so I won't be working Friday night. Tommy, a little WAC, is breaking me in for this shift then she goes on furlough Saturday night. I'll be very busy then.

I hope the colds are better and Granddad is a lot better. You really should see me in these coveralls, quite a sight.

Love,
Frances

Marianna AAFB, Florida
Wednesday Morning (4:20 a.m.)
February 23, 1944

Dear Mother and Dad,

As you can see back on the 11 p.m. to 7 a.m. shift. I had KP this morning and now today we change shifts. Working on Sunday does mix me up. I've completely lost track of the days, they all seem to run together. Maybe I'm just not use to it yet.

We worked Sunday, and then because of KP I was off last night. I persuaded Mary [Umholtz] to go to the second movie with me. It was the first one for me in over a week. The 3-11 shift is easy work but it certainly does cancel out your social life for the time being. In fact it was the first time I'd had on my dress uniform in 8 days and that is a change for me because ordinarily I was in Class "A" all day long. But that was when I was a white collar worker. You will have to excuse the mistakes, but my eyes are beginning to close.

A course in Malaria that I missed while I was on furlough had finally caught up with me. I had an hour of physical training, and hour of Malaria and an hour of First Aid to take yesterday, that was in addition to the regular shift I worked. There we are at a disadvantage because the extra hours must come out of our free time, while with most of the office workers; they simply leave their work to attend.

Then after KP all morning, I had two more hours of Malaria to take this afternoon, and the last hour tomorrow. I will probably have a chance to sleep about tomorrow afternoon. The Army is really making me work.

I stopped at "The Beam" office this afternoon between classes. Mr. Huff [our civilian's husband and a warrant officer] came in and dumped three pairs of coveralls in my lap. He had promised to try and get me some. So he did. They are slightly worn, but who cares in the Army. I think they are size 34 and that is enough for me. Now I can give Mary's coveralls back. I told him that now I was a "woman with a wardrobe." It was an awfully nice thing for him to do.

By the way, see if you can get some sweat shirts for me in Indianapolis. They have some light weight ones here but I really need heavier ones too. A heavy white one to wear underneath my coveralls. The Army hasn't provided the WACs with them. I'm lucky to have the coveralls now. If the sweat shirts come in men's sizes I will probably take a small.

I have about run down. I am so glad Dad is better. He'd better take care of himself.

Lots of love,
Frances

Marianna AAFB, Florida
March 1, 1944

Dear Mother and Dad,

I am on the day shift this week, 7 a.m. to 3 p.m. so I am living a little more like a human being. My soreness is all gone but I still find a fair size bruise on occasion where I've collided with some part of an airplane. If you could only see me in my baggy pants and heavy field boots. Chuck Lowrie calls me "Boiler-maker DeBra." So you can imagine how I look. It is a good 15 minute walk to the Hanger and since I make it four times a day, I get exercise. And I am enjoying it, feel better too. The only thing that bothers me, my appetite has increased. How on earth will I ever lose weight for those summer skirts? But that must take care of itself. Right now I am busy getting to work; I can't worry about trivial items.

We've had the usual peculiar Florida weather. Sunday [I changed to the 7 to 3 shift] it was sweltering and now today it is so cold I have to wear the "Flight Jacket" I've been issued. It is warm as toast, but I look slightly like a Teddy Bear in it.

Roberta [Harrison] and I would like to visit in Miami in April. I think we can swing a three day pass unless my new job proves so important that they deny it to me. That I can't imagine.

Much love,

P.S. My hours are so irregular that the Orderly Room seems to have lost track of me, consequently I've missed several inspections and retreats. I am undoubtedly becoming a genuine GI.

Frances

Posing in front of a tree covered with Spanish moss, Marianna, Florida, are (left to right): Ceil Gould, Janet Farnkam, "Charity" Childers, Hazel Reicheld, Beth Bermand, Mary Kaufman, Nellie Hahn, Frances, Ellen Gray, Roberta Harrison, and Jane Gragiali.

6

OVERSEAS TRAINING

[OVERSEAS TRAINING]

Tallahassee, Florida
March 19, 1944

Dear Mother and Dad,

Sorry, I couldn't write before this but I've been too busy—brace yourself. Thursday afternoon, I was asked if I would accept overseas duty and now I am on my way to Fort Oglethorpe [Georgia] for training. Everything has happened so quickly, I'm still in a daze.

Lt. Sayre called me in Thursday afternoon and asked me if I wanted to go overseas. They had been asked to recommend someone for #70 (Drafting) and I said yes. So my clothing has been checked (they took away my suntans, so it is a cold climate, glory be) and gave me a steel helmet and field equipment.

Mary [Umholtz] will be sending my suitcase and civilian items home. I was too pressed for time. I'll let you know a little later if there are a few things I may need.

I had a "booster" tetanus shot this afternoon and the cooks made a wonderful chocolate cake for me at mess tonight. They have all been so good to me. I really hate to leave them, especially Mary and Roberta [Harrison].

We took a roll of film this afternoon, so you'll be receiving some pictures when Mary has them finished.

I'm pretty tired now, I leave for Dothan [Alabama] on the bus at 11:45 and should be in Chattanooga [Tennessee] at 4 p.m. tomorrow. Helen Miller (she was in South Dakota) is there for training too. She is in Detachment E and I'll be in Detachment C. So I'll have one friend on the Post. I hope this isn't too much of a shock.

Very much love,
Frances

✖   ✖   ✖

TRAINING AND EQUIPMENT

There were a great many changes all of a sudden. I turned in my barracks bag and was issued a duffle bag. The duffle bag was larger, heavier material and more secure than the barracks bag, which was closed only with a drawstring. In the coming months, I learned the complicated process of living out of a duffle bag.

The rest of the field equipment was a steel helmet, helmet liner, and cap. The inside of the helmet liner could be adjusted to fit the head, and the helmet cap was a knit wool cap with a bill and was worn under the helmet liner. It could also be used as a fatigue cap in cool weather. A good many of our items served a double purpose.

I had already been issued a mess kit and canteen with cover, to this was added a pistol belt and first-aid packet, then two wool olive-drab army blankets, a shelter half (tent) with poles, flashlight, and gas mask. Also included were a can of waterproofing (for shoes) and a can of insect powder. We carried all of these items and more for almost two years. Later I heard that the waterproofing could be used to cook over, like Sterno, but I never had the occasion to try it. I used the insect powder in the winter of 1944 and 1945 when I picked up fleas riding the Paris Metro. It got rid of the fleas. We had received typhus shots, so there was no worry about that. In wartime Europe typhus, carried by fleas, was a great danger without the shots.

We had been told that a large percentage of the WACs had volunteered for duty overseas and since we were an all-volunteer service that was a reasonable response.

But the orders were only for me—so after disposing of civilian items I was sent on the bus to Fort Oglethorpe, Georgia. The army always seemed to send me alone, and it is a very mixed sensation to arrive at a new post and not see a single familiar face.

It also was unusual since I was in the air force and as a rule the air force never let any of its personnel go. But for overseas duty I was transferred back to the army. In discussing this with others I found that a good many of the WACs in this shipment came from the air corps.

This picture of Frances in her WAC uniform and wearing her purse according to army regulations was taken by her father when she was in Danville on leave. His shadow appears in the bottom right corner of the photo.

I met a staff sergeant and a first sergeant who had taken demotions to private in order to join what turned out to be the first really large shipment of WACs overseas.

I arrived in Chattanooga, Tennessee, which was familiar to me since I had basic training at Fort Oglethorpe. What part of the post we were on for the overseas unit I don't know. We were pretty well restricted, and a great deal of the army always looked the same anyway.

✖   ✖   ✖

Fort Oglethorpe, Georgia
March 20, 1944

Dear Dad and Mother,

I arrived here yesterday in the rain. Our barracks are comfortable; they look much nicer than they did last June. Maybe it is because the temperature is lower.

I have met some nice girls, especially the one who sleeps below me (yes, I am in an upper bunk). Six of us are in one group and we all seem to like the same things, so that makes it pleasant.

There are a couple of things if you can manage it. Never mind the sweat shirt, but I do need a couple of ties. Just like the one you gave me at Christmas, a sewing kit (all GI thread) and a package of needles. If Emma can find any stray bobbie pins in the City, I can certainly use them. That is all I can think of at the moment. But I hope she will be able to get them immediately.

The suitcase, Mary will be sending to you. I hope collect. So if you ever have an extra Angel Food cake, send it to her and Roberta, they'd love it and I won't have much need for one.

I can't think of anymore that I can say now. Perhaps, after I become accustomed to the restrictions I can write again.

Love,
Big Sis

P.S. the address PFC Frances DeBra
A-514210
Company 4, Detachment C
Fort Oglethorpe, GA

[OUR LETTERS WERE CENSORED FROM THEN ON]

✖   ✖   ✖

FURTHER OVERSEAS TRAINING

We were issued field jackets, also called combat jackets, and pants. These were made of a tightly woven waterproof material and could be worn alone, or for added warmth we had a jacket and pant liner made from a lovely soft, thick, wool felt. Later in Paris, I often wore the felt jacket and my olive-drab slacks when off duty. They were very comfortable. We were issued field boots that laced up, covered the ankle, and were double soled, the upper sole leather and the bottom one rubber.

There were two sets of long woolen underwear, two wool flannel shirts, and our lovely white towels were exchanged for olive-drab ones. We still had our blue-and-white striped cotton flannel pajamas but mostly I felt my soul was colored khaki or olive drab.

We were told to send everything breakable home. Fortunately, I had a polished steel mirror. We were also instructed to leave behind writing cases and address books—the address books were not to fall into enemy hands! I rebelled there and took a very small one, deciding that I could eat it if necessary. I knew I could never remember all of the names and addresses.

A part of the training was the proper way to pack a duffle bag. We practiced placing all clothing into a special envelope fold. Then into the duffle bag went the GI raincoat folded in envelope shape and placed on the bottom. The shelter half was folded in half lengthwise and used to line the walls of the duffle bag. Then the two army blankets were folded and fitted inside the shelter half. This left the middle of the bag to be packed with everything else in a special way. We became great packers and with practice the duffle bags resembled sausages, not a wrinkle anywhere. Teamwork was required when the bag was about half full, one girl climbed into the bag and supporting herself on the shoulders of two others, tramped the contents down. Then with a really full bag we used a piece of rope to pull the eye over the hasp to fasten it.

All this effort was necessary because before adding the overseas issue we already were equipped with the GI raincoat with attached hood, utility coat with lining, two sets of Class A uniforms, cotton shirts and ties, overcoat, fatigues, rubbers, cotton flannel pajamas, underwear, two pair of service oxfords, and of course our stiff dress hats. So there was a good deal to pack.

We had leggings that were almost too long for my legs. At one time they tried to fit us with field packs but the straps were too long—even shortened as much as possible. We wound up with a heavy pack not on the shoulders but somewhere in the middle of our backs! So we did not have to struggle with those.

Our duffle bags and our musette bag were stenciled with our names. It was at Fort Oglethorpe that I lost my knife, a Girl Scout pocketknife, the blade of which my father always declared was made of PURE TIN whenever he tried to sharpen it. I still had my sharpening stone. My father felt a girl was not equipped to go out into the world without a pocketknife and whetstone. However, as an artist I was accustomed to having a pocketknife to sharpen pencils because I had always used a variety of drawing pencils with different types of lead, so it was regular equipment with me. I missed it until I could get another knife.

✖   ✖   ✖

Danville, Indiana
March 23, 1944

Dear Frances,

Well, it was sort of like a shot out of the blue sky but you know Mother and Dad will make the best of it and wish you lots and lots of luck. Just got your second letter this morning and immediately called Emma as she was going up into the City this evening and asked her to see if she could get those things. The tie I sent you came from Sears but it is so hard anymore to get things from there I thought perhaps Emma could go up to Strauss [men's store] and perhaps get about the same thing. She said she thought she could get you some Bobbie Pins.

We had some bad weather Sunday, sleeted, snowed and rained—everything I think but it is pretty nice now and I think it will be better. By the way, I gave my first pint of blood Saturday here at the Blood Bank. It wasn't bad at all and I did not have any ill effects that I know of. My arm hurt some for a few days but it is OK now.

If you need anything else, money or anything, let us know and we will do our best. Will close for this time and let Daddy write a letter. We will be looking for your things and I will be sure to try to send the girls an Angel Food cake. If they don't send your things collect I will send them the money. Lots and lots of love and good luck. Hope we hear from you several times yet.

Mother

Danville, Indiana
March 23, 1944

Dear Old Big Sis,

Well here at last is a letter from your Daddy. I'll bet you had almost forgotten that you had a Daddy. You know what the mouse said to the elephant when the big fellow kidded him because he was so little and no account. The mouse excused it all by saying, "I've been sick." I'm lots better now but Boy oh Boy, I have swallowed a barrel of pills and taken so much cod liver oil that I kinda like it now. I took a tablet before each meal, and then there was my VIMMS vitamin tablet three times a day, the cod liver oil and the Entrenol tablets twice a week. When they all hit together, I had to take three tablets and wash it all down with the cod liver oil. Is it any wonder that I am finally getting well in self defense?

So you are finally getting ready to go overseas. Well I am mighty glad you are going to get the chance for you have always wanted to go. Of course you don't know where you are going but I hope it is to England where you will speak the same language. Who knows, you might even run into Freda's uncle who wrote me all of those letters. He lives just across the Mercey River from Liverpool.

You will never know how proud we are of you. I guess your going overseas loosened up

Mommy's pocket book a little. Before she had been slipping the Red Cross a $1 now and then. This time she gave them $2 of her money, $2 of my money and Little Sis gave them $3. You see we are depending on them to look after you. From now on we will really back them up for your sake if nothing else.

I went up to the Hatchery and ordered 25 baby chicks today. The earliest they can deliver them is May 10. They are booked up that far ahead. I wanted to get a rooster and set some eggs for our own hens but Mommy wouldn't listen to it. She said chickens

Sooner or later these chickens ended up on the DeBras' dinner table. In one letter Rupert noted, "The meat shortage is getting so bad that everyone is raising chickens."

already hatched were trouble enough without bothering with an old setting hen.

I wonder if Gwen Goodwin will be sent along with you when you go across. It might be nice to have someone with you from the old hometown. I can't think of anything more to write except to tell you how gosh-awful proud we are of you. So I'll just slip you a little ice cream money and say Good Night to the grandest Big Sis in the world.

Love,
Daddy

✖ ✖ ✖

FOOLISH MONEY

From the time I started art school in Chicago, Daddy often enclosed a one dollar bill in his letters. He would call it "ice cream money" or "foolish money," insisting that it was not to be spent on anything practical. It was just for fun and in those days of the late 1930s and early 1940s foolish money was hard to come by. Almost every penny was spent on necessities.

Drawing pencils were ten cents each, a sheet of Strathmore charcoal paper five cents, and the fabulous French-made Michalet paper cost fifteen cents. My first large set of soft pastels—eighty sticks and made by Mengs in Dresden, Germany—I purchased at Favor & Ruhl Art Store in the Chicago Loop for $2.40. I skipped lunches for two weeks to save the $2.50 for my wonderful sable No. 8 Windsor & Newton watercolor brush. I still have it.

Art schools in those days were composed of students who went to school on a wish and a prayer. There were no student loans and precious few scholarships. The money for art school tuition was up front and money for supplies next. Food, clothing, etc. came along down the list. Never was a tube of paint discarded until it had been squeezed and squeezed and then finally spilt open to extract every particle of paint. Charcoal and pencils were used down to the last usable nub. When a hole in your shoes became too large for a paper insole, rubbers were worn—rain or shine.

So Daddy's foolish money was always something special.

✖ ✖ ✖

Fort Oglethorpe, GA
March 23, 1944

Dear Mother and Dad,

I undoubtedly have the best family in the world. I knew you'd feel that way about it but still I liked the letter because I heard others talk about the way their parents felt. They hardly dare to tell them anything and I am mighty grateful I can depend on you.

We've really been busy. I had KP yesterday, a full day this time. I guess I've been pretty well toughened up working at the Hangar. Only my hands were sore but most of the girls looked pretty well tuckered out.

There is very little I can tell you about what we are doing and it cramps my style but I feel very well. Keep me busy and I'll be happy. I won't be able to see Roberta's home in April after all. I was ready for that 3 day pass.

I have met another Hoosier. The girl who sleeps next to me is named Benedict (we call her Bennie). She lived in Indiana until she was 17 then they moved to Washington D.C. but she is still a Hoosier at heart. She has been stationed in Texas and is very nice.

I had a letter from Peg [Allison Nightingale], she and Bill are finally settled. He started school last week. It is for two years and then he will be some kind of electrical engineer. She says Pete [Edna Peterson] and Park's [Helen Parker] boss is about to be drafted and Pete will take over the office. It is a good thing Peg is there because I almost never hear from Pete. They seem to be very busy.

I have a box to express home. It contains my make-up case and several other items. It will come collect and insured. By insuring it, I hope they will treat it a little more gently but it is probably a vain hope. I trust the charges won't be too much and that the mirrors aren't broken. I may want some of the things later.

Lots of love,
Frances

Fort Oglethorpe, GA
March 28, 1944

Dear Dad and Mother,

The letter from Daddy and the package both arrived today. Thank you—the ties, Bobbie Pins and sewing kit are exactly what I wanted. Emma is a wonderful "picker-upper." Later I may want something in the way of cosmetics, soap and hose but I'll let you know.

Roberta sent me some photos that Mary just finished. The day I left the Field we had one roll of film in our possession and we took all of it of the WACs. I was glad to get them because otherwise I would have no pictures of Marianna. As soon as I take another look at them I'll send them along. I intend to have one elegant scrapbook after the War. I've met some wonderful people and made a good many friends.

My suitcase should be along any day now. Keep your eye on the two robes because the Army doesn't seem to make up its mind about giving me one. Roberta has already forwarded my "Readers Digest" from the Field, so I am all set.

On KP Friday I saw Gwen Goodwin. She is in another Company here. However there is little time to look her up so we merely said Hello and chatted for a few minutes.

That was news about Mamma's blood donation. I haven't an idea when I'll be able to give more but believe me I'll try to when I have the chance.

We've had fairly hot weather so the "ice cream cone" dollar is a definite asset. You can be sure that is just what it will be used for. Thank you.

More Army business now, so Good Bye.

Lots of Love,
Big Sis

✖   ✖   ✖

Left to right: Roberta Harrison, Frances, Ellen Gray, and Jane Gragiali, Marianna, Florida.

CAMP SHANKS, NEW YORK

On March 31, 1944, we were put on the train and sent to Camp Shanks, in upstate New York somewhere along the Hudson River. This was a staging area, last stop before leaving the country.

There we had further training in gas mask drill. We were sent into a chamber filled with chlorine gas, put on our gas masks and walked out again—we were not to run. We learned that phosgene gas smelled like new mown hay, and we were never to carry anything else in the canvas bag that contained the gas mask! Like GIs everywhere this was disregarded. However, I only carried unboxed Kleenex in mine because I didn't think that would hurt the mask. Maybe a few times in Europe I stashed away a bottle of India ink in it.

We were given instruction and practice in climbing down a cargo net, which was supposed to prepare us to leave a sinking ship—a cheering thought. And finally in the last week between April 2 and the 8th we sent everything home that we had the slightest doubt about.

Our dog tags were also replaced, eliminating the name of the next of kin; again I suppose to keep names out of enemy hands! Now I can look back on an inconsistency. Halton Brown's had his mother's name and full home address on them, and he was certainly in greater contact with the enemy than I was.

This is where I met "Stew" and Anne, who were first cousins. They were also my roommates in London. Stew was from Texas and played a wonderful piano by ear. One had been a staff sergeant and the other a first sergeant. They took a bust to private to go overseas, as a good many WACs did. Since I was still a private first class, I had no sacrifice to make.

✺   ✺   ✺

Camp Shanks, NY
April 8, 1944

Dear Dad and Mother,

This is the barest kind of a note because the lights are about to go out. But I wanted to tell you that air mails for me are still 6¢ and I hope you'll continue to send them.

Tell Emma the Christmas shirts pack beautifully. I am ever so proud of them. They make me feel quite dressed up.

We are being fed entirely too well. Dad's prediction of 15 pounds for me will have to go up if this continues. The cake in the Mess Hall is about as good as Mother's and that is saying a great deal.

Time for bed now. I just want to tell you again that you are the "best family" anyone could have and I'm very proud to belong to you.

Much love,
Big Sis

7

LONDON

THE HMS QUEEN MARY

On April 9, 1944, Easter Sunday, we left Camp Shanks and boarded a riverboat for the trip down the Hudson River to New York, the port of embarkation. It was a lovely spring day. We wore our utility coats, helmets, and pistol belts with canteen and carried our gas masks and musette bag. Our dress hats, which we hated and could not be packed, were hung from a button of our utility coat. It took several hours to go down the river. This was fascinating since I had never seen that part of the country before. I remember thinking that a helmet was my Easter bonnet.

We boarded the ocean liner, Queen Mary, *about 5 or 6 in the evening. We walked up the gangplank to the music of "Pistol Packin' Mama" and "The WAC Is a Soldier Too."*

At the dock, the Red Cross gave us ditty bags. They were made of cotton, dyed olive drab, with a drawstring, and were to be used for toilet articles. I used mine for that until I purchased an English-made towel at our PX in London, which I made into a drawstring bag for carrying such necessities. After that I carried the ditty bag to the PX for my weekly rations in London and Paris.

We ate K rations coming down the river and the first night on the boat. Our duffle bags were in the hold of the ship, and we were restricted to certain areas.

Our sleeping quarters were in the main deck staterooms. They were paneled and decorated with beautiful inlaid wood designs. There were luxurious bathrooms. The decorations were all art deco. The cabins were filled with bunk beds, stacked three deep and very close together. I was assigned a lower bunk. The water in the bathroom was saltwater and even with soap made for saltwater, it left you feeling unwashed. Of course, in such crowded quarters the bathing was minimal.

Monday morning, we were taken to our mess, which was all the way down in the bottom (well very far down) of the ship. We were told the swimming pool had been floored over to make it.

There we were introduced to the caste system of the British forces. The rations for officers and enlisted personnel were quite different. But it was a British ship and staffed by the British navy, so their customs prevailed.

Our breakfast was a lovely brown meat in gravy, which turned out to be creamed kidneys! Not usual American fare. There were also thick slabs of bread with marmalade, which I could eat. On shipboard there were two meals a day, breakfast and an evening meal about 4 o'clock. I managed to go to one evening meal the whole time that I was on the Queen Mary.

As we sailed out of New York Harbor on Monday morning, we were allowed up on deck and I saw the Statue of Liberty grow smaller and smaller in the distance.

The next day—seasickness hit me. I really didn't know what it was at first. I was all right the first twenty-four hours and then the movement of the boat did me in. I was very dizzy, which I understand is a form of seasickness. As long as I lay down with my eyes closed I was fine. Fortunately it was a smooth voyage, otherwise I would most certainly have ended up in sick bay, as some of my friends did.

We spent a good deal of time on our bunks, but we were required to turn out for lifeboat drill, which meant filing out on deck and lining up at a designated lifeboat. This took about half an hour. It was a good thing it wasn't any longer because that was about my limit to remain upright before I became really sick. Lifeboat drill, however, had to be attended unless you were in sick bay.

The Queen Mary *carried a full division of soldiers and assorted WACs, Red Cross, and Special Services troops. A division numbered about thirteen thousand or fourteen thousand men. On some of the troop ships there were not enough bunks for everyone, and the men had to sleep in shifts.*

Normally, this ship made the crossing in four and a half to five days, but we zigzagged two extra days dodging submarines, a disturbing thought. The Queen *was such a fast ship (35 knots) that it sailed alone, without convoy. We were told that we went as far south as Bermuda and very far north.*

The one advantage to seasickness is that you don't have to worry about the boat sinking; you actually hope that it will sink and put you out of your misery. There were no pills for seasickness then—we just suffered. The waters of the North Atlantic were so cold you could only survive in it for about ten minutes. I certainly did not anticipate climbing down a cargo net.

The time was spent on my bunk, there really wasn't any place else. We usually had plenty of paperback editions to read, but I kept my eyes closed and wished for a lemon. Chuck Lowrie, the cartoonist at The Beam, *who was from California, had told me about the flowers in the desert and the Giant Sequoia trees. That was something I really wanted to see, so I lay there and thought about the towering redwoods. It was something to fix my mind on—an antidote for seasickness.*

Although someone always brought me a thick slice of bread with jelly or jam on it, which was all that I could get down, I did crave fruit. A couple of days before we landed I was given a lemon and it was wonderful. The lemon juice was just what I wanted.

The Red Cross girls and Special Services troops, who wore officers' uniforms, ate in the officers' mess and tended to look down their noses at us. They had fresh fruit in their mess because we could see them carrying it back from the dining room. My chief worry was whether I would be too weak to walk down the gangplank with all of my equipment. Fortunately the seven days ended and I was still on my feet. This answered a question in my mind. I had always heard that the five-day passage in peacetime received an extra fare that people were glad to pay—now I knew why!

We entered the Firth of Clyde about 4 o'clock in the afternoon of Sunday, April 16. It is still a vivid picture in my mind—the sky was opalescent, to an artist's eye, even a seasick one, overwhelmingly beautiful.

The next morning, we were lined up in the hall on the main deck with our duffle bags tagged and ready to be carried off when we debarked. We didn't have to carry them off, thank goodness. They were a sight to behold, smooth and stuffed tight, without a wrinkle or a dent. A colonel going past us shook his head and said, "How on earth do they pack like that?" We could have told him. It was an art and lots of teamwork.

I was able to walk down the gangplank, a triumph of mind over matter.

SOMEWHERE IN ENGLAND

We left the ship and rode in the familiar army trucks to the train stations and boarded an English train, with the sort of compartments we had only read about. Small sections with two facing seats, each seat holding three or four passengers. The long aisle outside the compartments ran the entire length of the car, a very odd, but not uncomfortable arrangement.

We rode from Scotland down into the middle of England without an idea of where we were going. The army only informed you of the destination when there was a compelling

Sketch of a WAC wearing a helmet. Shortly after arriving in London, Frances realized that when an air-raid siren sounded it was not a "practice alert."

reason. We arrived at Litchfield, which was a redeployment center or in GI a "repple-depple."

We were "billeted," it didn't take long to start using British terms, in old army barracks of several stories, made of brick and very Victorian, high ceilings and tall, tall windows, the kind that are seldom made now. I could easily imagine British regulars, the "Tommies" in dad's Barrack-Room Ballads by Rudyard Kipling, stationed there. Daddy loved the poems and used verses of them as the introduction for many of his weekly newspaper feature articles.

Our cots held straw ticks. We slept on this type of mattress for many months. It consisted of a long bag made of ticking and filled with loose straw and fastened at the end. When fresh, there was a certain amount of fluff to the mattress but as time passed it became molded to the shape of your body.

The first night, suddenly we were awakened by the wail of an air-raid siren. Looking at each other, we said "It must be a practice alert!" Then we realized that they didn't have practice alerts in England. We began to understand that now we were out of the States and in a theater of war. It was a short alert and then the all clear sounded.

And the darkness! Total blackouts were new to us and the utter absence of any light gave an added dimension of strangeness.

✗   ✗   ✗

[V-MAIL APRIL 18, 1944 LITCHFIELD, ENGLAND]

Mr. R.S. DeBra
203 North Tennessee Street
Danville, IN

PFC Frances DeBra
A-514210
WAC Detachment
APO 3 7599
C/o PM New York, NY

[SOMEWHERE IN ENGLAND]

Dear Mother and Dad,

As you can see, I arrived and am in excellent condition. Several times the boat and I had a slight disagreement. It went clockwise and I went counter clockwise. I was dizzy a good part of the time.

England is wonderful. The scenery is lovely and I've enjoyed every moment of it. Daddy's letter about the applesauce cake nearly broke my heart. I expect to find one waiting for me when I see you again.

Love,
Frances

[REDEPLOYMENT DEPOT]

Litchfield, England
April 21, 1944
Dear Family,

I sent you a V-mail yesterday because they were handy and I just had time for one. I am curious to know how the time of arrival compares with the Air Mail.

It was quite a trip. Your daughter was seasick but dry land was the remedy for that.

Our little English steward, by the name of "Charlie," was a great help. He slipped us crackers and apples when we weren't up to the Mess Hall fare and one evening he gave me a lemon. I can't explain it but it really hit the spot.

The trip down through England had beautiful scenery. The country side is just about as I had imagined it, very green and very like a garden. [Of course it looked like Indiana to me too but I didn't mention that.]

The houses seem to have been here for always and every bit of the land looked loved and tended. We were warned not to laugh at English trains because there was a reason for their small size but I liked them. The seats were very comfortable and the speed excellent.

The chief problem was me, Army equipment and the width of the aisle. You'd love to see me in my "battle dress" as Charlie called it. There is a certain amount of equipment we must carry with us and after I have strung to the right, left and back of me I felt like a decorated Christmas tree. I look at it in a pile on the floor and can hardly believe that I can carry it away at one time. If I could remember that I am a different circumference "dressed" than normally everything would be fine. But one day I expect to find me and a field pack firmly wedged in a doorway.

Our reception at Litchfield was splendid. We came in about 10 o'clock in the evening and there was a wonderful meal of roast beef waiting for us. They even placed a band in the Mess Hall for music. We really felt we were welcome.

I went to Service today at the Post Chapel. The Chaplain showed us a flag carried by an English Regiment at Bunker Hill. The American Troops here are raising money for a stained glass window in the church. So perhaps, finally the two countries will become fast friends. At least everyone does try to make everything as pleasant as possible.

My money has been changed into English coins. It is very confusing. I'll have to stretch my hand out and say "How much is it!" We have been so restricted I've had very little chance to spend any. I'll probably drive you wild asking for items to be mailed to me so you had better ask about postal regulations.

You will only need the 6¢ Air Mail stamp for me, even though it is overseas. It is fortunate because I will send all my letters that way when possible.

Lots of love,
Frances

✖   ✖   ✖

POSTAL REGULATIONS

As members of the armed forces we could always send letters anywhere without stamps by printing FREE in the corner of the envelope where the stamp usually was placed and writing our serial number and unit as the return address. This mailing privilege and the free movies on every post wherever we were helped when a soldier was without funds. The free mail outside the United States went regular mail by boat instead of by plane as the six cents air mail did.

The V-MAIL was a splendid type of mail, written on a printed form and photographed. The negatives were flown back to the States, the photostat developed in a reduced form, placed in an envelope, and mailed to the address. Halton Brown used those many times when he was in the line and only V-MAIL and pen or pencil was available.

The regulations for parcels required that there be a request from the soldier before the post office in the States would accept it. Packages could not be sent from the States without authorization. Eventually every few letters I included a note at the end requesting several items that my family usually sent. This way they always had a letter to authorize the box they wanted to mail. My letter was stamped and dated with the time at the post office.

✖   ✖   ✖

[BUS TOUR TO STRATFORD, WARWICK, AND KENILWORTH]

Litchfield, England
April 24, 1944

Dear Dad and Mother,

I am still enjoying England and trying not to miss a thing. The money does not seem so strange now and I am able to recognize most of the coins and figure at a slow rate of speed. The paper money looks so different; I think we don't quite realize that we are spending money.

I attended services at the Litchfield Cathedral, and then I went on a Red Cross Bus Tour. We went to Kenilworth Castle, a ruin but still Sir Walter Scott, Warwick Castle and Stratford on the Avon.

We were served lunch in a Town Hall and the plate held potatoes cooked four different ways, that also brought home to us where we were.

The houses are preserved as nearly as possible in the original state. A building only 200 years old is considered a "new comer." These were 500 or 600 years old. We saw the Church where Shakespeare was buried and the Avon River is just as lovely as the pictures.

The tours were arranged for the American Troops at the "repple-depple" [we never called it anything else]. It gave us a chance to see a little of the countryside and a part of historic Britain. It was a scenic section that nearly everyone loves. Since we were bound for London, it was our only opportunity to see some of rural England.

Stratford remains in my memory. This was April and spring in England is always lovely—the gardens and flowers around Ann Hathaway's Cottage and the house where Shakespeare was born were beautiful even to uneducated GI eyes. There were low, low ceilings in the room where Shakespeare was born. The Church where he was buried was at the edge of the nearby and evenly flowing Avon River. Somehow in America we aren't used to a close proximity to a stream. England was different in many ways.

I bought Post Cards like mad. So you will be able to see a little of it. You can imagine me with my eyes wide open so that I won't miss a single thing. I am a perfect "rubber neck."

> Lots of love,
> Frances

PFC Frances DeBra
A-514210 WAC Det
F-3 Sec. HQ SP TRP
APO #887
C/o PM NEW YORK, NY

London, England
April 26, 1944

Dear Mother and Dad,

At last I can give you my permanent APO # (Army Post office). As you see I'm stationed in London and thrilled no end. I have seen so many things I've read about.

I did receive Emma's letter with her pictures but the other mail seems to be trailing us. I've heard tales of people receiving a sack full of mail at a time, so that maybe my good fortune. At least now that our assignment is semi-permanent the mail should come through.

Our quarters (billet now instead of barracks) are grand. There are five WACs in my room and we actually have plenty of floor space and elbow room. It is such a change after all the various places we've stayed since leaving the States. We still live out of our "duffle bags" to a great extent but I'm becoming accustomed to it. However I never imagined that I'd be happy to see a good old fashion Army foot locker again.

Yesterday was my first day on the job and I'm sure I'll like it. The people I'll be working with seem to be very congenial and the office is very well equipped. I feel myself most fortunate. This is the highest American headquarters in the European Theater.

I have been shopping for clothes hangers as I left mine behind in the States and they are essential for our uniforms. My biggest problem is tired feet. There is so much to see and we have a great deal of daylight in the evening.

I now have a ration card that entitles me to certain purchases at our PX (Post Exchange). We can have 7 packs of cigarettes (which I don't need, but always buy to give away), two boxes of matches, one package of gum, and two candy bars and one cake of soap per week.

We consider ourselves fortunate in contrast to the British people. Their rationing is much stricter than ours. But there are a few items that you can send me. I'll give you a list of things I'd like if you can manage without too much trouble. Send them along whenever you can because packages take every bit of a month.

First starch because there seems to be none in England, a jar of Tussy deodorant and the big bottle of Dorothy Gray lotion which I left there and always use Kleenex for packing. We use our one cake of soap a week for everything so I would like a cake or two of Saymans soap.

I'll be able to write more now that I am settled. I'm getting homesick for mail because it has been awhile but I always know that it will come eventually.

> Lots of love,
> Frances

✖   ✖   ✖

CHARLES STREET

When we arrived in London, we were billeted on Charles Street. This was a very old street in Mayfair a few blocks long and running from North Audley to the south end of Berkeley Square. The street had slight twists and angles, a common feature in old cities. The street was lined with town houses, lovely Georgian architecture with the usual English half basement, ground floor and then the first floor. Our room was on the second floor, which would have been the third floor in America. We were in Company B, 41 Charles Street.

My roommates were Caroline Chaffee from Missouri, "Stew" (short for Stewart) and Ann, two first cousins from Texas, who were in my shipment from Camp Shanks and Hope, who only was with us for awhile. She went on with the Forward Echelon that moved to France after D-Day.

Our room was large enough for five army cots and a couple of open closets for our uniforms. Our musette bags hung from the bottom of the bed, shoes were under the bed, and everything else stowed in the duffle bag. Now that was interesting, when all of your possessions, underwear, toilet articles, and all personal items continuously go in and out of a duffle bag.

I began to sew my own drawstring bags by hand. I made a large one made from an English towel that I bought at the PX for my soap, toothbrush, hair brush, cosmetics, and etc. and carried it back and forth to the bathroom. I later purchased a chamois skin (not rationed) at Selfridges Department Store from which I made three small bags for little items. However, I remember a shelf in the closet that was used for our "Hobby Hats." We didn't wear them but they were kept safe.

The blackout curtains in our room never failed to intrigue me. Later I found out that they were all made to a pattern, for the ones in the Gobels home were the same.

Our room had large windows, about three feet wide and six feet tall. The heavy, dark curtains were lined and inner lined. There was no nonsense about perhaps meeting in the middle. These were two full curtains for each window. The outside bottom edge had a ring sewed to the corner. The curtains were closed and overlapped. The rings were fastened over hooks on the outside edge of the window frame. This stretched them tight over the edges. This was a complete blackout, not a crack of light showing. After all the bombing the British had endured there was no margin left for error.

Charles Street was about eight or nine blocks (and I use the term loosely when describing a route in London) from Grosvenor Square where I worked. The army headquarters on the northwest side of the square, bounded by Brooks Street and North Audley Street, had been a very elegant apartment building. Our WAC mess was in the basement, so we walked to breakfast, worked, and ate lunch there, then supper before returning to our billet.

The section I was assigned to was G-3 Plans and Training, a fairly small section. The drafting room was on the fifth floor and on the southwest corner of the building. A corner room, it had been a lovely living room with a baronial fireplace. Now the walls were covered with large-scale maps and drapes were hung over them—the door was kept locked.

My drafting board faced a west window and looked out over a bombed-out corner. A few blocks away I could see a barrage balloon trailing cables. We were told that they hovered over London to prevent the German dive bombers (Stukas) from strafing. We were also told that they would all be lowered when the invasion finally began.

The technical sergeant in charge of the drafting room was Frank Martello from New York City and a professional architect. He had been in England over two years, and he told me that one winter they were so cold they burned furniture for heat.

13 May '44   London
              outside the Drafting Room
              Barrage Balloon in the distance
(Corner of North Audley St & Upper Brooks Street)

The description Frances wrote for this sketch is: "London outside the Drafting Room Barrage ballo[o]n in the distance [upper right] (corner of North Audley St & Upper Brooks Street)"

There were two other men in the drafting room. A corporal who was soon released to go with the forward echelon and a British civilian who was left behind when we went to France. So I guess I did replace two men. Sergeant Martello and I became good friends. Visiting the Architects Club when he first came to London, he met a British architect whose daughter he later married.

Drafting in the army covered a wide range of topics, from name signs on desks and doors, organizational charts, information placed on maps, Bigoted material (a step above Top Secret), and anything else needed.

GROSVENOR SQUARE

Many of the American officers were enamored with their British counterparts. In our headquarters, only the officers were allowed to use the lobby and the passenger elevators. The enlisted personnel were restricted to the back stairs and the freight elevator. This was changed when we moved to Paris. Some of the officers adopted the use of the British swagger stick, a small baton carried under the left arm, which served no useful purpose whatsoever.

The American Embassy and the American Red Cross buildings were also in Grosvenor Square. Grosvenor Square was a rectangle with the park an oval enclosure that in wartime was boarded up and thus inaccessible. This was in the heart of Mayfair, just to the east of Hyde Park and a very fashionable part of the city.

The area around Grosvenor Square was filled with service personnel, so many that by mutual consent saluting was only performed in a face to face encounter. Otherwise we would have been saluting endlessly.

I frequently met Admiral Harold R. Stark, the commander of the general headquarters for American naval forces in Europe. A very fine gentleman, with gold braid up to the elbow, he always walked alone in contrast to the many army officers who had a retinue of half a dozen lesser officers trailing behind them. I was always pleased to salute Admiral Stark, he smiled and I am sure would have tipped his hat to me if we hadn't been in uniform.

In fact, in Paris where we were allowed in the front elevators and stairs, the chief of G-3, General George S. Eyster, and the head of the judge advocate section did always touch their overseas caps when WACs were in the elevator.

✖ ✖ ✖

[A LETTER TO MY SISTER ON HER BIRTHDAY]

Charles Street, London
May 3, 1944

Dear Sis,

Today is your birthday and again I am late. I've been keeping my eyes open to get you something special and to tell the truth I am still looking. If the package is a month or so late, you'll know it was really meant for your birthday.

That was a good letter and also the picture. I can't quite decide which of the two snapshots I like better, so I'll put it in the folder with the other one and then when I pull it out to show someone my family, they can judge for themselves.

We are having the most wonderful weather here. My case of "Spring Fever" started in February and grows progressively worse. You should see the flower sellers on the street with their roses, violets and lilies of the valley. It is hard to resist them. So to make up for it, I sit down and polish my buttons and shoes again, even though I know the shine can't possibly take the place of the flowers.

I am still walking over London, trying to see as much as possible. I've gradually become accustomed to the city pavements. After the cinder paths of Florida it was hard on my feet at first but I'll soon become use to the hard surface again.

After the Art Galleries, I am looking forward most to hearing the London Philharmonic Symphony. At long last I'm near enough to an orchestra to be able to hear it on occasion. I know I'll enjoy it. Finding my way will be a problem but with my trusty City map it shouldn't be too hard.

I just received a letter from Peg [Allison Nightingale] and one from Pete [Edna Peterson]. Peg works at Marshall Field now, back in the phonograph section. Pete says that Peg and Bill [Nightingale] know over half the people in the neighborhood already. That sounds like Peg, doesn't it.

> Happy Birthday,
> Big Sis

✖ ✖ ✖

BUTTONS

Another British custom engaged my attention. I had to take all of my brass buttons, douse them with lighter fluid, and then set it on fire. This burned off the lacquer with which the buttons were coated and which of course was formulated to make polishing unnecessary. From then on we had to use a polishing shield, paste polish, and a brass brush every few days to keep our buttons shining. For inspections, the degree of shine was supposed to be blinding. I never achieved it. Shoe shining I was used to—the regular army men in the Signal Corps in South Dakota had given me proper instruction in the spit and polish of shining shoes. But buttons!

✖ ✖ ✖

Charles Street, London
May 8, 1944

Dear Mother and Dad,

You have been keeping me supplied with letters, and I do appreciate it. As yet, I can't tell whether you know that I have landed but I hope you do.

I am still sightseeing trying not to miss any of London. Yesterday was my day off but since the other WACs worked, I started off alone.

[Headquarters operated seven days a week, so we had our day off at odd times.]

I saw St. Paul's Cathedral. It is magnificent. It is a miracle to see it still standing. But the bomb damage was slight in comparison to the whole structure. I'd like to see it with the stained glass windows in place as it would be normally.

[The earlier fire-bomb raids destroyed great sections of the old city around St. Paul.]

I found the British Museum "Closed for the duration" and that was a disappointment. But I expected it and would have been surprised if it had been open. Still I managed to see the Summer Exhibit at the Royal Academy, painting and watercolor. They were quite good

The mess hall at 20 Grosvenor Square, London, 1944.

and I was glad to see it alone. Most people aren't interested in it the same way I am and soon tire of the pictures. So I've found it best to make "solo" trips.

I walked and walked and enjoyed myself immensely. I did go down Fleet Street (Dad would know about that). Every time I pass something I've heard about I smile to myself.

We have no ironing facilities but the charwomen have been doing our shirts. The two I got for Christmas are certainly a blessing. I wear them day in and day out since the collars look fine without starch.

The food in the Mess Hall has been excellent, much greater variety than I had expected and certainly much better than the British people have. I am very glad I now like beets, cabbage and other odd vegetables. Remember I always said "I'll eat cabbage when it is necessary." I even enjoy sauerkraut!

I do hope you've found someway to send the hand lotion because between you and me, one of these days I'll dry up and blow away. It is impossible to buy here. Be sure that everything you send me is packed with Kleenex (if you can get it easily) because it is non-existent here. I still have some that I brought with me but with the constant colds that Americans seem to have in this British weather, I'm using it up rapidly.

One thing I like over here—we have whole wheat bread. The Army in the States served White bread and I hate it.

Lots of love,
Big Sis

For the Postmaster:
Please send me some hand lotion or cream, Kleenex and candy.

Frances DeBra

(Will that take care of it?)

✖ ✖ ✖

PHOSPHORUS

When we arrived in London, the fire-bomb raids were still fresh in the memories of the people because the phosphorus fire bombs had burned a substantial portion of London. At every stairway landing and at other locations there was a bucket of sand and we were given instructions about phosphorus. I learned to my horror that it would burn through anything, landing on the roof of a five-story building, it could burn its way to the ground, through concrete and metal. So if a piece of it landed on an arm or leg it would burn all the way through the flesh. This was a great and unwelcome revelation to us, fresh from the States where such things were unheard of. Fortunately the fire-bomb raids were ended and the buzz bombs and V-2s took their place. Still very deadly but without the terror of a substance that could burn through anything!

✖ ✖ ✖

Charles Street, London
May 15, 1944

Dear Dad,

Of course I would have gone to the Circus with you. I haven't seen a really good one for a long time. Janie [Baranowski] and I rode the Ferris Wheel in Deadwood last summer at the Rodeo and had a good time but as for an honest to goodness Circus I'll just have to wait for that.

Thank you for the extra dollar. I did use it for a "spot of tea" this time. I worked Sunday and therefore had Monday off. Woodie [Marjory Woodring] and I roamed around the "City" and at tea time stopped for that very thing.

Something else happened to your money, the English people are forbidden by law to accept our money in payment for purchases so I stopped at the Bank in Berkley Square to have it changed. While waiting in line [I had accumulated three dollar bills by this time] an American pilot in front of me offered to buy them, to use as "Short-snorter" bills. So there is no way of telling where in the world your dollars will go.

Yesterday was a wonderful day. We found some small bookstores up by the British Museum and I bought several picture postcards ones with famous paintings on the reverse side. They are marvelous and much finer than the ones we usually get. I'll never forget what a collection Miss Hendrix [my first art teacher] had. So I treat myself to them, ever so often.

We started at Trafalgar Square, saw the pigeons and began walking along the Strand. Most of the afternoon was spent along Fleet Street and the old section of "The City" around St. Paul's. Remember the nursery rhymes about the bells of London. "Oranges and Lemons say the Bells of St. Cements."

Then we passed the "Old Cheshire Cheese" Tavern, where Dr. [Samuel] Johnson went and also the grave of Oliver Goldsmith. You were right; the whole place reeks of history. I have a card for the Westminster Library now. It is not far from Charles Street. We are allowed to check out books. Perhaps some of the English History that I've read will straighten itself out in my mind.

Tell Emma that a whole month of Ballet performances start here this week. I'll have the time of my life if I can get tickets. I can use a sleeveless sweater and Emma is an angel to start it for me. Let me know when it is about finished and I'll request it.

Please send the pocket knife to me. I feel lost without one, "Stew" the Texan in our room has a beauty. I borrow it when necessary, but she still feels that I will hurt myself or the knife. I haven't decided which it is. Imagine me who had a pocket knife there many years! I suppose I should be highly insulted especially after lending her my whetstone. I didn't leave it behind.

The air mail letters are coming right through. I seem to receive my mail in bunches but I don't mind. The last one to this APO came in about seven days. But, as yet no Republican. [The *Danville Republican* was the county paper where my father worked.] Papers and magazines are slower, but since the letters are the most important, it is all right.

Thanks for the "foolish money" and the letters. I hope mine are coming through also.

Lots of love,
Big Sis

Charles Street, London
May 1944

Dear Mother and Dad,

Letters have been arriving from all of you now; it was rather bad for a time when our mail kept trying to find us. One day last week, I received 21 letters. Thirteen were from Janie—she writes me in spare moments, two were from Emma and so on down the line. It does seem odd to be receiving mail that was written two months ago before I left the States.

This is a much delayed "Mother's Day" greeting. I have a lovely card for it in my scattered possessions that I got last November to use. Still you know I love you and I will try to make up for it after the War.

Do you realize that Dad's birthday is the marker for my first year in the Army? I am going to celebrate the day on general principles, it has seemed an age.

Don't worry about my lost package. I imagine it is trailing me somewhere and there is nothing in the world that we can do about it. However, I hope to see it someday because my favorite watercolor brushes were in the box.

I would like to have the onion skin paper so please send that to me. Don't bother with envelopes because I can buy the stamped air mails at a near by Post Office but thin paper is impossible to get.

Friday night, I went to the Box Office to get tickets for the Ballet. I have seats for two different performances. I've given up trying to persuade anyone to go with me. Now I take off alone and enjoy it just as much. On the way back, I stopped and bought a bunch of violets from an old lady on the corner. They probably looked foolish clasped in my GI glove but I couldn't resist them. They are still in a glass of water at the billet here.

I liked the "Blondie" comic strip. Last week we had fresh eggs in the Mess Hall for breakfast. Believe it or not, I ate a fried one—the whole egg and enjoyed it. Daddy said the Army would change me. It has but I would not have guessed it about eggs.

> Very much love,
> Frances

Charles Street, London
May 23, 1944

Dear Dad and Mother,

Yesterday I received some mail, a letter from Phil, two from Janie and one from you. It contained a "foolish dollar" from Dad. I'll feast my eyes on it for awhile. American money is beautiful in our eyes, although I am becoming use to the money here. I am not a lightening calculator but I do manage to pick the right coin from a handful of change.

Sunday I went sight seeing and saw Westminster Abbey, Big Ben, the Thames River and of course Piccadilly Circus. London is a fascinating place. I am very grateful to be stationed here. I love to walk home through the streets. They twist and turn in the most surprising fashion. You can never be quite sure what will be around the next corner.

I went to Windsor & Newton today to buy paper and paints. After using their brushes for many years, I felt a tingle go up and down my spine as I walked into the shop.

I helped with a laundry detail yesterday afternoon and bounced over half of London in a truck but I managed to see London Bridge and Buckingham Palace as we zoomed past.

Iva and Rupert DeBra on their porch in Danville, Indiana.

[The place where we took the laundry was run by "Cockneys" and truly I could not understand a word they said. It might just as well have been a foreign language.]

A letter from Pete came today. She says that Peg works part time at Marshall Fields now and looks fine. Webb [Larsen] (Parks [Helen Parker] future husband) is on his way overseas and Pete's boss expects to leave for the service very soon.

I haven't received the Republican yet but it may be due to a mix up in the mail. Please change the address to this APO for me.

Love,
Frances

✗   ✗   ✗

WINDSOR & NEWTON

Windsor & Newton, a legendary art store, was on Tottenham Court Road near the British Museum and Soho Square. The original store was destroyed in the fire-bomb raids, but it reopened across the street.

My first art teacher started me out right with their brushes (student grades but still good sable), Watman watercolor paper, and Windsor & Newton paints. There were no brushes for sale so it was fortunate that my brushes eventually caught up with me. I had paper, paint, and sketchbooks, and we always had ink, pencil, and pens in the drafting room, so I started to draw again.

MAPS FOR THE INVASION

In the drafting room, a few days before the invasion, I worked on a series of maps of the Cherbourg Peninsula and northern France. They showed the invasion beaches and the expected time of advances on D-Day +10, +20, +30, etc. I knew this was a vital secret. We were very conscious in those days about not allowing any slips that might have disastrous effects on our troops. We were all on edge wondering when.

About this time, allied daylight raids started going out over London. There were hundreds and hundreds of planes in the sky almost as far as the eye could see.

We had been told that when the invasion started, the barrage balloons over London would be brought down. We were so excited I don't believe we thought to look.

× × ×

Charles Street, London
May 25, 1944

Dear Dad and Mother,

Yesterday was your Birthday and also the end of my first year in the Army. It hardly seems possible in one way and then again it really seems like a whole year.

So again, I have nothing for your birthday present and no idea what to buy for any of you. Emma's birthday just past, yours and Mother's coming up before long. Every bit of clothing is rationed here—other articles just aren't and about the only things left are antiques. How would you like a few of those? I'll find something eventually but I want you to know I hadn't forgotten.

[Also I was still a private first class with a Savings Bond taken out every month, leaving very little loose change for me.]

I saw the Ballet Monday evening; they danced Swan Lake and Twelfth Night. It was really good. I enjoyed it so much. I have another ticket for June 2nd because the season is only 4 weeks long. Emma would certainly love it.

At the intermission I sat in my seat very calmly waiting when what should appear but a little waitress with a tray and cups of coffee. I've seen soft drinks and peppermint candy sold before but nothing like that, "Solid Comfort" I call it.

Your letters are coming in six days now and I hope that mine do as well. As yet no sign of my TIME or READER'S DIGEST. Both publications were notified so I will probably get them all at once, then I'll have reading matter for days. As long as the letters get through we have no complaints.

Our weather has been quite lovely but the accounts that I receive from Marianna indicates that it is very hot there. I shouldn't wonder it was verging on the hot side when I left. Somehow, all along I had the feeling I wouldn't be spending the summer in Florida.

I do want the snapshots. My little pocket folder which I silently thank Emma for every day, was all I brought with me.

The clipping of "Hash Marks" are from a column in the Stars and Stripes. The first good newspaper I've had a chance at since I've been in the Army and I take full advantage of it. I thought you might enjoy them. We do. In fact, quite often they (Hash Marks) hit the nail on the head so neatly it almost hurts.

Thank you for the dollars. It is nice just to take a good long look at an American bill for a change. Of course, my purpose is to wish you a very "Happy Birthday."

> With much love,
> Big Sis

PS I have to add postscript. "Stew" and Ann just came in from a 24 hour pass. They spent it at Windsor and came back with a small hot plate. So now, please send me any of the following:

Nescafe or powdered coffee

Cheese, the packaged type

Cans of tuna fish

Anything else along that line which we could cook over a hot plate. Thanks loads and don't bother with it too much. I just received a letter from Janie in 3½ days, air mail. Happy Birthday Again.

> Fran

8

BUZZ BOMBS

[BUZZ BOMBS]

Charles Street, London
June 9, 1944

Dear Dad,

That was an elegant picture of you. It made me feel very much at home, backyard and all. As you know by now, the second front is on and with the radio you probably know more about it than I do but I am sending you the Stars and Stripes of the second day. I thought you would enjoy it.

Tuesday (June 6) was my day off. I ate breakfast and went to the Tower of London for the 11 o'clock tour. We waited in line a few minutes then the guide (a Beefeater) came over and we asked him if he was the guide to take us through the Tower. He replied instead that [General Dwight D.] Eisenhower had just announced the landing on the coast of France then he went right into the History of the First Tower. There was not a ripple of excitement from anyone so of course I didn't believe it.

Before the tour was finished a few casual remarks from some of the service men made me realize that it was true. I have never seen less excitement in my life. The only visible sign of anything unusual were the headlines in the newspaper. Golly, I have never seen such cool people. When Peace is declared, they will probably say, "Hmm, is that right" and go on about their business.

I talked to a couple of RAF gunners I met in town and they told me the Declaration of War was the same. I suppose, if we supply the dash, they are the steady ones—good people to have on our side.

The box from Florida finally arrived so you needn't worry about it any longer. I really didn't expect to see it, ever. Mary [Umholtz] did a beautiful job of packing, especially since it was only suppose to go to Georgia. The cologne bottle broke and a box of bath powder. I brushed "Pink Clover" powder from articles for two hours and we had a lovely scented room for inspection, otherwise everything was in good condition.

My Easter cards were in it so I sent them out anyway. I hope I won't be here to need them next year. I was especially happy to see my watercolor brushes. There is nothing at all like a good brush!

Inspection tomorrow, so this is button polishing tonight. You should see me. I "glisten."

Lots of love,
Big Sis

Charles Street, London
June 9, 1944

Dear Peg [Allison Nightingale],

I've intended to write ever since your last V Mail arrived. I found my way to Albert Hall and am having a field day—as far as concerts go. Sunday night I heard on, the Russian Festival series with [Pytor Ilich] Tchaikovsky's 6th Symphony and Petrouska. Last Wednesday I heard "Lieutenant Kije" by [Sergey Sergeyevich] Prokofiev. It was good, has it been recorded yet?

On Saturday the 10th, the "Promenade Concerts" at Albert Hall starts and will continue until August 12. I will really take advantage of it. My sojourn in South Dakota and Florida makes me appreciate the concerts I can attend.

I also heard from Pete [Edna Peterson]. She said you had a new "Perm," as they say here and looked scrumptious.

You have heard the news, of course, about D-Day. We have waited so long for it and now, no one here is excited. It almost disappointed me. I guess I expected the English to act like Americans but there was not a ripple, at least visible, of excitement.

Tell Bill [Nightingale] "Hello" and I look forward to your letters. The next time you are in O'Connells, you might have an extra hamburger for me. We have regular sessions, when we all describe our favorite food.

Lots of Love,
Frances

*Mail call. Mail kept Frances
connected to friends and family.*

[MEETING THE GOBELS AT THE SAVOY THEATER—HAMPSTEAD HEATH]

Charles Street, London
June 12, 1944

Dear Mother and Dad,

Your package arrived in excellent condition and I was glad to receive it. Thank you. The hand lotion was a welcome sight, my dry hands! It was a bang up job of packing and thanks for the Kleenex and air mail stationary.

I had a very interesting weekend. Saturday I had tickets for the last performance of the Ballet at the Savoy Theater. It was Swan Lake. As I sat waiting for the curtain to go up, suddenly someone stopped beside me and said "Are you alone?" I replied, "Yes," and a very nice English girl [Margaret Gobel] said "Then won't you come and have coffee with me and my sister at intermission?" Of course, I did. Her sister, Betty [Gobel], was a little girl of 14, who is taking ballet. I talked to them then and after the show.

They were both very nice and asked me to visit them in their home. So, of course I shall. They asked me quite a few questions and said I was the first American girl they'd talked to. On my next Sunday off, I shall cautiously find my way there. It was very kind of them.

Sunday morning (day off) I got up and had breakfast at the Red Cross Club with Caroline Chaffee and we actually had a fried egg. It tasted good. You would be amazed to see me enjoying a whole fried egg. But we have them so seldom, it is a treat.

In the afternoon, I attended a piano recital at Wigmore Hall, which was just north of Oxford Street. Without a radio, I take advantage of every opportunity for music. It was an enjoyable concert and as I left, the Manager stopped me and said anytime I wanted to hear a concert I would be admitted without charge.

In the evening, Ann and "Stew" my roommates and I took a bus ride. We decided to go north to Hampstead Heath. It was a lovely spot and after walking over the grounds and hearing part of the Band Concert, we started back. To tell the truth, we went in the wrong direction and walked all over the English countryside.

Soon it started to rain and we finally ended up climbing an iron fence, cutting through someone's garden and at long last we found our bus. Three desperate WACs finally arrived back in civilization. It was funny, especially since the sun started to shine just as we got on the bus. I need a pressing job on the suit.

I mailed Daddy some "Yanks" and "Stars & Stripes." Yank is the Army magazine and "Stars & Stripes" is the Army newspaper. Both of them are good. I thought he would enjoy reading them, especially now that the invasion is on. You'll notice the last "Yank" is entitled "Liberation Issue."

What was the size film at home that Dad couldn't use? Ann has a camera which uses 116. I am glad Emma is drafting all the time now. Someone has to win this war and I am counting on her. It was a good picture of her and the cat; it made me homesick all over again.

Lots of love,
Frances

✖ ✖ ✖

THE GOBELS

Margaret Gobel had red-gold curly hair and the much admired English complexion. It was her sister Betty's birthday, and she had brought her to the ballet as a birthday present. There was standing room only and they stood in the back of the theater for the entire performance. The Savoy Theater was much smaller than the usual American theater. My seat was about three rows from the stage, and I felt intimately involved in the performance, it was so close.

I learned later that Margaret had a heart murmer that kept her out of the British forces, otherwise she would most certainly have been in uniform.

✖ ✖ ✖

Charles Street, London
June 17, 1944

Dear Mother and Dad,

I suppose by now, you have seen the papers, heard the radio and are wondering about it here. We're not to say much about Hitler's newest menace, the V-1, which we call the Buzz Bombs or "doodle-bugs." It is all right and you are not to worry about me for an instant. They take the best possible care of us and I try to use my good sense when ever possible.

I sent a box to you today. On my day off, I stopped at Thomas Goode & Company to look at the china. Some of the pieces were beautiful, of course it is all Pre-War, and nothing is being made now. The two Minton bowls are for Mother, the plate also Minton, is for Grandmother. The small box with rose buds is for me, I am sending it home for safekeeping. The saucer is for Emma. The box was packed at the Company and I hope it will arrive safely.

I sent Peg, four Spode Serving plates to take care of a long delayed wedding present. I hope she likes them. So many things are off the market and silver is a little too expensive for me.

I have a 24 hour pass and am spending tonight and Sunday in Chingford with Margaret Gobel. They have been very kind to me.

Remember, not a <u>worry</u>
Frances

✖   ✖   ✖

BUZZ BOMBS

On June 12, the first of the flying bombs came over. They were a small pilotless aircraft, a cigar shape with stubby wings. They flew 200 or 300 miles an hour and at an altitude of a few hundred feet. They were filled with large quantities of explosives, had a predetermined course, and a cutoff mechanism that terminated their flight. When the engine stopped, the aircraft went into a steep dive and detonated on impact, causing devastation where it hit.

The news report said that they were falling on southern England, and they were certainly over our heads but we were not allowed to mention London in our letters. They came over at irregular intervals twenty-four hours a day. Sometimes they were spotted and the air-raid siren sounded and sometimes not. We could hear one in the air over our heads going putt-putt-

putt and then suddenly the sound ceased. We learned to hold our breath and count one, two, three. Usually at about the count of twelve we heard the sound of the blast and then started to breathe again. We were told that if we heard the engine cut off, the bomb would always glide past us, but it was the ones we did not hear that were dangerous. I'm sure that this was true, but tell it to your nervous system!

We simply lived with them. We were ordered to carry our helmets with us everywhere, and we did. After two months in England we were well aware of the destruction caused by flying glass. After I determined that I could remove a stocking and use it as a tourniquet, I felt easier.

We had been standing reveille in the street in front of our billet every morning but one of the companies had several WACs wounded by a buzz bomb, so the practice ceased. They received Purple Hearts.

I attended several of the Promenade Concerts at Albert Hall. One night the air-raid siren sounded and in a few minutes I heard the familiar putt-putt-putt overhead. I looked up and saw the entire dome of the hall was made of glass. I shivered at the thought of what a disaster it would be if the V-1 hit. However, the buzz bomb flew on, and the concert continued without missing a note.

GOBELS—CHINGFORD

The Gobels were very kind to me, inviting me to their home in the suburb of Chingford, which was in north London and near Epping Forest. I went there first with Margaret; she came into London and took me out to Chingford. I returned alone after being put on the right bus. The second time I went there with a girl in the Canadian Forces. I believe she was a cousin of Margaret's. She picked me up at Charles Street, and we spent several hours there on Sunday.

Later I went alone. If we had a twenty-four-hour pass we were allowed to draw rations from the mess hall when we visited an English family. The cooks let us select what we wanted, so I usually took tea, sugar, and canned fruit, especially grapefruit. The English were very strictly rationed, so the extra tea and sugar were a help. Margaret said that they had not tasted grapefruit since the start of the war.

Margaret's father was a contractor and worked in the city. This is the small section that contained the law courts, financial firms, and other related companies. The Gobels had two cars, a very small one that they used and a larger one that was up on blocks in the garage. It *didn't look very large to me but I realized that it must have been a luxury model. Sizes were so different in many things between England and the United States.*

Her father had been able to obtain bricks and had built a brick shelter in their living room, with four single bunk beds. They slept there at night. This was truly a luxury because they were safe from falling debris but were still comfortable at home. They had been through a great deal of bombing, and Margaret slept in coveralls instead of night clothes, just in case.

They always had typical English tea, which was poured into a cup at the same time the milk was poured. It took two hands, tea in one and heated milk in the other. Never having had tea with anything except sugar or lemon, it was different for me but I liked it. That was the only way I had tea all of the time I was in England, and it was very good.

KITCHEN POLICE

In London, the WAC mess hall was in an English basement (one half below ground and one half above) under the headquarters building where I worked. It was a large dining room filled with tables. The hall leading to it where we stood in line had wooden plate racks for the china just inside the door to the dining room.

When I was on KP I walked from Charles Street, wearing my green-striped fatigue dress, light sweater, fatigue hat, and utility coat. We arrived a little while before breakfast. We served ourselves, and there was a very strict rule that we ate everything we took, nothing edible

went into the garbage. Jam and jelly were always put directly on the bread. In the summer of 1944, the British were very conscious of the fact that a great part of their food, and all of ours, came in on ships that ran the U-boat gauntlet, so there was no nonsense about waste.

After breakfast the dishes were washed, the floor mopped and the tables reset with sugar, salt, and pepper. At other stations we were usually near enough to our billet to rest there for a little while during the day. However, in London it was too far to go back and forth. So, on KP as at work, we arrived before breakfast and stayed until after the evening meal. It was not hard work but very wearying.

A WAC in the green-striped fatigue dress that was worn for KP duty.

The cooks were very pleasant, and Lieutenant White, the mess officer, was tops. One of the cooks always had a flower tucked in her cap over the ear. It was a cheery note.

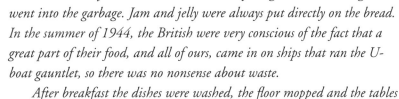

[VISIT TO THE GOBELS]

Charles Street, London
Middle of June, 1944

Dear Mother,

The box came yesterday in fine shape, not even a dent on the corners. Thanks so much. I should have enough Kleenex and Tussy to last awhile. Thank Dad for the pocket knife, it is really sharp and I did need it. Everyone in my room says to tell you the candy is delicious, and it was. The divinity was as soft and fresh as if it had just been made. Mary and Roberta [Harrison] wrote me from Florida praising the Angel Food Cake you sent to them to the skies. I hope you will meet them one day. Roberta even gave me a scolding for not writing you. Doesn't she know the mail was held up? It sounded just like Roberta.

Saturday, I had KP. It was about as usual. They are very nice to us here in the Mess Hall, even though it is a long day. We have excellent food, much better than I had expected. But when I get back home you can put me on a diet of cheese, eggs, fresh vegetables and fruit. I'll ask for nothing more.

Sunday, I went to visit Margaret Gobel, the English girl who introduced herself to me at the ballet. We had a good time. We walked around the town, saw their garden (they have never heard of popcorn). Mrs. Gobel cooked a lovely supper. I had Yorkshire pudding with the beef roast for the first time. I've heard about it and it was good. She cooks her new peas with a sprig of mint; it gave a delicious flavor to them.

We listened to the radio and then I left. They gave me a bouquet of roses from the garden. I can't imagine a nicer family. They have a son in the Army; Margaret tried to join but was rejected on the physical. They told me to consider that my home while I was in England. It was such a warm welcome.

I'll certainly go again; it really made me feel good. We meet some people in London, a big city of course, who aren't especially glad to see us. I believe the average Englishman is like Margaret. They would like to know us, if they only knew how to go about it.

That is most of the news, things are about the same. We do settle down into a routine when the Army leaves us in one place long enough.

Thank you for the Comics. I always enjoy "Blondie." How is Emma coming with the sweater? Winter is coming you know.

Love,
Frances

P.S. You might send me some soap—P&G or Swan. We get one cake of toilet soap every 2 weeks, but I need something for laundry.

Thanks
F.

Charles Street, London
End of June, 1944

Dear Emma,

The writing paper came in the mail last night and I have an idea that you are the one to thank, any way I am grateful. It has been a long time since I've seen paper as nice as that. Congratulations now that you are back at work and drafting full time.

I heard from Peg yesterday. She does a good job of keeping me informed about Chicago. She blithely asked me to send her some Irish linen if I found any, for Bill wanted her to have some. Doesn't she know there is a War on? There is nothing I'd like to do more, except for the fact, I can't buy one single square inch of cloth—it is all rationed.

Last Thursday was my day off and I went out to Richmond, a suburb of London, with a couple of my roommates. We poked through a couple of antique shops and I came out with dirty hands. The things I'd like to buy on my PFC salary!

I hope my letters are coming thru now. Yours have been very slow but I knew that there was a mail tie-up. I am enclosing a few English coins so you will know what I mean. A six-pence, a penny, half penny (or ha'penny, as they say) and a farthing (¼ of a penny).

Caroline says, the custom is to alternate the facings of the monarch on the coins. Victoria is looking left—Edward to the right—George V to the left—but when we got to George VI, he thought his left profile was the best!

If perchance you run across some Nescafe (instant coffee) send me a couple of cans. It makes much better coffee than we usually get and I am still a "coffee fiend."

Lots of love,
Sis

P.S. Could you put in a couple of paint rags if Mother has some, cotton if possible? Also a couple of kneaded rubber erasers, if attainable they certainly aren't here.

Thanks loads, squirt.
F

[SKETCHES AT THE RED CROSS—PEWTER PITCHER]

Cpl Frances DeBra
A-514210 WAC Det
G-3 Sec HQ COMD ETOUSA
APO #887
c/o PM New York, NY
Charles Street, London
July 5, 1944

Dear Dad and Mother,

Now you can see I've been promoted. One of the Army PFCs is a T/5 but you can call me Corporal. Lee [Noyes], one of the fellows in the next room at work, is a T/4 and gave me a lovely set of stripes. It is suppose to be good luck for someone else to give you a set. I sewed them on and now I hardly know myself. Stripes, brass buttons, ribbons and what have you. I feel that I fairly "shout" as I walk down the street, but that is the Army.

Sunday I worked, so yesterday was my day off, 4th of July and all. Of course it isn't a holiday here but the Red Cross Club made a celebration of the day. Woodie [Marjory Woodring], a WAC from Kansas, was off too and we fooled around together.

I had breakfast at the Service Women's Red Cross Club. Scones toasted with jam and were they good! I think I like them better than baking powder biscuits and that is saying a great deal. We did a little shopping, sketch books for me and then looked in some second hand book stores on Charing Cross Road. This time I restrained myself.

The cooks in the Mess Hall are wonderful. The Hall was decorated with flags, we had music and fried chicken—not quite as good as Mother's—but we did feel as if the day was celebrated adequately.

After lunch, I sketch a bit at the Red Cross, Woodie acting as model, and then we walked down to Westminster Abbey. She had never been there, and I always like to go again.

Ann and "Stew" were in Windsor on a 24 hour pass, again. They brought each of us an antique when they returned. Caroline, a small silver 17th century box, because she collects them and Hope and me small pewter pitchers. I like mine very much. One of these days I'll have to pack it up and send it to you to keep for me. But now I take it out and look at it every so often.

Our mail has been slow again and I haven't heard from you for several days, but I know I'll have a letter when it does come through. I hope everything is all right.

Of course you have read the news about the Russian Front. We sit around saying "Gosh, do you suppose we could be home by Christmas?" More likely next spring, I imagine. But whenever it is, you will have me on your doorstep for awhile.

Peg says Bill doesn't care to listen to records after 10:30 pm the way we use to do, so she says she tells him, she'll move back with me. "Poor Bill," I know exactly what he is going through.

A [Danville] REPUBLICAN came a couple of days ago that was only 5 weeks old, they eventually catch up with me.

Lots of love,
Frances

P.S. Woodie just dropped in and wants me to say "Hello" for her. She didn't tell me yesterday was her birthday until late last night, but I think she had a good time, so it is all right.

From:
M. Nightingale
3844 Broadway
Chicago, IL
July 17, 1944

Dear Fran,

Spending lunch time as usual listening to music. "Warsaw Concerto" finally came out in Symp-form on Columbia and it is the same one Bill heard in London two years ago almost. My, how we do get around. My latest purchase is Earl Hines "Boogie Woogie on St. Louis Blues." I am saving one for Alice and one for Young—who unexpectedly came to town last night for 10 days. One of those pool things where he isn't permanently assigned and so got another furlough. Nice, huh? Two in three months but of course it took him 8 months to get the first. The clothes situation is terrific, I'm not a 14, too plump, not 16, not fat enough, not 15, not shortwaisted enough, so I am not buying clothes and as I have no shoe coupons, no shoes and we're hunting for a house and will buy it and pay for it like rent. I hate to pay out $35 a month and not get much, so we're looking and hope to move November 15 or so. After election anyway. Six rooms so I can get Mom's furniture all used so you'll get a home to bunk in yet. Also my biscuits are divine. I actually make 'em and they taste de-lish. Write soon about birthday and Christmas.

Peggy

Charles Street, London
July 16, 1944

Dear Emma,

Your postcard came in last night's mail and I know you've had a wonderful vacation. Mamma's package came in the same mail and I think it was one of the nicest boxes I have ever received. Kleenex, cheese and tuna fish, you should have heard the sighs from my roommates. They all love tuna and you know I appreciate the cheese. Also, thanks ever so much for the hose. I was just about to write and request some. So far my GI rayons have been doing very well, but you know—one runner and suddenly you have them in every stocking.

I started knitting a pair of gloves on the Air Field, wailed and lamented for months because they were in the box Mary mailed to me. It finally arrived and I, foolishly, stuck the needles with the knitting inside my helmet. When the first night alert sounded, weeks ago, we grabbed our helmets and raced for the shelter. All of the needles broke in two when I removed them in a hurry. So now instead of green needles, I have bright red English needles to finish knitting the gloves.

We can buy red cherries from push carts now and we do take advantage of it. Any fresh fruit is delicious. Be sure to tell Mamma that I am all in one piece and staying far, far away from the "Buzz Bombs."

Love,
Big Sis

Margaret Nightingale
3844 North Broadway
Chicago, IL
July 18, 1944

Dear Corporal,

Congratulations and all that—I imagine—Can you say what your duties are that give you the uppance or is it a military secret? I started one V-Mail to you yesterday and then rec'd your $2 and will immediately look for film and lipstick. I'll call Phil and Alice and tell them the news and also will write when the package with the china arrives. It sounds wonderful, but you are a goon-child for sending me money. Anytime I can't fix you up, I'll inform you of such but as long as it is the little things in life you want and need. Please give me the pleasure of sending them to you. Also I'll get hold of the TIME and see what they are up to and get the subscription straightened out if possible. They are funny sometimes, but I'll do some double coaxing and we'll see. I'm waiting for Nancy to meet me for lunch. I'm at Helsings on Washington, the new one, so holding a booth is a matter of glaring as usual. Be good and keep well. We're all fine and dandy.

Love,
Peggy

Charles Street, London
July 20, 1944

Dear Peg,

The house sounds wonderful and I'll take you up on the bed, at least for a little while. You may have to lead me around; I'll probably forget what Chicago is like. I know you will like owning a house. Remember the elaborate plans we kept making for the use of your Mother's furniture?

I thought I had told you about my work. I'm in the drafting room of G-3 (Plans and Training) pushing a pencil again. I have finally remained in one spot long enough to have a chance at a rating. Bill can tell you about the "Army."

As to the birthday and Christmas, we always appreciate hard candy. And if you really love me, how about sending a couple of cans of KIWI shoe polish, mahogany. I got some at a North Michigan Men's Store when I was there on furlough. If you can't get KIWI, Esquire is okay. These GIs are hard enough to polish with a good paste and I don't know what I'll do when my present supply runs out.

I can hardly wait to try your biscuits and hint, hint is any of the oatmeal for cookies left. After all, I only got the burnt cookies from the ones you made to send to Bill.

Lots of love,
Fran

Charles Street, London
July 24, 1944

Dear Dad and Mother,

I hope Momma enjoyed her week at Battleground and I'll bet you were glad to see her come back. The place always did fall apart a little when she was gone. I'm glad you sent the popcorn. I'll take it out to Margaret's and we will pop it. She may not care for it but I will. Did Emma enjoy her vacation? I loved the postcard she sent "Hope to see you soon"! Yipe, so do I.

For your information, our "Tin Hats" are the brand new, poke bonnet style helmets. As yet I haven't used mine to wash in but you never can tell. It would be handy.

By the way, I've never received the TIME overseas edition. I've written them several letters but so far "no soap." We see very few late magazines. One of the largest departments stores "Selfridges" actually has on sale the New York Times Newspaper from May 24th. How is that for late news?

The Nescafe makes elegant coffee, if it isn't too much trouble to find, you can send me another jar. Caroline had some cookies from home and last night we had a cup of coffee and cookies.

In case anyone is interested, I could use a couple more shirts like the ones Emma got me, size 13 and about a 28" sleeve. They have been a God send. I often wonder what I'd have done without them.

The snapshots you sent me are honeys and I do like getting the letters. There is nothing like an ocean to make one homesick.

Thanks for the dollar; I am mighty foolish with it.

Lots of love,
Big Sis

P.S. Here they paint their buses red and their fire engines gray! Golly!

Charles Street, London
July 26, 1944

Dear Mother,

How was the Battleground trip? I know you had a nice time, in spite of Daddy's comments about it. Thanks for the picture of you. I really enjoy the snapshots; anything from home is extra nice. It isn't so much the fact that we have to be away from home that bothers us but the fact that we never can tell when we will be able to come back. I'll have to pass up that furlough I would be having about now. Janie [Baranowski] writes that she plans to take hers in the fall when the weather is nicer. She has the right idea. I don't suppose she has exactly enjoyed spending the summer in the heart of New York City.

Margaret, the English girl is on her "Holiday" as they call it. She also sent me a card. They plan to have me out the weekend that she gets back. They have all been very nice to me. I wrote to Peg to send me a lipstick for her. They are very difficult to get here.

The WAC Mess Officer, Lt. White, has given me permission to sketch in the mess hall and kitchen. The other morning I did a small one, of the Lt. and several KPs peeling onions. It was really funny. Just standing near I got enough fumes to cause my eyes to water and the poor onion peelers almost had a knife in one hand and a towel in the other. I have been sketching and enjoying it. The two year layover did no harm after the first rustiness wore off.

I am sleepy now and it is time to go to the shelter. Do you remember our Girl Scouts hike and how I hurt my back sleeping in a pasture? Well, now I know. I could sleep on a rock pile; I only have my doubts about a good bed.

Lots of love, Frances

UPPER RIGHT AND ABOVE: *WACs performing KP duty. Frances received permission from the mess officer to draw the personnel in the mess hall and kitchen.*

✖   ✖   ✖

AIR-RAID SHELTER AT BERKELEY SQUARE

At night, after the buzz bombs started coming over, when the warning siren sounded we went to the shelter. This was located under a multistoried building at the south end of Berkeley Square.

We were only a few blocks from Hyde Park, which had a concentration of ack-ack antiaircraft guns. We were told that we had five minutes from the time the air-raid siren sounded to reach the shelter and be under cover. By that time the guns began to fire and the flack and debris falling from the sky made being outside very dangerous.

When the siren went off, we would hurriedly get out of bed, leaving lovely white sheets, pull our coveralls over our flannel pajamas, don our utility coats, grab our helmets and blankets, and run down three flights of stairs and about a half block to the shelter. By the time we arrived there, my stomach was in knots.

After a few nights of this, we decided it would be better not to get between those lovely sheets and simply make our way down to the shelter at bedtime. It would be months before we slept between sheets and in any sort of comfortable bed as a regular thing.

At the shelter, we slept in about the third basement down. It was a large room with bunks made of vertical steel pipe, and three or four bunk beds stacked one over the other. The beds were constructed of steel ribbons about an inch wide and woven into squares that were about six inches apart. That was it. We slept there, usually with a pillow and our two blankets, but on the bare steel slats.

The overhead lights were on all night as people came and went. How we slept, much less rested any, I'll never know, but we did.

✖   ✖   ✖

Charles Street, London
August 2, 1944

Dear Dad and Mother,

We have had nice weather recently, not especially hot, but warm enough that with a little imagination we can say it is summer. Tell Emma not to forget about the sleeveless sweater she planned to knit for me. I know it is August there, but here I can feel winter coming on. I will be able to use it under my blouse (Suit Coat). The climate is so much damper here and the heating facilities so much less the only thing to do is put on more clothing. The very thing Daddy always preached.

Woodie and I went to a movie tonight. We stopped in at the Rainbow Corner Club. The Red Cross Club on the corner of Piccadilly Circus, you may have heard their radio broadcasts. We both dearly love doughnuts, so we stopped for some of them and coffee. As we were sitting there, a soldier on his way out stopped at the table and said simply, "You can't know how good it is to see an American girl." We smiled and thanked him; he said good night and walked out. He was in fatigues, helmet and very muddy leggings, so I knew he'd been somewhere, probably "classified." But it made me feel very good inside. If the GIs only knew how proud we are of them, I don't believe they would tease us as much. But now and then something like this comes along and I know the whole "she-bang" was worth while. Just as, when the fellows pass us in trucks, wave with a grin and yell "Hi, Yank!" Then I am mighty proud of my uniform.

Time to be ambling down toward the Shelter.

Much love,
Big Sis

Charles Street, London
August 7, 1944

Dear Mother and Dad,

I received another ribbon today, the Good Conduct Medal (red and white ribbon). This, with my WAAC Service Ribbon, and the European Theater of Operations ribbon, I have quite a row across my chest. To tell the truth I feel a bit sheepish about wearing them. Decorations are always associated with something really important and it is a cinch I haven't done much yet.

I suppose it is all right but when you see some of the fellows who have actually been in all sorts of combat and are minus practically all insignia, it gives me a peculiar feeling.

While reading "Yank" this morning, I came across an item about how people feel in the States. In their opinion, the War must seem practically over. I wish it were! But from our point of view, they shouldn't pick up their chips quite so soon. We can see how slowly the miles go by and I can imagine how a fellow at the Front feels.

Wee, I am sounding off as usual, but I keep thinking back to my furlough and the opinions I heard expressed then. Not that I want to see anyone at home deprived of anything but they certainly have no idea of what the War really is. When I think that it could have been me sitting there, too, I feel pretty grateful. This has been a painful and boring experience for me but I wouldn't have missed it.

The Gobels have invited me for the weekend. I go out about 7pm and stay until tomorrow night. Margaret has had her Holiday and her Mother and sister are on one now. So I'll see her and her father. They certainly are nice to me.

Thank you for the absentee ballot application card. I will return it immediately. And I will be looking for the box with the Birthday cake. I won't care if it is as hard as a rock, it will be eaten just the same. I've had an Angel Food Cake for my birthday ever since I can remember. This is no time to spoil a record.

Lots of love,
Frances

P.S. Have you written TIME? I think about not having the magazine, and I see red. They make me mad.

F.

Charles Street, London
August 13, 1944

Dear Emma,

It was a nice weekend. I went out to the Gobel's directly from work and they waited Tea for me. Tea in England is a very flexible meal, anytime after 2 pm.

Mr. Gobel started work on his greenhouse and Margaret and I took a walk. We climbed to the top of Chingford Mount and I could look down on London and see St. Paul's Cathedral away in the distance. It does not become dark until 10 pm here, so we had all evening.

I did enjoy myself immensely. When Margaret found out my birthday was coming she promptly invited me for the weekend again.

Tonight Woodie and I intend to try a Polish Restaurant up on Oxford Street. I really should have Janie along.

I hope your coming vacation or "Holiday" is everything you hope. I am very proud of you and your work. I always mention whenever possible, "Now, my sister is working for Allisons. Oh, yes drafting."

Love,
Big Sis

P.S. Tell Dad that I received my first overseas edition of TIME yesterday. It was July 24.

✖　✖　✖

OVERSEAS TIME *MAGAZINE*

My overseas Time *was a pony edition printed especially for the members of the U.S. Armed Forces overseas. It had about thirty-four pages and included almost all of the usual departments. It measured 8¾ inches by 6⅛ inches, was folded lengthwise, and came by first-class air mail in a long envelope. I felt I had a window on the world that included many aspects that were missing from our military publications.*

✖　✖　✖

Charles Street, London
August 18, 1944

Dear Dad and Mother,

Your letter came saying the china arrived safely, so that is one thing off my mind. I mailed a parcel from the Red Cross today. It contained my iron, which I am sending back since the current here is 220 volt. With it is a box labeled souvenirs which contains a little of <u>everything</u>.

The pewter pitcher from Windsor, two silver spoons, my drawing set and slide rule, a good many gallery postcards of paintings I would be seeing if the museums were open. Also a large map of London.

They tell me I have a package waiting in the mail room. I wonder whether it is from you or Jane. She is sending me more vitamins. I should be in good health since Woodie sees that I take them faithfully.

Last weekend at the Gobels I helped pick raspberries and looked over the garden in general. I think Mr. Gobel is as proud of his garden as Daddy is of his chickens. They are always interested in the things we grow in the States.

The beans were ripe and we had some for dinner. I have never seen such beans. They climb on a string to about 6 feet, grow to be 6 inches long and have a beautiful scarlet bloom. I thought they were flowers until Margaret started to pick the beans. They are sliced into strips and the taste is very good but they are very different from ours.

Mr. Gobel gave me a handful of seed. He says they'll be all right for next spring. If I don't have a chance to send them home they will be in my duffle bag. Golly, what beans!

I am glad you decided not to sell the north lot. I have always liked that land around the house. I may not have gotten around to saying it but I have always intended for you to have the War Bonds that are in Dad's and my name. It is certainly little enough for everything you have given me. They are yours, to cash in or keep as you see fit.

Lots of love,
Big Sis

Moved to Park Street, London
August 22, 1944

Dear Mother and Dad,

Last week we were unusually busy. On Monday I had KP, Wednesday was my day off so Woodie and I went sightseeing. Walking up Fleet Street to St. Paul's Cathedral, we passed the Cheshire Cheese Tavern built in 1667 and the favorite haunt of Dr. Johnson and Dickens. It was about 12:30 and we decided to stop in for lunch which had an excellent roast beef and Yorkshire Pudding.

At St. Paul's we climbed to the Whispering Gallery and on to the Stone Gallery. From there you can see all of London and the Thames River spread out before you. It was a beautiful day and a perfect spot to view the City.

Thursday and Friday we packed up and moved to a new Billet a few blocks away. Now we are on the 5th floor and it is some climb.

Saturday night, I took Margaret to see "The Marriage of Figaro" by the Sadlers Wells Opera Company. It was sung in English and very good. She has a brother named Bill, about 20 years old, who is a dispatch rider for the British Army. He was home on leave and came along with us.

I went home with them since I had a 24 hour pass. The first thing, yesterday morning, Margaret opened her eyes and said, "Many Happy returns of the Day" then handed me a package. It was a book by one of her favorite authors. This was followed by the morning cup of tea in bed.

We have had lovely weather for the past week, but yesterday it rained. So most of the time was spent indoors. We played Snooker (pool), darts and they tried to explain Cricket to me.

For tea there was a Birthday Cake, a square one with a light and dark layer with chocolate icing and candles. In this land of rationing, this is a rarity!

When I was ready to leave, I was "bumped" an old English custom. Instead of spanking, you are picked up by the shoulders and feet, and then your rear extremity is bumped on the floor. Since I was a guest, I was bumped on a cushion.

After I got back to the billet, Woodie gave me a good old United States spanking. So it was a fine Birthday.

You mentioned canning a bushel of peaches, they say "bottling" here. I found that peaches are 10 shillings ($2) a peach, a bushel would be worth a small fortune.

Thanks for seeing about the sweater because winter is definitely on the way.

Love,
Frances

✖   ✖   ✖

PARK STREET

On Charles Street we billeted in town houses, but on Park Street it was more of a mansion. There were a number of WACs who had been billeted there all summer. This was also nearer Grosvenor Square where I worked. Of course, I saw only a small part of the new place, but the first floor (second floor to us) had an elegant drawing room that ran the length of the house and had street-side windows along one wall. It was filled with army cots. There was a beautiful and large mirror over the mantel, and I could only speculate about it and the air raids. Later, Lee, whom I roomed with in Paris, said she lived there and they did not go to a shelter all summer, simply stayed in bed.

The billet on Charles Street, London.

The new room for Caroline and me was up under the eaves, a garret. Quite nice—I am sure it must have been servants' quarters. We were there only about ten days before we went to France.

✖   ✖   ✖

Park Street, London
August 25, 1944

Dear Dad and Mother,

You are angels, both of you, the money order came today and it was most welcome. In other words, I needed it.

The packages with the cake arrived last Tuesday. It missed my birthday by a mere two days! You should have heard my roommates' cries of delight. The cake was delicious and in very good condition, frosting and all. Emma is a good packer. Needless to say the walnuts, lemon and butterscotch drops also hit the spot. Hard candy is appreciated. We get candy bars at the PX, four per week in our ration.

Thank you for sending the sweater, I know I'll be using it soon. A parcel is in the mail containing the book Margaret gave me, two small art books that Woodie found somewhere and the package of beans from Mr. Gobel. They are called "Scarlet Runners." He says they grow 6 feet tall and will need some sort of support. I hope I will be home to help you plant them.

A letter from Roberta and she is on the list for overseas after a month of telegraphic training. Today, on my way back to the billet, I met "Tommie" the WAC that I worked with at the Hangar in Florida. She has been in England for a couple of months and was in London for a few hours.

I have to get ready for inspection tomorrow. Woodie was on KP today, oh her aching back! Thanks for the Birthday present. You are mighty nice people.

Lots of love,
Big Sis

✖   ✖   ✖

CANDY RATION

Our candy ration consisted of very peculiar English brands. We knew the British had been at war for a long while, and everything produced was reduced in quality but they were odd. "Chuckles," a jelly type candy, is impressed in my memory and the others defy description. Once in a great while we would get a Three Musketeers, but nothing like Hershey Bars, Milky Way, Clark Bars, or Butterfingers.

In fact it was a puzzle to me why I had a craving for them. Then it dawned on me that there was very little that was sweet in our diets, dessert was usually a half cup of canned fruit cocktail, and I suppose I felt the need for something really sweet.

✖   ✖   ✖

Park Street, London
August 27, 1944

Dear Peg,

Your package arrived yesterday in fine shape. Thanks a lot. I know the English girl will love her lipstick and the film is very gratefully received.

So thank Pete, Park [Helen Parker] and Bill for me. Tell Bill I'll be able to get the shillings, six pence and half crown but no crowns, they have long since disappeared, American coin collectors.

About the shoe polish, just send a couple of tins of KIWI mahogany. I have my own shoe kit but it is impossible to find that shade of polish here.

I saw "LaBohome" last night, sung by the Sadlers Wells Opera Company. It was good and I enjoyed it. I wish you could have heard it also. I am still music starved. I can hardly imagine what it would be like to get dressed in the morning to the sound of the "Breakfast Club" again.

We will attend the Service at St. Paul's Cathedral this evening. I enjoyed the one at Westminster Abbey very much. You should have heard the Organ. Wow, cold chills up and down my spine.

Mother sent me an Angel Food Cake for my birthday and it was only two days late. Can you imagine? I had no idea that she would send one. But we couldn't have my first birthday without one, so, icing and everything.

Love,
Fran

✖   ✖   ✖

*Frances titled this sketch
"London 'Fatigues.'"*

"ENGLISH FRIENDS"
FORTY-EIGHT-HOUR PASS

*When I had occasion to reach Margaret Gobel by phone, there was a special procedure
to follow. The public phones in England had a button, a little like the one on the CB radio. I
talked and then pushed the button so that I could hear her, a little confusing for an American.*

*Toward the end of August we expected to move to France, but for a few days between
regular work and the time the planes were scheduled, it was possible to get a forty-eight-hour
pass. I knew Margaret was on holiday at Canvey Island, and she had told me to phone her if I
could get away.*

*I called and she gave me the directions for getting to Canvey. This was the start of my
only solo experience with the British railways. I went by Underground to the Fenchurch Street
Station, which was in East London and just north of the Tower of London. From there on,
kind people literally passed me from hand to hand.*

*While waiting in a long line for my railway ticket, a lady came up to me and pointed
out a vacant ticket window, telling me that I was "Forces," so I had my ticket very shortly.
In Britain, everyone queued, lined up for everything, and it was the very worst breach of
manners to break into a queue!*

*After being directed to the right train, which of course had compartments, other kind
souls told me what to do with my ticket and about the conductor. Then someone else alerted
me when we reached the station at Canvey.*

Canvey Island was a small island in the mouth of the River Thames and only a short distance from the north shore of the river. Margaret met me at the train and we walked to her aunt's house. The island was small enough that it was possible to walk everywhere.

Her aunt, Mrs. Wyatt, was Margaret's father's sister, and she was very kind to me. I received a Christmas card from her for many years after the war.

Her daughter, Margaret's cousin Eileen Wyatt, was there also. The three of us slept in a large bed on a feather tick up under a slanted roof. It was very comfortable.

Margaret took me to "South End." It was a few miles away and very near the mouth of the Thames. We took the train again to reach it. It was a typical British resort spot. We went into a milk bar for some refreshment. Until then I had been drinking tea the English way. It was very good, and I felt "when in Rome." Also one time at her home Margaret had offered to make me a cup of coffee and reached up on the shelf for a dark brown bottle of liquid labeled Camp Coffee. I refused and drank tea. But at this time it was late August and cold. I spent most of the summer in England shivering. So, I ordered coffee at the milk bar. The proprietor put the coffee in an electric blender and shook it up like a milk shake and then poured it out for me pale and frothy. I have always been a strong black coffee drinker! Outside I remarked about it to Margaret, and she said, "They shake everything up in a milk bar." They certainly did.

In the evening we went to a place where a dance was being held, something like a town hall. Eileen was there with "Long George," a very nice chap, who was there on leave. All ages of people were at the dance, and everyone seemed to have a good time.

The next day we walked over the island, visited the beach, and the church. I was struck by the sight of so many tombstones in the churchyard of young men in their late teens. It was motorcycle accidents, Margaret said. Speed and the narrow, winding roads were to blame.

Margaret loved Canvey; after the war she married and lived there. On Sunday afternoon they placed me on the train, and I reversed my journey back to London and the billet on Park Street.

After I returned, we packed the contents of the drafting room and sent it on ahead. I left several lovely large drawings in the paper cabinet, expecting that in France we would have the same furniture. Later, I discovered that all items such as drafting tables, etc. went to a huge supply depot, and articles and furniture that we needed were drawn from that supply.

To tell the truth, just about the time I left the army, its systems and methods of operation started to make sense to me.

✗   ✗   ✗

9

SOMEWHERE IN FRANCE

SOMEWHERE IN FRANCE
CROSSING THE CHANNEL

Our English money was changed to French currency and our orders were "to proceed to Headquarters Com Z (forward) and take station there." On the first of September we were all packed and in our battle dress—helmet with liner, long underwear, woolen socks and field boots, wool shirts, field jacket and pants with felt liners, and leggings. This was topped off with a gas mask and musette bag. The duffel bag, fully packed, was with us.

We were driven in trucks out to the air field, prepared to take a flight over the Channel. It was my first experience with a plane flight. As it happened, the weather was not favorable and the air field was blanketed with fog.

In the last few days, we had seen the fog rolling in frequently, so in some ways we were glad to leave. A blackout combined with fog is beyond belief. I stayed inside.

We were trucked back to our recent billet for the night and then on the second of September, back to the air field and into the C-47s. These cargo planes had a row of bench type seats, lined up along the sides.

There were nine planeloads on our orders. I was in Plane #4 with Captain Florence Clark, the G-3 Administrative Officer in charge, and thirteen WACs of G-3, plus five others from the Signal Corps.

Lee Noyes, the WAC I had become friendly with on KP, was in Plane #5, so we had spent most of the previous day at the air field getting acquainted. She was with the Judge Advocate Section.

It was a short flight; my chief emotion was overwhelming thankfulness that I did not have to cross the English Channel in a boat!

IN CAMP AT VALOGNES

We landed at an air field near Cherbourg. The desolation and ruin of the harbor and countryside was an awesome sight. We rode in army trucks to the camp at Valognes. This was the forward echelon. We were all under canvas, the sleeping quarters, the mess tent, and of course the drafting room.

There was a luminous quality to the air caused by the mist that simply hung there suspended all of the time. When I went to bed, I only removed my shoes, and they were stowed safely away in my closed duffel bag. Otherwise they would have been covered with mildew by morning.

Our tents for sleeping contained five regular folding army cots, which were placed upon a wooden palette about four inches high, and just slightly larger than our cots. To keep reasonably warm, I placed my shelter half on the cot, arranged the blankets very carefully, and folded the rest of the shelter half over the top. This was the first and only occasion I had to use the shelter half that I carried with me all the time I was overseas. This time it kept the damp cold from the underside of the cot and did help.

To tell the truth, I had three blankets. We brought two wool army blankets with us from the States, and at sometime in the summer of sleeping in the shelter, I managed to acquire a grey English blanket from the supply room. It was a treasure, and I kept possession of it until we finally were ready to sail for home.

There was a latrine tent, and I used my steel helmet to hold water for washing but we did precious little bathing that week in camp.

The mess line was outside, and we ate our meals sitting on benches in tents. The honey bees buzzed around the orange marmalade served in the morning. We watched to be sure we didn't get a mouthful of bees.

We did very little drafting work under those conditions, but the man I replaced in London and who came to the forward echelon was there. He obtained a map case for me in which I carried my watercolors and sketchbooks from then on. He had also acquired a Thompson submachine gun, so the drafting room felt safe.

It was still light in the evenings, so one night after supper, Lee and I with a couple of men from her section walked a little ways from camp to see some of the countryside, especially the hedgerows. We had read about them and understood that they were unbelievable. They were! The fields were quite small, and they were bordered with mounds of earth built up about five or six feet tall. On the top of this, hedges grew up and up, a thick and matted barrier not to *be penetrated by livestock or anything. There was a gate across the gap that made an opening for the field. I wondered how on earth the crops received enough sunlight, but I suppose they did.*

While we were strolling down the road, I became increasingly uncomfortable. My intestines churned and quivered—diarrhea. Thinking the camp was an impossible distance away, I continued walking and carrying on a conversation. At long last we reached our tent area, and Lee and I said good-bye and went in a direct line to the latrine. She had been in the same condition. The next day, we found that our companions had also suffered the same pangs.

The culprit turned out to be the chicken à la king of the evening meal. Everyone was sick

to some degree, at least everyone who had consumed the chicken.

MPs escorted WACs down the hill to the latrine all night. As we staggered out of the tent, a kind arm came out of the darkness to support us down the hill, waited, and then helped us back to the tent. That's how we found out the MP guards were stationed around our tent area. Wonderful—those MPs!

By the next day we were pretty well recovered and it was a laughable matter—the entire camp with "the GIs."

✕   ✕   ✕

Frances and Lee Noyes in the camp at Valognes, France. Referring to this photo in a later letter, Frances wrote, "I have my eyes closed as usual, and don't be alarmed I was wearing almost all the clothing I owned. I am not quite that pudgy."

[IN CAMP AT VALOGNES, CHERBOURG PENNISULA SOMEWHERE IN FRANCE]

September 4, 1944

Dear Mother and Dad,

Moved again, as you see. I can hardly believe that I am here. If Daddy wanted a picture of me in my "sun bonnet," he should see me struggle with the lacing on my leggings. That is really "grim" as Margaret [Gobel] would say. We wear woolen shirts, long underwear, pants, leggings and jackets. It is quite an out fit and I feel exactly like an overstuffed Teddy Bear.

Our section of France is just as damp as England was and I do mean damp. At least half of the time there is a very fine mist in the air.

We live in a tent, big affairs with five WACs to a tent, and sleeping on camp cots. I sleep very well. I suppose my weeks in the shelter prepared me. Now, I roll up in a couple of blankets with ease. After the War, a really good mattress will be wasted on me.

Our food is good. There is an outdoor mess line and we eat sitting on benches in tents. My struggle is always with the mess kit. It has too many parts. I arrange it one way and then change my system entirely for the next meal. It requires a knack.

I managed to get a 48 hour Pass to see Margaret. She was visiting her Aunt and a cousin. They live on a small island in the mouth of the Thames River. It was a very lovely spot.

We walked along the sea wall and the beaches. The beaches at Canvey are made of cockleshells. The wind whips down over the island constantly.

They took me to an English dance the first night. Then to South End, a sort of resort town a little way from there.

No people could have been nicer to me. I'll never forget it. I told Margaret what Daddy said about the watermelon. She said if she ever did get to visit Canada, she would drop in on me. I consider that a promise.

I have about run down. My pad of paper is so damp; the pen has to be pushed across it. I hope you can read it. Please keep on sending me Kleenex. I can tell by my dripping nose that I'll need it.

Lots of love,
Frances

10

PARIS

PARIS

Once again, on September 9, we packed up to move, this time to set up American Army Headquarters in Paris. This was just two weeks after the liberation of the city. G-3 Section was very fortunate, we flew to Paris. There was a very fine T square about four feet long that I could not bear to leave behind in the woods, so I took it with me. Besides the gas mask, musette bag, and map case, I had a T square over my shoulder. No one objected, and we did need it when we arrived in the new quarters because we were very ill equipped for a time.

On arrival, we were trucked as usual to new living quarters. These were marvelous. The Hotel Windsor-Reynolds was a double hotel at 14 Rue Beaujon. I was in the Windsor. It was a few blocks from the Champs-Élysées and the Arc de Triomphe. The little Square Balzac was in front of it. I was placed on the fourth floor in a room with Gerry Garrison and Mildred Murphy, two WACs also in G-3.

The hotel was fairly new and designed in the art-deco style. The rooms all had lovely private baths. There was one bed in the room and two army cots, an inlaid wood wardrobe, and French doors that opened out onto a small balcony. The regular furnishings had a desk and lamp with a straight chair and two upholstered easy chairs.

We were among the first WACs in the city aside from some in the forward echelon, which may have been there earlier. We were certainly tired and dirty when we arrived. But there was electricity and water, which flowed hot now and then. We were very fortunate, the Metro was not running and only certain parts of the city had electricity.

It was a small elegant hotel. The front desk preceded a lovely lobby with a small salon that contained a grand piano and one of the most beautiful chandeliers I have ever seen. The dining room opened off of the lobby, and the elevator was just past the front desk.

The elevator was not the usual American sort. It had an open wrought-iron art-deco cage. The stairway spiraled up around the elevator cables. Four or five people were a load for it. The operator was a Frenchman, Rene Jensen, who became our friend. He had been in the First World War and had a withered arm. He spoke excellent English. We could always count on him for help and advice. The elevator would ascend and descend slowly, slowly at a snail's pace. It had none of the swoosh and power of modern elevators. This one moved at such a slow rate it left you feeling that you could easily step off and on at will. For a few flights we would take to the stairs, but the elevator was temperamental and at times would be out of service. Then we appreciated it, slow or not.

The orderly room was on the second floor, just off the elevator. In common with many French buildings, the first or ground floor had a lofty elevation, the equivalent of about two ordinary stories.

We ate in the hotel dining room; the regular hotel staff did much of the work. There was a mess line to fill our plates, but the waitresses filled our goblets with coffee and water. I am sure the WAC cooks were used and Lieutenant White was the mess officer, but we used hotel china and cutlery. The only really odd item, there were no cups and saucers. Something must have happened to them because we drank our coffee from thin-footed crystal goblets the entire year that we were there. However, considering the hotel had housed German occupation troops for a long period of time, everything was in good condition.

For the first two or three weeks rations were very slim. The army had moved so swiftly after Normandy that the supplies were behind us. It was the only period of time in the army that I remember leaving an army mess still really hungry. This lasted about ten days until the supplies caught up with us. The men at the front were the primary concern—gasoline, ammunition, and supplies for them had priority.

The second night, we walked down to the Red Cross Club at the Concorde in a blackout, although not as total as those in England, just to have some Red Cross doughnuts. The Red Cross doughnuts in France bore no semblance to what we normally considered a doughnut. I can well understand the old term for them—sinker. As far as I could tell, they were made of flour and water, and then deep fried in fat. There was no yeast and certainly no sugar at all. We were really hungry! It was a pretty good hike down the hill of the Etoile to the Concorde and then back up the Champs-Élysées again.

This was less than two weeks after the Germans had left Paris and burnt vehicles were still along the river with the remains of barricades. There were fresh scars in the bark of the trees along the Seine. All over the city for weeks, the French flag hung proudly from balconies, frequently coupled with the Stars and Stripes. In our drafting room, which was on the fourth floor of the Hotel Majestic, one of the French windows that faced Avenue Kleber had a bullet hole in it.

We wore our field uniforms for several days after we arrived. Gradually we acquired enough equipment to set up a working drafting room. This consisted of Technical Sergeant Frank Martello and me.

For several weeks Frank had been on tenterhooks because his English wife was expecting a child and she had flatly refused to move out of London. He had the worrisome thought of the buzz bombs plus the V-2s, along with his normal concern for her and the baby. Fortunately everything turned out all right and General George S. Eyster gave him a pass back to London after the baby arrived.

Lee Noyes, my new friend, and Lucille Verzano, another WAC in the Judge Advocate Section, came to Paris several days later in a truck convoy. The convoy used the Red Ball Highway, a network of main roads that the army had designated to move supplies to the front. The roads were one way, some going east and some west, and the trucks moved over them twenty-four hours a day. So convoys were simply moved over to the side of the road and stopped whenever the supply trucks came through. It took a day for the WAC convoy to cover the distance from Valognes to Paris. The girls were really tired when they arrived. The first days were pretty unscheduled because there was little work we could do yet, so I was able to meet Lee and direct her to my bathroom for a good bath. She and Lucille were billeted in another hotel.

We walked to the Eiffel Tower one of those days. We could see the tower, but without maps, we had trouble getting to it. The streets started out in the direction of the tower, and then suddenly we would find that we were going in a completely different direction. After many zigs and zags we finally arrived.

Along with a number of other GIs, air corps, and other assorted personnel, we started up the stairs to the first level. This was 190 feet and 300 steps, and even though we were in good condition, the last several flights of stairs were climbed with much huffing and puffing. The view was magnificent.

✖   ✖   ✖

France
September 10, 1944

Dear Emma,

I just received your letter written on my Birthday. Thank you, Sis. It was a nice Birthday. The Gobels saw to that.

Mother said that you had decided to go to Central Normal College for awhile. I know you'll enjoy it and it is a good idea.

They have moved us out of the mud and tents into billets with four walls and a roof. To tell the truth it is quite a relief. I love the out of doors life in the summer but right now winter is too close.

Our billets are quite nice. We are in a Hotel and I am using one of the nicest bathrooms I've had in quite sometime. There is nothing to compare with the first hot bath I had when we got here. I scrapped off the mud and just <u>soaked</u>.

French people are very nice to us. I wish that I could speak the "lingo." We are picking up a few words and phrases and I hope our vocabulary will continue to improve. It is really comical to see me and a couple of French people try to get something straight. By the time I get home I'll be waving my arms to such an extent, it will not be safe to be near me.

I am expecting Lee, a WAC from Minnesota to be in soon. As yet, Woodie [Marjory Woodring] and Caroline Chaffee are billeted somewhere else.

Work is about the same, except, whenever we move it takes time to get set up again. In fact, I arrived here with a T-Square over my shoulder. It is our only one to date. We use what we can until the drawing boards and etc. catch up with us.

I believe I will like France and I am looking forward to letters when our mail finally comes.

Lots of love,
Frances

Hotel Windsor, Paris
September 15, 1944

Dear Mother,

Today is your Birthday and now I am allowed to tell you where I am. The city is perfectly beautiful, in spite of having been taken over from the Germans so recently. I feel certain that later when more places are open and more people return, we will be able to see a little of how it was before the War.

There is a different feeling here. We have always heard how unlike the English, the French were, so to move from London to Paris I can see the contrast. I liked London very much and I am sure I'll like Paris, too.

Frances sitting in front of the Eiffel Tower. Frances was promoted to sergeant while serving in Paris.

There are still signs of Paris having been a recently occupied city. Food is still quite scarce. We are fed in civilian restaurants taken over by the Army. We have a very few fresh vegetables or fruit, but the rest of the food is good. But as far as civilian restaurants, they just aren't. Maybe later I'll have an opportunity to have some real French Onion soup for instance.

We are well taken care of, for our Hotel has lights and we actually had hot water a week ago. Let me tell you, that is a luxury. The city is still strange but the main spots are beginning to look familiar. Several days ago, Lee and I climbed to the first level of the Eiffel Tower over 300 steps! But the view was superb. Maybe someday, I'll be able to see Paris from the very top of the Tower.

Our mail is still delayed. I just received the V-Mail Emma wrote me August 9. But soon I hear it will be straightened out and I hope to get stacks of mail. I am really looking forward to the sweater Emma sent.

A very Happy Birthday Momma, even though it will reach you late. I hope to see you on the next one.

Much love,
Big Sis

✖ ✖ ✖

FRENCH COOKING

During the year I spent in Paris, we were forbidden to eat in civilian restaurants and cafés. This was a matter of necessity. There were great numbers of American troops on duty there with extra buying power to outbid the French people.

Then as the war continued, Paris was the destination for all of the soldiers with a pass or on convalescent leave. They were accommodated at the Red Cross and in the army transient mess halls in the city. The troops would have devoured civilian supplies very quickly.

The same principle held for the regular mess halls. All of our food came from the States unless there was a surplus. There was one surplus. Beets! We had beets in the mess hall every day and sometimes twice a day. Beets have never been my favorite vegetable, but I could eat them. These, however, were simply plain boiled beets, no Harvard beets, or pickled beets, just boiled beets. I continued to tell myself they surely had valuable vitamins and minerals that I needed. The day came, after many months, when I really could not swallow another one.

✖   ✖   ✖

Windsor Hotel, Paris
September 23, 1944

Dear Mother,

I just received your last letter or I would have answered sooner. I know it is late to tell you what I would like for Christmas, but to tell the truth I have no idea. There is nothing in particular that I need. The magazines are wonderful, now that my TIME has caught up with me. I can use a few pairs of hose but no cosmetics because I have nearly enough anyway.

But food, that is different. Here in France, we are not allowed to buy food because of the shortages. We do get a little hungry for American items.

If you can find a fruit cake in a tin, that would be wonderful. Any sort of tined food, nuts, dried fruits, candies (any kind) especially hard candies or mints. Cookies or any sort of food which can be kept and used for snacks.

Frances on the roof of the Hotel Windsor in Paris.

This will probably reach you about October 14 with our mail still tied up. I really don't need any extra money; your birthday present to me came at such a good time because we were on the move. Usually I have plenty.

I received a letter from Margaret Rodney and a birthday card from Virginia Belle, which I will answer.

I'd better finish, so this letter will reach you in time.

Lots of love,
Frances

✖　✖　✖

AIR RAIDS IN PARIS

In the fall at various times, usually at night, the air-raid sirens would sound. We were ordered to go to the basement of the Hotel Windsor. Wearing our utility coats over our flannel pajamas and carrying our helmets, we filed down the steps to wait until the all clear sounded. Blackouts in France could not compare to those in London.

✖　✖　✖

Hotel Windsor, Paris
September 29, 1944

Dear Peg [Allison Nightingale],

I've had two letters from you, so I thought I'd better answer. Our mail was in such a jam for awhile that I became pretty low in spirits but now it is coming through (even though it is from August) and I feel better.

Your news about the house on Fullerton sounds Okay and thanks for your kind invitation concerning the use of house and wardrobe. Who knows, I may have to take you up on it. However, did it ever cross your crazy head that I might not settle down in Chicago after the War, much as I do love the place? I've been away a long time. But at least, I'll make tracks for you as soon as possible. From where I sit, it looks like a long, long time yet. How long I'd hate to guess, but some day!

Paris is still wonderful. It is nearly dark at 7PM, so I have very little time to sightsee in the evening. We saw a Special Service show here last Monday. It starred Fred Astaire and top-notch French acts, including the quintet from the "Hot Club of France." Peg, the guitar player was out of this world. When they played, "What a Lovely Way to Spend an Evening" my toes fairly curled. It was wonderful. All of the acts were good but I would have been happy just to hear the music. I am still starving for music and it has been a month since I've seen a movie. How I will enjoy a radio, when I get home.

The food situation is much better and now our PX is operating. But we still have no hot water, in fact it is not even cold water, it is ice water. The coldest I've ever felt come out of a tap. Someday, I expect the girls to chop me out of the basin with an ice pick. Still we hope.

I solemnly promise not to open the Xmas box even if I have to carry it in the bottom of my duffle bag.

Tell Pete [Edna Peterson] I will take her up on her offer to help me shop after the War. I have almost forgotten how I look in other shoes. I will be completely out of touch.

My English friend wears a 9 ½ stocking, the same size as I do and I know she would love to have some hose.

I did vote, weeks ago, before I left England. I hope that answers a few of your questions. I've about run down now. Your letters mean a lot to me. Tell Bill [Nightingale] "Hello" and take care of yourself.

Much love,
Fran

× × ×

WASHING IN COLD WATER

For weeks we did all of our washing, clothes, hair, and baths in cold water. To wash my hair, I got everything laid out and ready then I washed my hair as quickly as possible, put a towel around it, and sat down with my head between my knees to keep from fainting. The ice cold water caused the blood to flow away from my head. This made me faint, but of course it passed quickly.

Whenever possible, we collected the packages of lemon crystals from the K rations, which were intended for a lemonade drink. We used these to rinse our hair. Hair rinses were nonexistent, and bottles of shampoo few and far between. We also resorted to vinegar from the chemist in England to cut the soap film from our hair.

× × ×

Hotel Windsor, Paris
October 1, 1944

Dear Dad and Mother,

I just received a letter from Jane [Baranowski] saying it had been 24 days since she had a letter from me. I am wondering how long it has been for you. I knew our mail was in a terrific state because Emma's August 9 V-Mail just arrived. Well, at least I hope you know by now that all is well (we even had hot water yesterday and after washing in cold water for weeks, it was absolute luxury).

I want to thank Dad for the foolish money and the clipping about Donald. It seems hard to believe doesn't it—the boys will certainly have some tales to tell when they get back. Just think Donald in the Pacific, Dick in China and me here, it is a small world.

I am enclosing a few franc notes that you might like to see. The franc is worth approximately 2 cents. The 5 and 10 franc notes are French money. The 2 franc one is our own, called "Invasion Money." There are very few coins, so you can imagine what a devilish time we have with change. I can have a billfold bulging with about 85 cents. I usually need an entire table top to make change. English money was a lot heavier but it did seem more substantial.

If you could send me a box containing Kleenex, cough drops, and a jar of Vicks, I'd be most grateful. As yet, I have fought shy of colds—but they are all around me and it is good to have Kleenex and cough drops when you need them.

If you have wondered about the poor quality of my letter paper, it is some that the Germans left behind them and all that I have at present. I do hope you weren't especially worried.

Lots of love,
Big Sis

✖ ✖ ✖

HOTEL MAJESTIC ON AVENUE KLEBER

The offices of our Section G-3 were in the old Hotel Majestic, which was on Avenue Kleber. This avenue radiated out from the Arc de Triomphe in a westerly direction, and the hotel was about two blocks from the Place de la Etoile. The hotel was a large stone building, six stories tall. There was a beautiful wide carved staircase. We were allowed in the lobby and front elevator here. The elevator was fairly small, so we usually walked up the stairs.

We often saw General James Gavin of the Eighty-second Airborne Division. He always took the stairs two at a time and had only one aide to accompany him. He was a very young looking general, unusual in those days.

General Benjamin Davis, the first black general, was also seen on the stairs many times, accompanied by a solitary aide. This impressed us, since we were always skeptical of an excessive show of "Brass."

Our drafting room was on the fourth floor, and the French windows faced Avenue Kleber. They were all beautiful French rooms, high ceilings, panels of red damask on the walls, and beautiful woodwork. Our furnishings were the usual drafting tables, tall stools, a coat rack, straight chairs, and a filing cabinet. A large part of my work involved a Leroy Set, a mechanical system of lettering.

We found stacks of German printing and realized that the German propaganda center had been in this building. The Gestapo headquarters was in the next block, on the Rue de la Perouse, nearer the Etoile and was a windowless building of cement blocks, three or four stories tall. We shuddered slightly as we passed it daily on our way to work.

Our billet, the Windsor Hotel, was about three blocks on the east side of the Champs-Élysées, and the Hotel Majestic was about three blocks past the Champs-Élysées to the west. We crossed the Champs about two blocks below the Arc de Triomphe. We walked the six blocks to work in the morning, back to the Windsor for the noon meal, and then back to the Majestic for the afternoon.

✖   ✖   ✖

Windsor Hotel, Paris

October 4, 1944

Dear Dad and Mother,

The first package arrived, it seems months that I have been waiting. The sweater is simply wonderful. I have been pretty cold at work, no heat of course. I can't work in my blouse (Army for jacket) so I've used my long sleeved GI sweater over the shirt. Now with the new sleeveless sweater and the GI both, I'm quite comfortable. Thank you.

The Kleenex arrived at a most opportune time. I was very nearly out. You know I will enjoy the coffee, cheese and film. Gerry, one of my roommates and I bought a hot plate. I still have some of the coffee you sent me in London and we make coffee nearly every evening. In this weather, with no heat, a hot cup is about the only thing we have to warm us up.

Yesterday noon, we had bean soup for lunch. It was delicious. It reminded me of Mama's "Thursday Beans." The French cooks we have are quite good even with our "c" rations. I can well see how good they would be in normal times.

I spent most of last evening just puttering around, ironed a shirt, shined shoes and started a mystery story. Tonight, I'll go with Lee to her hotel for awhile. I have never seen it. Tomorrow is my day off and I hope to see a little more of Paris. The Metro still does not run on Sunday, but we expect it to soon.

I just came back from Mail Call. The letter from Dad, containing a "Foolish Dollar" said you had been without mail from me for 3 weeks. I was afraid of that, but I hope the letters catch up soon. I am very well, so I hope you weren't too worried.

Much love,
Frances

✖   ✖   ✖

DRAFTING ROOM

It was cold in the drafting room. Sometimes without heat those huge stone buildings would be colder than the air outside. My hands were so cold sometimes that they were stiff. The light was a bare bulb that hung from the ceiling just over my drafting board. So I would cup my hands around the light until they were warm, go back to work until they were really cold again, and then repeat the procedure.

MARIGNY THEATER

The Marigny Theater, on the Avenue Marigny, was just off the Champs-Élysées and a little north of the Place de la Concorde. This was an Allied Entertainment Theater that brought in popular bands, variety shows, and plays from the States and England and also featured local French talent. I saw the Sadler's Wells Ballet from London dance there and heard Glenn Miller's band.

There were tickets printed with the date, and these could be obtained free of charge from the orderly room. We also had a Northwest African Air Force garrison cinema on the Champs-Élysées. It was only a few blocks from our billet. The uniform you wore was your admission ticket. We saw American films there. Sometimes we went to the French movie houses and saw American movies with the dialogue dubbed in French!

✖　　✖　　✖

Hotel Windsor, Paris
October 16, 1944

Dear Dad and Mother,

I've been a little slow keeping you up on the news, but some how everything has settled down into a rather sluggish routine. The rainy season for Paris has begun. We all have colds, just enough to make us sore and aching. I have been dragging around and now I find myself with a good case of the "sniffles." At that, I have fared so much better than a good many of the girls that I can't complain. Maybe the vitamins that I have taken so long for Janie has something to do with it. Anyway the hot plate and a hot cup of coffee at night, really helps out.

After the amount of rain we've had the last few weeks, I'd say London has nothing on Paris, as far as humidity is concerned.

More WACs are arriving everyday. The other evening, as we came back, we found the stairway up to the Orderly Room jammed with tired muddy girls. Most of them now are coming directly from the States and they are really worn out when they get to our Hotel.

So far everyday I've had off, it has rained. My sightseeing of Paris has been curtailed. The Metro does run everyday now and helps us cover more territory.

Yesterday morning (Sunday) Lee and I wanted to see Sacre-Coeur in Mont Marte, but too much rain. We would have been drenched. So I stayed at the Hotel and did odds and ends.

In Mother's last letter, she said you hadn't heard I'd received the sweater. I hope by now you'll have my letter about it. I did get the box and I think the sweater is wonderful. It is just right and has been much admired.

The enclosed picture is one I had made months ago in London. It is a matter of months for almost any photographic work here. I thought you might like it.

Love,
Frances

Hotel Windsor, Paris
October 24, 1944

Dear Dad and Mother,

The package containing the shirt finally arrived today. Beside the package I had five letters. The box was in fairly good shape, the shirt fine (thanks to Emma), the Kleenex, candy, "Blondie" strips and cheese, greatly appreciated. I did grin when I saw the tissue because I have had a drippy nose for weeks and my supply of Kleenex was at rock bottom.

Peg wrote a fine letter, she always rambles on in the same way she talks. I wrote at one time asking when I could receive some oatmeal cookies. I always watched her make them to send to Bill and she would only let me eat the very, very black ones that were burnt beyond recognition. In this letter she said Bill planned to make cookies for me soon. So, Peg evidently picked out the right sort of man.

They are still looking for a house to buy. She mentioned one in La Grange that they liked. She added that they had an extra bedroom on the first floor for me, because I'd been complaining about the stairs I have to climb here. She seems to have my life planned out for me after the War.

You talk of chickens and eggs then Janie tells me about the Southern Fried chicken dinners that she has there in New York.

I haven't had a "shell egg" since I left London and certainly have no prospects of any in the future. The other day one of the messengers, Bunce wandered in. We always talk about American Drug Stores and food. He told me after the War instead of the usual pin-up girl, in his room he intended to have a picture of two beautiful fried eggs!

Jane also told me she was sending me some Vitamin C for my teeth since no fresh citrus fruits are available. It won't be Janie's fault if I am not healthy.

More gray rainy weather, I understand that this is the rainy season. Saturday night Lee and I went to the GI movie theater. Yesterday, which was Sunday I worked, but she went sightseeing with some people from her Section. It was cold last night, so I stayed in and ironed shirts, and enjoyed puttering around. Incidentally I had a couple of cups of hot coffee to warm me up. If we do not have heat this winter, the hot plate will probably be our salvation. With it, we can get a hot drink before we go to bed. And believe me, with the small number of blankets that we have, it is always best to go to bed warm.

If you find any packages of bouillon cubes or any condensed soup, anything we can add boiling water to, send it on. Also if possible send something in a wooden box, a Kraft cheese box, because I would like to mail some perfume home and packing is non-existent.

The September 17 TIME came yesterday, so I am only about a month behind with my news. I always enjoy getting it and will love having it for next year. When it does arrive I am a very envied person.

One more request I'd like to make. Can you get me a pair of lined leather gloves? I can tell from the weather now that they will be almost a necessity. The Army gives us light leather dress gloves and a pair of woolen ones. But in this damp rainy cold weather I will need a pair of lined leather ones. Please buy them with some of the money I send home and if you have any difficulty in finding the right kind write to Peg and ask her if she can get them at Marshall Fields. She says the store has good stocks of almost everything. I would write to her directly but she always bawls me out when I send her money for something. Do what you can, right now I get so cold at times I think my hands will drop off and it isn't winter yet!

Lots of love,
Frances

✖   ✖   ✖

PERFUME

After the stores returned to normal, for wartime, we became aware of "Parfum." This was Paris, there were no beautiful clothes, but there were still bottles of French perfume. The GIs soon became at home in the world of fragrances—Chanel No. 5, Guerlain, Worth, Lancôme and my favorite Jean Patou.

We were informed that a scent could only be judged by smelling it on the skin, not sniffing from the bottle. Skin chemically changed the scent. Bunce arrived in my drafting room one day saying "I have Chanel No. 5 on my left wrist, Guerlain "Le Blue Huere" on my right wrist, Lucien Lelong behind one ear, Jean Patou behind the other ear, and various other lovely odors on my elbows and perhaps my heel!" The WACs may have been clothed in olive drab, but they wore very expensive perfume.

HOTEL WINDSOR

The Hotel Windsor was staffed with French personnel. The jobs were coveted because the waitresses were allowed to take leftovers home with them. One of the waitresses was a favorite of ours. She was so cheerful and helpful and looked healthy, with a high color in her cheeks, but some time later we were told that she had died. The poor food of the war years had taken its toll.

✖   ✖   ✖

Hotel Windsor, Paris
November 14, 1944

Dear Mother and Dad,

We are still having damp rainy days and I am beginning to believe the winter season in Paris is not their best one. We would probably notice it less if the buildings were heated and we hear tales that they soon will be. As yet it isn't unbearable. Our greatest difficulty is caused by the head colds which hang on and on. I waited until the middle of October and then caught mine. Now, every really rainy day, I begin to sniffle again.

Last Friday night, Lee and I shared a box at the Opera with four men from my section. The Opera was "Romeo and Juliet." It was the first time I'd seen it and the French certainly know how to stage a performance. We enjoyed every moment of it. Between acts, I sat at the front of the box and sketched. Nothing of any importance, but right now I am working on quick sketch, so it was good practice.

Yesterday Caroline was off and managed to get tickets for "Thais" next week. It is difficult to get the tickets because the Opera House is so far from us and consistently sold out every time I go. The French take tremendous lunch hours. In England, it was "Tea" in the morning and afternoon with everything stopped for it. But the French usually take their lunch at home from 11 AM to 2 PM and simply close up. It is wonderful for them but plays havoc with any shopping at noon.

Sunday afternoon, we took a walk along the Seine, from the Eiffel Tower to Napoleon's Tomb. It was a nice day except for an overcast sky but we have had very few sunny days the last month and a half.

All along the river bank we saw very old men fishing. They all had the same expectant air the fishermen had along Lake Michigan. No one to date has seen a fish pulled out of the water.

In the evening, Lee and I took a chance on the GI movie, not knowing what the show was and it happened to be "Lady in the Dark." We had both missed it in London, so we enjoyed it. I have yet to go to a French movie house. I understand that most of them are our movies with French subtitles. That seems odd, but since I have been over here, I see how wide spread is the distribution of American films. So perhaps I won't be too far behind with my movies.

Saturday, of course, was Armistice Day. It was some celebration. Early in the morning the crowd began to gather and by 10 o'clock it had reached sizeable proportions. The Arch makes a magnificent back drop for parades, so I don't wonder that the French have as many as they do. I believe everyone from the baby to Aunt Susie was there. They brought camp stools to sit on and even step ladders. It went on for hours. I think everyone in Paris took their turn to march up to the Arch and put a wreath on the Tomb of the Unknown Soldier. We made ever so many detours on the way back for lunch and dinner. But the crowds were so colorful and happy that I pushed and shoved with the best of them.

My TIME magazine continues to arrive and I do enjoy it. We are expecting a Reader's Digest to make its appearance soon. The October issue, not the November. That will give us a little added reading material, but the "pickings is pretty slim." I spend most of my free time drawing. I'll be a wild woman when I actually get into a Library again—an American one.

I want to explain about the "three penny bit" pieces. I had them ready to mail and Woodie was sending a package to her family. Nothing would do but that she should include them in her package and have her Dad send them to you. So that is how it came about.

Election Day is over. I cast my ballot back in August before I left London and since the amount of news we've had about it was limited I didn't get as hot and bothered as usual. Thanksgiving is nearly upon us. It will seem odd to be spending a second Christmas away from home, but since that's the way it is I'll make the best of it.

Lots of love,
Frances

✖   ✖   ✖

THE OPERA

The grand marble staircase with the bronze figures holding branched candelabra and the soaring marble columns led to the foyer. There were heavy red velvet drapes in the boxes and a style of elegance that could only come from the nineteenth century. We were introduced to the custom of a glass of wine from the bar at intermission.

The stage was enormous. When I saw Faust *there were horses and a forty-piece band on the stage. In the winter of 1944 and 1945 there was no heat in the opera house, and I felt great sympathy for the ballet troupe that danced on the chilly stage in thin gauzy costumes. It was cold, and I was wearing a full uniform with a coat.*

✖   ✖   ✖

Hotel Windsor, Paris
November 19, 1944

Dear Mother and Dad,

Thanksgiving is nearly here and we've been reading about the wonderful meal we are supposed to have, turkey and everything. I'll bet we do, too. I talked to Lt. White, the Mess Officer, the other day and she wants me to help with the decorations for the dining room. I told her I'd be glad to help. She is a very nice person. In London, I sketched her and five KPs peeling onions. She wanted the picture and I gave it to her—thinking that any Mess Officer who sat down and peeled twice as many onions as her KPs deserved the best. Since then we have been good friends and I know if it is in her power, we'll have everything for Thanksgiving. It still won't be Mother's mincemeat and pumpkin pie though.

Last night Caroline and I started for the GI movie. It was Bogart in "Conflict" and we heard that it was good. We went for the second show, but after waiting in line for nearly an hour, I decided it wasn't worth it and we came back. We had a cup of coffee and some fruitcake she had received in a snack box and enjoyed ourselves twice as much.

I still hate to stand in line. It seems to be about all you do in the Army. After awhile you get to the place where almost anyone can line you up and you'll stand there for hours, whether you know WHY or not. I guess we are a little like Mammy Yokum's Pappy "already broken in spirit." However, "Dragon Seed" is scheduled for tonight and Lee and I will try to make the early show this time.

Our heat is greatly improved. We have a little in our offices and hot water at the Hotel all week. So if I am very cold in the room at night, I wrap up in a blanket and go on reading.

The weather is still cold and damp, always seems to rain at least a part of every day, but I think we're a little more use to it by now.

Could you help me with another matter? No civilian shops will repair shoes, simply because they do not have the materials. The Army QM (Quartermaster) handled it for a while but now we're unable to send them there either. The heels of my Service shoes are worn down past the usual repair mark. If you can send me some composition heels in a package by First Class mail, I am sure I can get them put on at a French Shoe shop. I need some about 3 ½ inch in diameter the long way. If you could send 2 or 3 pair it would be wonderful. First Class is necessary because all the packages are stuck in the Christmas rush. I sometimes think about all I do is ask you for something.

The enclosed snapshot was taken when Lee and I were in the "woods" at Valognes. I have my eyes closed as usual, and don't be alarmed I was wearing almost all the clothing I owned. I am not quite that pudgy.

Much love,
Big Sis

Hotel Windsor, Paris
November 29, 1944

Dear Dad and Mother,

The mail has been so slow in arriving the last few weeks due to the Christmas packages no doubt, that I have almost lost interest in letters. However, I did receive one from you both in the last week so I can't complain.

We had a fine Thanksgiving. I worked that day but our dinners were scheduled for the evening and the cooks did themselves proud. We had turkey, potatoes and gravy, dressing, salad, apple pie with cheese, coffee and wonder of wonders "a piece of fudge" made by the cooks. It was all very good. White tablecloths, paper napkins and candlelight. We ate and ate, saying it was almost like home. I stayed in that night, although my roommates went out. I was very thankful later when I heard the rain start.

In case I haven't mentioned it, this is absolutely the rainiest town I've ever been in. It rains a part of every day, and they tell me April is the rainy season. I should live so long.

But aside from the rain, it is still a charming place. We heard the Opera "Thais" last Monday night and then I was invited to the Ballet on Wednesday. Both were good. Now, if I had a radio maybe I could manage to get through the winter. I must say, the last three months have zipped by. I hope the rest of the time passes as quickly.

We do have some heat now. Hot water at the billet and a little heat in our offices. It is much better. Although I will be grateful for the bed socks and it is very kind of Grandmother to knit them for me. As far as wearing them—you bet I will. I have been wearing an ordinary pair of GI socks to bed since I've been overseas. Remember, I slept in a cool London shelter for weeks and summers are not especially hot here.

I do mean to answer your questions. I haven't made friends with any of the French people. Language is a terrific barrier. And I know Paris isn't London, so I am careful about going around completely alone. Lee goes with me quite a bit. She is from St. Paul, Minnesota, by the way.

That is about all of the news. I do still take the vitamins that Janie sends me.

Lots of love,
Frances

Sgt Frances DeBra
A-514210 WAC DET
G-3 Sec HQ COMD
APO #887 ETOUSA
C/O PM New York, NY

Hotel Windsor, Paris
December 4, 1944

Dear Dad and Mother,

The first Christmas package from you came yesterday. The box was pretty battered so I opened it. It contained candy, nuts and Kleenex, that is wonderful. The Kleenex is always handy. How did you happen to think of candy corn? I love it and everyone to whom I offered it, also said, "Whee, candy corn!" It was a universal favorite. The candy and nuts may be gone by Christmas but we are really enjoying them.

We were given Typhus shots last week and I nursed a sore arm for a day and a half. Still, I can't complain because I know they are for the best.

Thursday night we heard "La Boheme" at the Opera Comeque. It was excellent. Even better than the performance I heard in London. Then Friday night we saw "Faust" at the

Opera. Not too bad, but not too good. Something failed to click between the singers and the orchestra.

We have had very mild weather the last few days; probably we're ready for a cold snap. There is quite enough heat and hot water. And a couple of days ago we were given beds and mattresses! It is wonderful. We are still sleeping between GI blankets instead of sheets but beds—ah.

My shoes continue to be a worry. They are taking no shoe repair until further notice. One day, my shoes may just give up the battle. I have always hated run over heels and you should see mine now.

Thanks again for the Christmas box. We all enjoy each others boxes, but we are still a "homesick bunch of Yahoos."

Much love,
Frances

✖ ✖ ✖

COFFEE IN A CAN

The Selfridges Department Store was only a couple of blocks from our offices in London. In one of my forays through the store I found that although tea was very strictly rationed, it was possible to buy ground coffee over the counter at will. So I took a pound of coffee to France with me. We had a hot plate in our room in Paris and someone had received a package containing a heavy tin can with a removable lid, like a syrup can. With a little experimentation I found out how to make boiled coffee on the hot plate. I started with the water and coffee, brought it to a boil and boiled it seven minutes, then cut the hot plate off. This left me with a strong cup of coffee and grounds floating in the liquid. It is a little hard to drink hot coffee and spit out grounds at the same time. Adding an egg or eggshells would settle the grounds, but eggs were unobtainable. Finally some one informed me that if I added a spoonful of cold water it would settle the grounds to the bottom of the can. It worked. So we made boiled coffee in a tin can whenever we had coffee. Nescafe was the favorite, but it was not always obtainable. Quite often someone going back to London on business would bring us back a pound.

✖ ✖ ✖

Hotel Windsor, Paris
December 12, 1944

Dear Mother and Dad,

It is my Sunday off and a lovely day. After breakfast I washed clothes and spent the rest of the time on my Christmas Cards. Yes, I know it is disgracefully late to send them out, but I only found the card recently. After my late, late Easter cards, I didn't suppose anyone would mind.

The Christmas box arrived a couple of days ago with the soup. It will be fine and I am very grateful for the Kleenex. We are suppose to get a small box every two months at the PX but it is always just luck if you receive it.

Roberta Harrison sent me a Christmas box and also one from Peg arrived. She has made such dire threats that I am afraid to open it. She might put the evil eye on me or something.

This afternoon, Lee and I were invited to the Opera "Manon" by one of the fellows at the office. I enjoyed it as usual. But goodness, those Opera Houses are drafty. The stage is so huge and we were seated near the front on the Orchestra floor, when the curtain goes up a cold gale blows right at you. I swear next time I will take a blanket along.

We left the Opera in a slight drizzle. A day couldn't pass without rain. We worked our way through the subway to the Hotel.

That subway! It always amazes me. I've never been so pushed and shoved in my life. Parisians individually are quite polite, but in a crowd! After living in London and Paris I am convinced that Americans have the best manners in the world. In fact, we're almost head and shoulders above them on every score except books on Art.

It was such a nasty night, we decided to stay in. I stopped in Woodie's room on the way back from dinner and saw her Christmas tree. She has her presents underneath. Of course, she knows what every single one contains, but it looks good.

Last Wednesday afternoon, we went to bookstores. I found two small copies of Van Gogh and Degas which I liked, but that was all. Next time I intend to go over into the Latin Quarter and try my luck.

On the way back, I stopped at a small Art Shop, old and musty. I intended to get a couple of tubes of watercolor paint. I've had no backbone when it comes to Art Shops. Of course, I will use them, but I hadn't intended to buy so many. They were very small tubes of watercolor.

Daddy's letter containing the money order arrived and I thank you very much. A package was mailed a couple of days ago. It is hard to say when it will arrive. A present for Mother, Emma and Grandmother and a small one for Daddy. You'll know it is on the way and I hope you like it.

I'll write to Aunt Beulah and give her a request for the Reader's Digest, although I haven't had one since September. Guess the copies are floating around in the Christmas mail. I will also send her my income tax statement that they mailed me from Chicago, because I can't make heads or tails of it. Maybe she can.

Mother mentioned something about sending me magazines. Would you, please. Especially back copies from last March will be most gratefully received. I sometimes think I'll go crazy for something to read and American magazines are special!

I hope I have covered everything. I am still waiting for the gloves—they are somewhere in the Christmas mail. They'll be along any day now.

> Love,
> Frances

Hotel Windsor, Paris
December 21, 1944

Dear Dad and Mother,

Another Christmas box arrived—this one contained cans of pineapple, tuna and juice. The fruit cake disappeared in a flash and the apricot juice was very good. The tuna, I think I will save until Christmas or New Year's and we will try to get some French bread to go with it.

We still have rain and more rain, but by now I must be use to the climate, since my last cold was almost two months ago. We were given the choice of working either Christmas or New Year's. I choose New Year's because I'd rather be off on Christmas Day which is on Monday. I'll also have next Sunday off, so with two days, I'll feel as though I were on vacation. I would have liked to go to Midnight Mass at Notre Dame but I am afraid much of Paris will have the same idea and there is also the problem of returning to the Hotel. The METRO stops running at 11:30 PM and there is only "Shanks Mare" left and it is quite a long hike up the hill.

Thanks for sending the shoe repair material. I've had one pair of shoes in QM for nearly two weeks and goodness knows when I will get them back. The pair I am wearing is really down at the heel.

I had Lobby CQ (Charge of Quarters) Friday night from 7 to 12 PM. You are a general information clerk for everyone who comes in. I took the book "Dracula" along to keep me awake and it did! It nearly scared myself into fits. That was the first horror story I've read in a long, long time.

Woodie has managed to get herself a small Christmas tree for her mantle. It looks elegant and she has a couple of small wooden shoes, the kind the stores sell to the children. They put them out for Santa to fill instead of hanging up stockings. I am still partial to stockings myself.

The bed socks arrived and I put them right on. I've had trouble keeping my pajama legs tucked into the other short socks and these are made to order. It was very good of Grandmother to knit them for me and they will certainly be used.

No gloves yet, but I expect them any day. They are probably in the Christmas mail.

Love,
Frances

P.S. Please send me coffee and candy or anything. Lee and Woodie are nuts about licorice.

Hotel Windsor, Paris
December 22, 9144

Dear Peg,

The time passes. I worked last Sunday and after work we saw "Saratoga Trunk" at the GI movie, after waiting in the rain for an hour. It was good.

Thanks for the clippers. It certainly takes me back to Chicago, The Tribune, Marshall Fields and the other stores. I suppose Fields is beautifully decorated as usual. We have felt so little of the Holiday spirit. There are decorations up here but very few. I think the chief lack is radio and magazines. I am just realizing how conscious the radio makes you feel that Christmas is approaching. The wooden shoes are adorable. French children put them out instead of stockings. They are painted and gilded in fantastic ways.

Peg, I feel I bother you incessantly but one more thing I'd like you to find out. What is the camera situation! It is difficult borrowing someone else's so I have decided to buy one if it can be found. I thought Fields might have a supply.

I want a folding Kodak, not too complicated, if possible. Would you see what is available? Something about $20 or $30. Since I see no immediate homecoming in sight, I would like to have a camera.

You are an angel, Peg. Let me know what you find out. Tell Bill "Hello" and that I am becoming very accustomed to dehydrated eggs.

Love Fran

11

BATTLE OF THE BULGE

During the Battle of the Bulge, a counteroffensive by the German army, we were censored and of course not allowed to write anything about it in our letters. Headquarters was flooded with rumors, each having a portion of truth in it. The Germans had dropped English-speaking paratroopers in American uniforms behind our lines. We were given to understand that headquarters was their objective. Soon patrols were organized to man the corridors and intercept any roving Germans. This continued for a few days and then common sense prevailed. It was fortunate because the guards were all drawn from the headquarters clerks, and generally speaking they were not accustomed to the daily use of firearms.

Leige and the supply depots were seen to be their goal because we knew the Germans needed supplies. A curfew was ordered for our troops, and from about 8 p.m. on we were restricted to our quarters. This made it easier for the MPs to spot any unauthorized American-dressed personnel in the city. Leaves and passes to Paris were canceled immediately, limiting the number of Allied soldiers on the streets.

We had planned to attend Midnight Mass at Notre Dame Cathedral as a consolation for being away from home another Christmas, but the German offensive canceled that. It was highly improbable that the Germans would have infiltrated Paris, but in a theater of war sometimes the impossible did happen.

✹　　✹　　✹

Hotel Windsor, Paris
December 23, 1944

Dear Dad and Mother,

The gloves did come and they are exactly what I wanted, very warm and the fit is perfect. Thank you very much. I have been strutting around being inordinately proud. Aunt Beulah is a very fine shopper. Please give her my thanks. I received Christmas Cards from all of you. Mine may be a little late but they will arrive eventually.

Tuesday afternoon I went to the little art shop here because I was short on paper. I came out with four new sketch books and some superb watercolor paper. It is all rag paper and handmade. The texture is fabulous and it takes color like a charm.

Wednesday was my day off, so Woodie [Marjory Woodring] and I went shopping. She had never seen Notre Dame, so we went there. It is a beautiful Cathedral and I always enjoy going back to see it. After that we walked along the Rud de Rivoli and shopped for a few things, small presents for my roommates.

It is odd that we have very little feeling that Christmas is almost here. The lack of snow, decorations and music, I suppose, but we will manage to have a nice one. That is all of the news, but I wanted you to know I had received the gloves because they were a long time on the way.

Lots of love,
Frances

✖   ✖   ✖

PRESENTS

I found some large sheets of plain paper and made my wrapping paper, drawing and painting designs on the paper with inks and watercolor. The presents were tied with regular mailing cord. We had no tape or ribbon, and there were no gift boxes. In fact, the boxes we received from home that were in usable condition were the ones we used to mail our items back to the States. There was literally no packing to be had through the usual channels.

One of the boxes that I received from home contained artificial Christmas trees. One was about three inches tall, and several others about one inch tall. I added a crèche I found in the department store and a couple of the small decorated and gilded shoes of the type left out for Saint Nicholas by the French children. We felt festive, if only on a small scale.

✖   ✖   ✖

Windsor Hotel, Paris
December 27, 1944

Dear Dad and Mother,

Christmas is over and I'll tell you about it. But first, thank you for the package I received today. The box contained stationary, cheese, candy, cookies and nuts. There was no date on the box and I wondered if they were the cookies mailed in September? I hardly think that they could be because they are so fresh. They are very good.

We had a very nice Christmas. I was off Sunday and Monday, therefore I will work next Sunday and New Year's Day. We were given a choice. Most of my friends worked Sunday, so I settled myself by a window and painted in watercolor for awhile. In the evening, Gerry [Garrison] and I went down to Caroline's [Chaffee] room for a small party, cheese and stuff, to which I did justice. After that I watched Gerry and Murph [Mildred Murphy] (my roommates) open their gifts. I only watched because I had promised Lee [Noyes] to wait until morning.

We had breakfast in our rooms and opened our gifts. Gerry gave me a pewter box and Murphy a little glass bunny (Lalique) and Lee a pin. Roberta [Harrison] sent me a box with several items from wash clothes and a tie, which I can certainly use, to Kleenex and candy. The girls in Chicago came up with odd items I had been needing like shoe polish, film and hose.

After our dinner of turkey, dressing, blueberry pie and napkins, four of us went to one of the hospitals to talk to the GIs. We sang Carols with them in a ward and then visited around until visiting hours were over. You would think they had every right and reason to be blue spending Christmas in a hospital bed, but their spirits are wonderful. They are all homesick of course, but almost to a man they would say, "Why, I'm not bad at all," but take the fellow in the next bed. . . . That is really tough!" And so it went until you feel that they are cheering you up instead of the reverse. Still I do wish that I could drop Peg [Allison Nightingale] into those wards for awhile every day, she would brighten the air.

Nothing special was scheduled at night. A few of our friends were up in our room to talk awhile, and that finished our Christmas. I did wonder just what you were doing.

I know you are wondering about the snapshot. It is another Christmas present for you. But I am finding it a little difficult to say as I want to. I wanted very much to tell you in person.

Do you remember a Charles Lowrie, who I worked with in Florida? My letters were undoubtedly sprinkled with matter concerning him. Before I left the Air Field for overseas

Chuck Lowrie (sitting) at work on The Beam. *Chuck and Frances worked together at the air base in Marianna, Florida, and he proposed to Frances before she left for England.*

duty, he asked me to marry him. I was undecided at the time, but now my mind is fairly well made up. Since it will still be a very long time before I see you, I wanted you to know.

I'll try and describe him—he is 27 years old, birthday August 15, blond, 6 feet tall, left handed and an excellent cartoonist. He is from Long Beach and a Californian through and through. His mother died when he was 13 and his father in 1941, he has no brothers or sisters.

I am giving a very poor description, guess I should add that he has a smile that caught a bit of the sunlight and that he knows very well how to handle a contrary female like your daughter. Which is no mean trick!

He is still in Florida in the Air Corp and since neither of us knows when we will be discharged from the Army, our only plan is that I'll visit California as soon as possible. After all, I'd like to see the spot where I will be living.

I can't think of more to say just now and I am a bit disappointed not to tell you in person. But I will be very proud when you do meet him, of you and him both.

Very much love,
Big Sis

✖ ✖ ✖

AMBULANCES

During the Christmas week a long line of army ambulances started streaming into Paris. I didn't know their route, but they came circling around the Etoile and down the Champs-Élysées on their way to the hospitals. Day and night for days and days, a continuing line of ambulances came into the city. Whenever we went to work and then back to the hotel we saw them, all bringing American GIs in from the front. I think we really tried to shove it into the back of our minds, but there they were—an oncoming tide of wounded soldiers.

✕ ✕ ✕

Windsor Hotel, Paris
January 7, 1945

Dear Mother and Dad,

A box arrived yesterday with Emma's name on it. It contained fruitcake, candy, orange juice, Vicks, cough drops and writing paper. Thanks so much.

I am thankful to say, at the moment I do not need the cough drops or the Vicks. After the first two months here, I've had very little trouble with head colds. But I need to have it on hand. I'll never forget the coughing spell a box of Caroline's Vicks drops helped me through. Gerry has had quite a cough, so I gave her one box of the Sucrets.

The sweater also arrived about two days ago. It is beautiful and fits perfectly. I am very proud of my sister. I wear the bed socks and on cold nights they are a blessing. We do still have some heat in our offices and the Hotel. Several days at the Holidays it was pretty cold, but now the weather is back to normal. My system seems to be pretty well adjusted now, so you must not worry about me.

Last night I moved, I have been living on the 5th floor with Gerry and Murphy, a couple of G-3 WACs. Now I am on the 7th floor with Lee and Lucille. Lucille Verzano is from the south side of Chicago. Now and then we talk about places we both know.

It was quite a move. We literally picked up my traps and carried them upstairs. Woodie came along at a good time and helped. Then after piling everything in the middle of the floor, I had the rest of the evening to find places to stow it away. It was a fortunate thing that I had so much help. I did hate to leave Gerry but I think it is a change for the better.

The New York Herald Tribune has resumed printing their Paris edition and believe me, I was happy to get the first copy. They are sold in our Lobby, at 5 francs (10¢) which is of course very high, but just to get my hands on an American newspaper again is a treat. Stars and Stripes is a great help but this is "honest to goodness" US news.

I am still grateful for the gloves; they are exactly what I wanted. The metal band on my wrist watch is broken beyond repair. Could you find me one of the black cord type of band? I believe you can get them with an extra cord also. Maybe you can send it in a letter. I do seem to be asking for things continually. You know that I am grateful. After that move last night, I will never complain at the sight of a suitcase or trunk. Barrack bags, "phooey"!

Lots of love,
Frances

Hotel Windsor, Paris
January 12, 1945

Dear Peg,

I have meant to write thanking you for the Christmas, nearly every day. Peg, everything was just right and I waited until Christmas morning to open it. The shoe polish is the right color and the film, wonderful. We were given a choice of working New Year's or Christmas, so I was off Sunday and Christmas. It was lovely. I loafed Sunday and Christmas Eve. We went to a party given by some of the girls we know in the Hotel.

Christmas morning, Gerry, Murphy, Lee and I opened our presents. I have a pin, a pewter box, a glass rabbit, I call him "Mac" and from home everything from a yellow scarf, shirts and tie, to a magazine subscription.

We had the promised turkey for Christmas dinner and all of the trimmings. In the afternoon we went out to a hospital to talk with some of the boys. You should have been there, Peg. You would have been a great help. You know me, it is still hard to talk to strangers, but I did the best I could. I believe they are grateful for anyone "who speaks United States." Their morale is something wonderful and I only wish I could have done more.

Last week, I changed rooms and now I live with Lee Noyles [Noyes], who is from St. Paul, Minnesota and Lucille Verzano from the south side of Chicago.

Last Sunday afternoon, Lee and I went to the Opera, "Boris Godonov." He died as beautifully here on the stage as he did on the records. But how cold it was! Fuel is so precious that none can be used to heat buildings of that type. So it was almost an endurance test whether the Opera would finish first or I would freeze solid. I wrapped up in my overcoat and looked longingly at the velvet drapes. The next time I am determined to bring a blanket.

We have had snow in Paris for the last few days and it is still falling. It is very beautiful but when you think of the suffering caused to a city without fuel and an Army at the Front, it is something to be wished away.

I received the box of candy from Bill [Nightingale] and I thank him. We nibble at it and imagine it is extra good because it came from Marshall Fields.

Love,
Fran

Hotel Windsor, Paris
January 22, 1945

Dear Dad and Mother,

I've had two letters from Mama asking if I'd received the sweater made by Emma. I certainly did, it came the first of December. We have heard of mail being lost or it may even be sitting in a post office somewhere. After all, I just got the October Reader's Digest. I believe I have received about five of the Christmas packages. Janie received the candy you sent her and the Gobels also. Margaret [Gobel] was especially thrilled with the hose.

I am glad you are pleased about Chuck. His full name is Charles E. Lowrie. I believe he has a couple of married cousins who live somewhere on the Coast but aside from his friends that is all. He owns a property with two houses, the rear one quite small, in Long Beach. He also has a car, I think a DeSoto. He went to art school and is an everlasting tease. I have also thought that California is a long way off. It is one of the very last places I'd choose to live myself, but he loves it there. At least you will be spending your winter vacations in the sun. We all liked the "Blondie" clippings. You certainly are my favorite family.

Love,
Frances

✗ ✗ ✗

SIEGFRIED LINE WORK

The G-3 section officers conducted briefings for soldiers from many different units. Some of the work I did was connected with this. Sometimes I assembled very large maps made of many sections—these were used on a wall. Often it was necessary to assemble them on the floor of the drafting room and then enter various sorts of information in the proper section.

The maps of the Siegfried Line were different. They were just a large paper size, but I transferred information such as the location of pillboxes, dragon's teeth, the antitank defense, and other data on several copies.

Dragon's teeth were waist-high concrete forms that resembled blunt teeth and were set in several rows, alternating the spacing to slow down tanks and mechanized vehicles.

There were only human copiers then. I have no idea where they went. It was very small, exacting work but essential. In particular I remember working on those maps and stopping at intervals to warm my hands around the bare light bulb that hung over my drafting board.

✖   ✖   ✖

Hotel Windsor, Paris
January 28, 1945

Dear Dad and Mother,

Not a very exciting week. We still have snow on and off. The streets are clear for a day and then the snow begins again. I wear my rubbers going back and forth through the snow, kicking up the slush.

Friday night, Caroline and I saw the movie "For Whom the Bell Tolls," I enjoyed it. Lee has quite a cold in her chest, so we rubbed it with Vicks. I have been fortunate perhaps it is Janie's [Baranowski] vitamins.

I read a good bit now that I have no conscience telling me I should be studying radio. I feel free to enjoy the books as I find them. The December 18 and January 1 issue of TIME just arrived. I keep pretty well abreast of new books and movies as well as the news. I received a letter from Roberta. She had a furlough at Christmas and was able to see Betty, her daughter. I do hope I have an opportunity to see her again after the War. She said she had mailed me some Guava jelly, which I love.

Enclosed are various income tax statements I have received. The last one demands payment by December 14, 1944. I can't make heads or tails of it. Will you pass it on to Aunt Beulah and ask her about it? If I do owe money, I'd like to pay it and have it over with.

I hope Dad is over the flu. I just received his letter regarding Chuck and I am glad you both feel that way. I am certain that he will be a worthwhile addition to our family.

Love,
Big Sis

✖   ✖   ✖

ON THE METRO

In Paris we used the Metro to get around. Our uniform was a free pass to ride, so I went everywhere within the city limits. I often worked on Sundays and had my day off during the week and so visited many places alone.

The subway trains had the exit and entrance doors in the middle of the car on both sides. One time I was one of the first into the car and that placed me against the far door. As French people entered behind me more and more people pushed in. For the only time in my life I was afraid that I might be crushed against the door.

Two wonderful American GIs near me saw what was happening and with one on either side of me they turned to face each other and placed their hands on each other's shoulders and made a space for me to stand between them. I had room to breathe.

When the car stopped I thanked them, and I have never forgotten it. Almost always the American soldiers were very thoughtful of us.

✖   ✖   ✖

Hotel Windsor, Paris
February 6, 1945

Dear Mother and Dad,

For lunch today, we had ICE CREAM! Do you know the last time I tasted it was back in the States in March. Nearly 11 months ago. It was really a treat and chocolate at that. We sit around and talk about "Hot Fudge Sundaes," but I really had not expected any until I got back home.

Lee and I went to a French movie last night. It was a "Disney Parade" and you should have heard Mickey Mouse and Donald Duck in French. It was amazing and as funny as ever.

Tuesday was my day off and it was so warm I thought spring had arrived. We walked down by Notre Dame, hunting book shops along the river. I found a printed portfolio of some Rembrandt drawings and a small box of Goya and one of Degas.

There was a notice on our bulletin board that several of the Art Schools are open, including the Beaux Arts! But so far all of the classes are during the day, so I am out of luck. If they ever have some evening classes scheduled, I will take as much work as I can. Remember how I always wanted to study at the Beaux Arts—and now I am just across the river from it.

I had a letter from Phil. He said he had just visited Bill and Peg in their new apartment. Then he told me about a new job that he has. I think it is drawing instruments and etc. for the Services. He seems to like it, and I know it will be good experience for him. Still the same old Phil, working 16 hours a day. I can dimly remember back to the days, when I, too, worked like that. In a Christmas rush, there is no choice.

Love,
Frances

Hotel Windsor, Paris
February 7, 1945

Dear Dad and Mother,

Sunday afternoon, Caroline took me up to the "Flea Market." It is on the outskirts of the City and is a push cart peddlers paradise—almost everything is sold—violins, movie cameras and rusty nails. The goods are spread out on the ground or in temporary shops and it stretched for blocks. We wandered up and down with our eyes bulging, trying not to miss a thing.

Caroline wanted some copper pots for their cottage and she did get several nice ones. It is open on Saturday, Sunday and Monday. I'd like to take Lee up there one day soon. It was fascinating, shoe laces or brass candlesticks, it is all there.

Last night when we got back to the room, we found that our mattresses had been changed. How wonderful the new ones are. The ones we had were a little like hollowed out cement.

Do you suppose you could find a camera for me? I've written to Peg thinking she could get one at Fields. I have decided I'd like to buy one. I want a folding one in a case for convenience. I have several rolls of film that you and Peg have sent me and I may be able to arrange a trade.

I will undoubtedly be here a good many more months and now that good weather is coming, I'd like to take a few pictures.

I know you would like to hear more about Chuck and I hardly know where to begin. He was born in South Dakota and his parents moved to California when he was small. His mother was Danish and his father Scotch stock. He went to Art School and came out in the middle of the Depression. I think he worked in the oil companies right before he came in the Army; he was a welder at Lockheed and at the shipyards. He has been in the Army three years. He enlisted as an Aviation Cadet and washed out of pilot training about the same time Dick Helton did.

He loves Los Angles because there is so much within driving distance, the mountains, Catalina Island, Pacific Ocean, Redwood National Park and the desert. He is the only person I've heard who can make a desert sound interesting. He does a good bit of ocean and salmon fishing and hunting. He likes to be out of doors. He likes electric trains and is a complete tease. Almost everyone likes him and he has a good disposition. He likes to handle his own affairs and definitely is not interested in other people's business and doesn't expect them to be interested in his.

I think we both want the same things from life and this is definitely a "for the next 50 years" affair. There is no one else, ever quite like him.

Love,
Frances

12

BLEAK WINTER IN WARTIME

MUSÉE RODIN

I found my way to the Musée Rodin. It was a fascinating spot. It was in the Hotel Biron, on the Left Bank, quite near the Invalides, which was Napoleon's tomb. "Hotel" in this case meant a mansion in the heart of the city and surrounded by a gray stone wall and formal gardens. It was cold, no heat, but with the bare-bones beauty that all of Paris possessed in those days.

Auguste Rodin, the sculptor, lived and worked there. It was a classic gray-stone dwelling with tall French doors and beautiful parquet floors. It was filled with Rodin's work—small unfinished pieces on modeling stands, bronze statues in all sizes, and other more complicated works. It was hard to believe that any sculptor could mold the human form into life poses that had a quality of draped silk folds. They were breathtaking. The monumental figure of The Thinker *was in the garden.*

✶ ✶ ✶

Hotel Windsor, Paris
February 17, 1945

Dear Dad and Mother,

I have received a good many [Danville] "Republicans" recently—they range from September to November, just a little late, but I enjoy reading them just the same. We have had what amounts to a spring thaw, warmer weather and rain. But after the cold dismal winter, it is a welcome change.

I have been especially busy this last week or so. In the evenings, I relax at the GI movie or with a book. I have read more this last winter, than all the time I have been in the Army.

Now for the news, I've bought a camera. A French make, used and Caroline [Chaffee] found it for me. It is a folding Kodak, shutter speed 150th of a second and a 4.5 lens. Not bad, eh. It takes 120 film and I have several rolls. When the sun stays out for a little while, I'll be able to send you some snapshots.

If by some remote chance you've already sent me one, it is quite all right, because I can get rid of it very easily. I wanted you to know that I had found one.

It is rumored that we will get the new "Off Duty" dresses for Easter. Spring wardrobe!

> Sleepy now, love
> Frances

✳ ✳ ✳

SAINTE-CHAPELLE

Lee Noyes and I went to see the Sainte-Chapelle built by King Louis IX (Saint Louis) in the 1200s. I had read about the architecture and the beauty of it. So one day we set out to find it. It was a bleak winter day with gray skies. After consulting the city maps and going down wrong streets several times, we finally found it.

There was a lower chapel and an upper one dedicated to the relic of "The Crown of Thorns." It was cold, probably as cold as the many times services were held there. The soaring proportions of the walls, slender windows, and exquisite detail were very satisfying to the eye. We were the only people around. I am sure in wartime there were no French sightseers and very, very few Americans.

But again, the quiet left me feeling how much history, tragic and happy had passed through it, leaving some sort of residue in the bare stones of the place.

✳ ✳ ✳

Hotel Windsor, Paris
February 24, 1945

Dear Mother and Dad,

I have just received your letter saying it had been six weeks since you had mail from me. That was really a shock. I am very sorry, because I can well imagine how worried you must have been. But it was the mail, because I have written at least once a week.

If it ever happens again, however, please never think such a lapse in mail might be due to my illnesses because in that case I know Lee or Caroline or Woodie [Marjory Woodring] would keep you informed. We keep an eye on each other, just as Peg [Allison Nightingale] and I use to do. So you can blame it on the mail. We still have transportation difficulties here in France and the ammunition and food still have the right of way.

Evidently you didn't get my letter asking for a black cord band for my wrist watch. The metal one finally gave up the ghost, and I've had to carry it in my pocket. If you can get one, it could probably be put in an envelope and mailed easily. You also said, you didn't know whether I had received the sweater. Well, those letters too were delayed because I did get it and a beautiful job Emma did. I also hope you know that I bought a French camera. So you needn't bother trying to find one for me.

Does that catch things up pretty well? The Sadler's Wells Ballet Company has been here in Paris for the past week. I have been three evenings and enjoyed it immensely. Last night Woodie and I went. We were seated in the first row of the second balcony and had a fine time hanging our heads over the rail at intermission.

Today is my day off. Lee and I were both off last Monday. We have so much work in the Drafting Room that I have worked several Sundays and now I am enjoying the "fruits of my labor." I certainly need it. Never let anyone tell you that bending over a drafting board is easy work because it isn't so. After a full day, my back feels as though I had been shoveling coal. But it is the thing I can do best, so I am glad to be here.

Monday, Lee wanted me to take her to the "Flea Market." We spent an hour wandering around. Then Lee and I had coffee and donuts at the new WAC Red Cross Club and saw a movie at the Garrison Cinema. It was "Hollywood Canteen." Can't say I cared too much for it, but at least I did hear the song "Don't Fence Me In." I read in TIME and the paper about this or that song which has been first on the Hit Parade and I haven't so much as heard them. It does give you a cut off feeling. You never know how much radio is a part of your life until you have been without one. By the way, Dad's LIBERTY arrived in fine shape. Thank you.

Much Love,
Frances

✗   ✗   ✗

THE FLEA MARKET

The flea market was located on a gently sloping hill. There were many hills in Paris away from the river. The array of items offered for sale or trade was extensive. A pile of small plumbing fixtures next to a heap of used shoes, then a section of semipermanent wooden buildings that contained antique furniture and pieces of choice lusterware. Almost anything could have been found if enough time was spent seeking it.

In wartime, cigarettes were a basic medium of exchange; nonsmokers were in a favorable position. The American troops were allowed, at one time, a carton of cigarettes per week on the ration books. Even an indifferent bargainer could buy many things with a couple of packs and a few francs. I was too timid. I gave my cigarettes away to people who could not afford to buy them or who smoked more than their ration.

✖   ✖   ✖

Hotel Windsor, Paris
End of February 1945

Dear Mother and Dad,

I have a letter from each of you to answer, so I'll start with the camera. I paid 1600 Francs or $32 for it and I think it is worth the money. I have a couple of rolls of film being developed now. I'll send you prints as soon as I get them. The prints, I can send but I am afraid negatives are a different matter. The Army has a special censorship on them, so most of us send the snapshots home and keep the negatives to bring back with us.

I also got a yellow filter for this camera. It screws tight on to the lens. I am hoping for some good cloud shots later this spring. But I know so little about the settings on the lens that I usually look up at the sky—squint and then guess at where it should go. After a few rolls of film, I'll have the knack of it.

We just received a shipment of pre-Christmas mail; I got a letter from Chuck [Lowrie], yesterday, dated December 8th. I am sure he would love to have cookies, candy or anything. He is such a nice guy. I am enclosing an extra snapshot he sent me. You'll be able to get a glimpse of that grin. The other fellow is the new editor of the "Beam." And incidentally those are the steps leading up to the front door of the "Beam" office.

We had beautiful weather Sunday and Monday. It is wonderful to have sunny days after all the dull dreary times. Lee and I heard the Band Concert (Army Band) Sunday night and last night went to a GI movie. Tonight, she and Lucille [Verzano] are both out, so I have peace and quiet.

Did you receive the shoulder patch I sent Emma several weeks ago? Blue, with a star, chains, etc. We are now authorized to wear it and I have it on my sleeve. This was the ETOUSA patch (European Theater of Operations United States Army). I sometimes think I will wear out the suit just changing patches. It is my 4th so far.

Lots of love,
Frances

P.S. Please send me film for my camera—120.

✳   ✳   ✳

SEWING ON PATCHES AND DECORATIONS

The sewing kit Emma found for me just before I shipped overseas was a lifesaver. We tried to avoid wearing the WAC stripes and ribbons. But one day a formal order was posted on the bulletin board saying we were to put them on and that our rooms would be inspected to be sure they were on all of our clothes. So we gave in.

Our reluctance was due to several factors. We felt we were not as important as the men fighting on the front. The Good Conduct Medal was passed out as a matter of course to anyone who behaved themselves, and we soon caught on to the fact that the bronze star attached to the ETO Ribbon, signifying service in a war zone, was passed back and forth between friends in headquarters. So the battle star on the ETO Ribbon could mean that one had truly been in a battle or that they were safely in the rear echelon. The green ribbon with yellow ends signified that the wearer had been a member of the WAAC, the Women's Auxiliary Army Corps, and we wore it proudly. Our stripes, except for the company cadre, denoted our pay scale and the importance of the job.

Therefore, in our eyes, the only important decorations we saw were the Purple Hearts, the Combat Infantry Badge, and a shoulder patch of a fighting division. From then on I sewed patches and stripes on for some of the men in our section. Emma had included a package of small needles for me, and I had a thimble. The regular needles in the sewing kits were huge— plus the fact that the GIs were usually all thumbs when faced with a needle. I did not mind since after the spring there was always spare time now and then.

✳   ✳   ✳

Windsor Hotel, Paris
March 3, 1945

Dear Dad and Mother,

We have been so busy; I haven't had a day off in several weeks, so you will have to excuse my slightly confused state. I have been coming to the Hotel in the evening, relaxing for a bit and then going to bed. Soon the rush will subside and I will have time to breathe. Yesterday a box arrived with cheese, tea, candy and cookies—oh yes, and walnuts. We liked the walnuts, they were delicious and the cookies were quite fresh. Now if you could only manage an apple pie.

The days are so much longer now with more light in the evenings we can see more of Paris. I have actually seen very little of it in comparison to what I saw in London. With the weather nicer I am sure we will perk up a bit and "catch Spring Fever."

I am very sleepy now, so perhaps I'd better finish. Never let anyone tell you drawing isn't hard work! Because I can ache from head to toe after a day of it—it is! However I wouldn't trade it for anything else and I have no trouble sleeping.

Much love,
Frances

✖   ✖   ✖

SKETCHES

I arrived in London without drawing or painting supplies. We were instructed to leave everything not essential behind. We did not know what our circumstances would be when we arrived at our station.

After getting my bearings in London, I had pen and ink and tracing paper in the drafting room, so my first drawings were in sketchbooks purchased in an art store and only in black and white.

I found an empty black japanned watercolor box in the regular supplies. I could purchase the half pans of watercolor, which were fashioned for the box. But there were no brushes. I waited until my own brushes caught up with me before doing anything in the nature of a wash.

In the long dark rainy fall in Paris, I began to use ink washes. The colored inks were supplied through the army warehouse. It was a medium very well suited to the landscape and mood of the city. At first, I used sepia ink lines with sepia and blue washes. It was cold, damp, and dreary and I felt that the French people's weariness and despair rose like a mist from the ancient streets and cobblestones.

Gradually, I moved into colored inks, not knowing that inks were dyes, which are always subject to fading and changing of color. After I found the shop with the handmade rag paper and the very small tubes of watercolor paint, I used straight watercolor in many of my drawings.

✖ ✖ ✖

Hotel Windsor, Paris
March 3, 1945

Dear Peg,

Did I tell you that I now have a French folding Kodak? I did not believe it was possible to get one here, but Caroline found one, so now I am all right.

There are several things I want to tell you. The "Saddlers Wells" Ballet Company from London is here in Paris performing for the Troops. I have seen it three times, they were modern ballets. As you may have heard, Glen Miller's Band has been playing in Paris and I heard it several weeks ago.

There as big as life was Mel Powell at the piano. He was good. Also Harry "Hot Lips" Levin is playing with the US Army Band stationed here. I heard him at one of the Sunday evening band concerts, and remembered our old "Lower Basin Street" days. But aside from those two, there is little to hear in the Jazz line as far as the Army is concerned. I lack your ear for picking the best from the local Jazz musicians. I have tickets for a piano recital of Chopin tomorrow night. I don't know the pianist but I hope to enjoy it.

You are dangling Paradise before my eyes in the form of a "Beauty-Rest" mattress. I'll take you up on it sooner or later. Say "Hello" to Bill [Nightingale] and the girls for me.

Love,
Frances

Hotel Windsor, Paris
March 8, 1945

Dear Dad and Mother,

I am still receiving your letters written when you had no mail from me. It is such a shame. There seems very little excuse for such a mail tie-up, but I am afraid we will have to put up with it for awhile yet. But never worry about me—because I know Lee or one of the other girls would let you know if anything did happen out of the ordinary. Lee watches over me, even more than Peg use to and goodness knows Peg concentrated on everything that was for my own good.

Saturday I wandered over to the Latin Quarter, around the Beaux Arts School and all of the little book shops, to take some pictures. The sun was shining brightly all morning, but as soon as I appeared camera in hand, it went behind the clouds.

Sunday, I worked, then after supper Lee and I went to Caroline's Hotel to return a book I had borrowed. We found her half way ill. I think it is only a cold, but we all have "winter fatigue" and she is taking longer to throw it off. Probably Jane's [Baranowski] vitamins have done more for me than I give them credit. Did I tell you the dosage? There is every day—two for my eyes, two for my teeth, and one huge one that contains all of the vitamins. I swallow five of those things before breakfast. She insists that is the proper time.

We have been so busy, the days have passed quickly. My two roommates are out, so I have peace and quiet. I wrote to Chuck one time and told him that most of the girls thought me a "stick in the mud." But he replied that he was one too, so we are probably two of a kind.

Love,
Frances

Hotel Windsor, Paris
March 12, 1945

Dear Peg,

The cookies arrived! Not crushed, just 35% crumbs, but believe me I like crumbs! They were good.

I went into the Day Room and the record playing was Bing on "How Deep is the Ocean." That brought back memories. Do you play the records much, Peg? I hope you are not being your usual generous self and giving them away. Because, after you, I think I should have a few years of listening to them first, and it has been so long.

I heard a marvelous piano recital last week. A Polish pianist—Malcuzyuski [Witold Malcuzynski]. It was an all Chopin program and I enjoyed it 100%. Otherwise, I go on about as usual. Paris has less to do than you imagine. The weather has been fairly nice, although I'll take Chicago anytime.

Peg, I am sorry about the snafu on the pictures. My poor efforts and the French method of developing leaves very little to show for my efforts. I'll keep trying. At least, I will have a new uniform to pose in. This was only meant to be a note, and my eyes are nearly closed.

> Love,
> Fran

P.S. That record made me homesick!

Hotel Windsor, Paris
March 17, 1945

Dear Dad and Mother,

The bracelet for my watch came yesterday and I put it on immediately. It fits. I will miss the old one, but perhaps it can be fixed.

I have received several of the REPUBLICAN and a LIBERTY. The READER'S DIGEST (Feb) is really a late issue. In our PX we can buy one from December.

I went to a class at the Beaux Arts School yesterday. There is a life class there on Wednesday and Saturday morning. I was given permission to work on Saturday and take my day off on Wednesday. Yesterday was the first class.

I would have given a great deal to know a small amount of French, for I would have liked to talk to the students. The girls were very nice, taking me out to an Art Store to purchase a large portfolio, full sheets of paper and charcoal. The usual supplies for life drawing. The class is from 8 to 12 PM. I would have preferred a quick sketch class with short poses. However it has the old smell of an Art School—linseed oil and paint.

Last Sunday night we went to a French movie theater and saw "Wuthering Heights." I enjoyed it, although it was strange to see the French titles flashed across the screen.

T/Sgt [Frank] Martello, the draftsman I've worked under since I've been overseas, left for a furlough to the States. He has been in the ETO three years and was given an opportunity to return. We were all more excited than he was. It is always thrilling to see someone you know go back to the States. I told him to look at the Statue of Liberty twice, one for me, and he promised that he would.

Lots of love,
Frances

✖　　✖　　✖

ÉCOLE DES BEAUX-ARTS

Attending the École des Beaux-Arts was the secret dream of every artist. Located in a very old quarter on the Left Bank, it was a pile of gray stone with an open court, two stories tall in the center. The court was filled with classic statues, casts, and originals. The school was built around the courts. There was no question of tuition. In France the art schools were state-supported and free of charge to all students.

It was very interesting, and I attended classes when my days off coincided with the class. The language barrier was an impediment. However, it was a psychological lift to even breathe the air of such a legendary place.

✖　　✖　　✖

[A LETTER FROM GENERAL GEORGE S. EYSTER, THE HEAD OF MY SECTION, TO MY FATHER.]

Brig Gen G. S. Eyster
G-3 Section HQ ETOUSA
APO 887 % PM NY

Dear Mr. DeBra,

Your daughter has worked in my office in the ETO as a draftsman and artist for nearly a year. I am on my way to the US at this moment by air on business. I told all of my people I would try and contact their families.

Your daughter is one of my most valued assistants—always cheerful and willing to work long hours if necessary. She does fine work and like all WACs is proud to be serving her Country.

You may rest assured that your daughter is well cared for, is well and doing a fine job.

> Cordially,
> George S. Eyster
> Brigadier General

Hotel Windsor, Paris
March 28, 1945

Dear Dad and Mother,

We have had sunny weather for several days this week, but now the gray weather is back. I suppose this is a typical spring, with rain sandwiched in, until summer comes. However, the sunny days are beautiful and Paris is a lovely city.

Yesterday, a momentous event took place, we were given sheets! Yes, actually. For 10 months, since the "buzz bombs" started hitting London, I have slept between two blankets. The smooth feel of those sheets was unforgettable. I stretched out and sighed blissfully.

We were issued the new winter Off Duty Dresses. It is a shirt-waist type in light tan. Mine needs a good many alterations, but I guess the Army is trying to help us look a little better.

I was issued my overseas stripes, but I haven't put them on my sleeves. You may have seen them; they are small gold bars, one for each six months overseas. They are worn on the left cuff of our blouses, with all of our ribbons, stripes and brass buttons, I feel like a Christmas tree. I am giving you advance warning, when I come down the street in the outfit for the last time, you'd better have a camera focused on me. After I take it off, it will be for good. I am giving a chunk of my youth to the Army.

But seriously, I expect to be over here for quite some time and I am reconciled to it. I can stand a good deal to get this War finished. I am glad you received the letter from General Eyster. He is a fine officer and I have always enjoyed working for him. He is the chief of our section, and I have certainly enjoyed the work here in the Drafting Room, more than anywhere else I have been placed in the Army.

Chuck has a new address again. Marianna was taken over by the First Air Force. Poor guy, he tried to get into another overseas shipment—they said they were taking nothing over

Corporals. He offered to take a bust in rank, but they said no. They didn't want his MCS (Classification No.) and also won't change his MCS for him. So there he sits, very disgusted with it all.

Love,
Frances

13

SPRINGTIME IN WAR-WEARY PARIS

CHESTNUT TREES IN BLOOM

In the spring the drafting room was moved to a small room on the fourth floor on the east side of the Majestic Hotel. Directly beneath my windows was a row of chestnut trees in bloom. They were small, medium-sized trees growing through a circular grate set into the sidewalk. In bloom they were a lovely sight, lighting the drab, weary-worn aspect of the city. But the ambulances still rolled into Paris in an unending stream, day and night. And we wanted to go home, oh how we wanted to go home!

✖   ✖   ✖

Hotel Windsor, Paris
April 6, 1945

Dear Mother and Dad,

Our Easter was a gray cloudy day, too cold for much Easter finery, and since I worked, my new off-duty dress stayed in the closet. I'll wear it one of these days.

After work we did walk a few blocks down the Champs-Elysées. Although the Parisians were out strolling they still wore their winter clothes with a few extraordinary hats here and there.

I do remember last Easter, boarding a ship in New York harbor. Walking up the gang plank is something not to be forgotten and walking down it is something to look forward to.

I am glad that Emma received the copper box. It came from the Flea Market and I thought she might like it. Since you are not able to buy Nescafe for me could you send me some coffee? I understand that it is not rationed and we can always make boiled coffee on our hot plate. I still cling to that hot cup of coffee if I feel low or hungry at night. Send any kind, can, bag or jar. I appreciate it very much.

Here are some snapshots we took and one that Chuck [Lowrie] sent me.

Very much love,
Frances

✖   ✖   ✖

FLOWER CARTS

With spring, the flower carts appeared on the streets. I have always loved lilacs. They are my favorite flower. The colors of the blossoms for sale ran from the palest pink, blue, and lavender to the deepest tones. The lilac branches were a little large for an army drafting room, so I usually settled for a bunch of violets. Flowers in the office in London would have been unthinkable, but by springtime in Paris, a small bouquet was quite acceptable. An armful of lilacs, however, would have very definitely been "out of uniform."

At Easter the altar of the Church of Saint Augustine, on Avenue Freidland and near the Windsor Hotel, was banked with white lilacs. It was a mass of blooms, ten feet tall, and curved around the altar. It was a beautiful sight, and the fragrance was a lift to my spirits.

✖   ✖   ✖

17 Hill Lane
Chingford E 4
London, England
April 11, 1945

Dear Frances,

Thank you so much for your parcel. It was so kind of you, but you really shouldn't waste your money on me. The stockings are grand and I can't remember the last time I had a bottle of perfume, so I'll be able to dress myself up now.

We had a letter from your Mother on Tuesday. I do hope I shall have the opportunity of going out to see you all after the War.

You must be enjoying Paris now—they say it is best in the spring. We have had some beautiful weather, too lately. Our garden is beginning to look nice again now, with all the spring flowers and fruit in blossom.

I went down to Canvey Island for Easter as Arthur was home from Ireland and Bill [Gobel] was on Holiday. Eileen [Wyatt] and I were out with them the whole time and we had a jolly good time.

We all went up to town on Saturday and saw Bing Crosby's latest film. It was good. I returned with them to Canvey for the rest of the weekend.

They all wish to be remembered to you and hope you will be allowed to come back for a leave. If they let you know suddenly, don't bother to write and ask, just come straight here.

Bill is in Palestine now. He at least has a motor bike so is content. He was 21 last Sunday. We hear from him two or three times a week and he seems very well. He was in Cairo for a while and had marvelous food, especially fruit. He said, he made up for all that he had missed during the War.

We can't grumble, for we are getting quite a lot of oranges and lemons now. They taste exceptionally good after having been without them so long.

All the family sends their regards and best wishes. We are all hoping, it won't be too long before you can get leave.

> Cheerio for now,
> Yours,
> Margaret

35 Grafton Road
Canvey Island, Essex
April 11, 1945

Dear Frances,

I received your parcel yesterday, and I really don't know how to thank you enough for it. You couldn't have possibly sent anything more wonderful than those silk stockings. It was like the thrill we used to get when we were kids at Christmas, getting something we had longed for, for ages and thought we would never get. I haven't got over the surprise even yet and the perfume is smashing. I'll keep it for high days and Holidays. It was funny, only Saturday, I was admiring a pair Margaret had on and thinking, gosh, wouldn't I like to have some of those. I am sure you must have known what I was thinking.

We had a rather hectic time last weekend, as it was one of the boy's birthday, we thought a bang up celebration was just the job. We were unlucky at getting any seats for a show, but managed to see the one and only Bing in "Here Comes the Waves" which we took a good view of, then had dinner at the Regent Palace Hotel. We couldn't get in any of the other places, bags of people queuing up, of which we took a very poor view. However, we eventually arrived home just after midnight. We would have been much later, only we were lucky enough to get a Taxi from the Station. Needless to say, we did not rise very early Sunday morning. We went out to Tea and played Table Tennis in the evening. On the whole we enjoyed ourselves.

The weather has been quite nice lately. It makes you feel that summer is on the way at last. The trees are a mass of pink and white blossoms and all the spring flowers are in bloom. Won't it be nice if you do get some leave soon, and if you do stay with Margaret, you must make a weekend or a few days down here again? You know you are always welcome and it seems quite a long while since you were at Canvey. We should love to have you again.

I am trying to get some early nights in to make up for the late ones I have been having, so must say Cheerio for now and thanks again for the parcel. All at home send their love.

Bags of love,
Eileen

Hotel Windsor, Paris
April 17, 1945

Dear Mother and Dad,

The weather is warmer and Paris with blue skies is a gorgeous place. I have a drafting board squarely before a large usually open window. In the evening, the sun streams in our Hotel room. The first thing we do after "evening mess" is place ourselves in the sun light. We can't seem to get enough of it after the long winter.

I had a letter from Roberta [Harrison] last week; she is at Mac Dill Field, Tampa, Florida. Now she is a Sgt. Isn't that grand. I was so happy for her. She wrote a very nice letter and her handwriting is perfect. I look at her letter, sigh and then start my scribble.

I sent a small package to Margaret Gobel and her cousin Eileen. I stayed there when on my 48 hour pass to Canvey Island. It was a couple of pairs of hose and a small bottle of perfume a piece. I received a letter from each of them, thanking me. I was given several pairs of hose for Christmas and they were so thrilled, that I felt undeserving of their thanks. Margaret had just received a letter from Mother. She would like to meet and visit us after the War. So, who knows?

I hope you received the snapshots. We are waiting for some others to be developed. Back to the subject of food, the Army gives us enough food, but it is so tasteless. I continually crave something salty, sour or sweet.

Love,
Frances

Marianna, Florida
April 18, 1945

Dear Folks,

The cookies arrived today and they were very good. Luckily I have the afternoon off as I'm on night KP so I'll munch on the cookies while I am loafing. The barracks are empty so I can eat them in peace; if the characters I live with were in I'd undoubtedly get one or two cookies and consider myself lucky to salvage that many.

A letter is a different way to meet a person, but Fran has spoken so much of you in her letters that I don't feel like a stranger. So in this letter and in future letters I'll just ramble on as if I had known you for years.

In my mind you have the sweetest daughter in the world and if I can measure half way up to her, I'll believe I am really doing something. Before meeting her I was completely satisfied just plodding along my own way. I had one Buddy on this Base I palled around with all the time. He became the editor of the paper shortly after Fran left.

When she quit the paper to go to work down on the Line I knew then that she was the one girl for me. One afternoon, she called up and said that she was shipping. To me, it seemed like everything in the world was crumbling. I couldn't believe it and strange as it may seem after all this time, it doesn't seem possible.

Shortly after she left, I went home on a furlough and I can't say I enjoyed it very much. I guess I feel the same way you do; I want her back in the States as soon as possible. In one of her letters she expressed the fear that about the time she was ready to come back, I'd be shipping. This will probably happen, I am long over due. Last Sunday, I finished 3 years in the Air Force and while sewing the "hash mark" on my blouse, I said a silent prayer that I hoped I wouldn't acquire another one. I have been on this Air Field 28 months and I am beginning to feel that many more months in this place and I will be ready for the crazy house. Ever since I've been here, I have tried to get out, but I met a stone wall of resistance.

We have changed commands three times = 1st Eastern Flying Training Command, then 3rd Air Force and now the 1st Air Force, just by staying in one spot. Now that I've finally sewed on all of my shoulder patches, it would seem perfectly plausible to change again.

I read in a Camp newspaper from an Eastern Flying Training Command that they are accepting enlisted men who are qualified for B-29 Super Fort Flight Engineer Training and former Air Cadets are eligible. The course takes 47 weeks to complete. In this course one has to take 10 weeks of preflight training. The preflight I had at Maxwell Field was plain murder. Never the less, if I get the chance I believe I'll take it.

Well, I guess I will close for now and get ready to go peel spuds. Please write soon and thanks again for those swell cookies.

Love,
Chuck

Hotel Windsor, Paris
April 23, 1945

Dear Dad and Mother,

A couple of cold gloomy days after the lovely weather we've had, it is a let down after the brilliant sunshine. My spirits seem to go up and down with the thermometer. In July, I'll be unhappy because it will be too hot, but right now I soak up the heat. Last winter was a little cool for me.

We are now authorized to have a furlough. Some people have already gone back to England or Scotland, and I have a very warm invitation from Margaret Gobel. But a furlough spot on the Riviera will be opened up soon and I think I would like to see the South of France.

The envelopes with the writing paper and the new LIBERTY arrived. It has an article of Paris WACs. Not too bad, but if you read it, take it with a grain of salt please. Conditions are not always as they are pictured.

I will never be sorry for having joined the Army or for coming overseas, but it certainly is stretching into a long War. I expect to be here some months yet and it is a struggle to remember that I will have a different sort of life someday.

We were issued a new suit last week, slacks, skirt and jacket. The jacket is copied from the British Battle Jacket. They look quite nice. It is very fortunate because our ODs [olive drabs] were certainly getting threadbare. I kept wondering how long mine would stay together.

I received an April 13 TIME yesterday. They are coming just about a week late now, and I consider it very late news.

Love,
Frances

✕   ✕   ✕

NEW UNIFORMS

The new uniform was comfortable and becoming. The jacket was patterned after the British battle jacket. General Dwight D. Eisenhower had adopted it, so it was also known as the Eisenhower jacket. The slacks matched and were worn with the jacket when we were traveling. They were made there in Paris for us to our measurements. We were still wearing the men's overseas caps, but we were allowed to wear the slacks, with shirt and tie, and the felt jacket, which had been the liner for our field jackets, as an off-duty uniform.

This was a comfortable informal uniform we had never had before. The only other pants we had were either the field pants or coveralls, and neither was suitable for anything except field conditions or work.

The skirt and slacks had buttons inside the waistband that buttoned into a flap inside the bottom part of the battle jacket. This kept the outfit from gapping at the waist and the shirt from showing. It made a neat appearance. This was fortunate for me because in the summer of 1945 my skirts were beginning to hang on me. And the new jacket had no brass buttons!

✕   ✕   ✕

Hotel Windsor, Paris
April 27, 1945

Dear Mother and Dad,

I saw a familiar face a couple of days ago—Paul Denson. Imagine, he has worked just around the corner from me for two months and our paths had not crossed. He has been trying to locate me. It was especially nice to see him. He told me about Scotland and I talked about London. We plan to take some pictures Saturday morning, when we are both off. His Billet is even about 4 or 5 blocks from mine. But that is Paris and the Army for you. He is the first person from home I've seen over here.

We were just issued the new WAC overseas cap, with yellow scarf and gloves, very spiffy. All these new clothes make me gasp.

I understand the WACs will parade on May 14 (the date of our founding) so if some one gets some good snapshots, I'll send them on. We should be quite a sight. The French aren't the only ones who can parade down the Champs-Elysees.

This is about all because the past week was just as usual. Paris maybe a hot spot for tourists, but not for a "working girl."

Much love,
Frances

✖ ✖ ✖

WORKING GIRL

The options for entertainment were limited. Paris was a city that had been at war for years. The only goods in the shops were the remnants of prewar stocks or "ersatz" products used only through necessity. The shoes with wooden platform soles must have been very painful for the feet of the women who had to wear them.

The Red Cross clubs were filled with thousands of soldiers in Paris on leave. We were a small boat of WACs in a great sea of soldiers. There were only seven or eight thousand of us in the entire ETO that spring of 1945, and that was the greatest number we ever reached in the theater.

At the Hotel Windsor, our dates stopped at the front desk and gave our name to the French man in charge. He called our room and informed us that we had a visitor waiting. We were also allowed to invite company to eat in our evening mess if we notified the orderly room in advance. We were still barred by army regulations from meals in any of the French restaurants.

The amusement park, Luna Park, had a tall, tall roller coaster, and in the summer we went to the American Legion Post Number 1 for hamburgers.

We waited in line for movies, walked all over Paris, sometimes in the rain, and sat on the benches, that were placed on the lovely wide boulevards and talked about going home.

✖ ✖ ✖

Marianna, Florida
May 4, 1945

Dear Dad,

Received your letter this PM and was sure glad to hear from you. We just cleaned the BKs for tomorrow's inspection, so instead of just loafing around thought I'd come over to the office and write a couple of letters.

The pictures were swell and as for myself I think it is a pretty nice family. In fact pretty nice is a gross understatement. I hope you can make out my writing OK. My mind is generally three jumps ahead of my hand.

I believe I'll be heading for the Coast on a furlough around the 21st of this month. I really don't care about going but my buddy who has been taking care of my business was drafted about a month ago and now his Mother is taking care of things for me. So this trip will be mostly spent straightening things out for her.

A boy who was in the Cadets with me was also going. He had arranged a hop (flight) for us to the Coast and tonight I found out he was shipping on a Station to Station transfer. So there goes the flight out the window and I'll have to take that blasted train which means four days out and four back.

I don't believe I've told you much about my section of the country. As most Californians I think the sun rises and sets on that State. Undoubtedly I am prejudiced, even though I can't be classified as a native. I was born in North Dakota but left there when I was about 18 months old. We went back there when I was 8 years old but one year was enough to send the folks hurrying back to the Coast.

Long Beach is about 24 miles south of Los Angeles and is located right on the ocean. It and San Pedro Harbor are the home base for the Pacific Fleet. You know there are large oil fields out there and within a radius of 10 miles we have about 7 large refineries. Now, with aircraft and shipyards it is a

Frances at Parc Monceau. Military personnel could ride free on the Paris Metro, giving Frances the opportunity to explore Paris.

pretty busy place. Normally, the population is about 165,000 but now it is nearer 300,000.

My place is about 10 blocks from the Ocean and I guess I miss the Ocean more than anything else. We do a lot of traveling out there on days off. To put 300 miles on a car on Sunday is not unusual. We are a bunch of desert rats, so we frequently go down to Palm Springs or up to the Mojave Desert. These take about 3 hours to reach. Then in winter we head for the mountains. We know all of the best fishing spots. We also get quite a bit of rain and plenty of fog.

Before I left to come in the Army I put my car up on blocks and gave the tires to my buddy. When I go home I always check it and it seems to be OK. When I get out I'll probably have to have the engine over hauled but I am glad I kept it. Cars are selling for a small mint now and I expect to drive it for a year or so after the War.

Fran said she couldn't drive but she is sure going to learn when this is all over and I can see now this is going to be an experience in itself. I just hope she is not too short for the brake and clutch. I drive with the seat all the way back, but with her it is going to be as far forward as possible. Guess I'll just have to pick a nice straight road and let her go her darndest.

I detect the same thing in her letters as you have. She is darn homesick but now with Germany on the rocks it shouldn't be too long before she is on her way back. This Army beats me. Here I thought she was going to release me for overseas and look what happened. Gosh, I don't think I'll ever live that down, if I stay in the States for the duration—ah me.

I understand the occupation troops for Germany have already been picked. It is the 15th Army. This Field will probably be open long after the others have closed—the only thing that is holding me is my job, they just don't need us.

I hope it is true that they will discharge us according to length of service. My three years should come in handy that way. If it is according to the point system I'll be up a tree.

I'll sign off now and go hit the hay; probably my next letter will be from California. Give my love to Mom and Sis.

Yours,
Chuck

Danville, Indiana
May 6, 1945

Dear Old Sarge,

Well, here I am again to chew the fat with you for a little while. Mommie and Little Sis stayed for Church. We all went to Sunday School but I guess I am sort of a heathen for I can't resist the temptation to get out in the sunshine when I get a chance. So I came home to write you before dinner; then I intend to get out in the sun this afternoon. But first I've got to de-louse the old setting hen. She is doing a grand job of setting on that one lone egg; won't get off to eat. She is going to be surprised when she finds 25 baby chicks under her next Friday morning.

The meat shortage is getting so bad that everyone is raising chickens. People at the corner of Tennessee and Main Street are raising chickens right under the window of that big house where Joe Hess used to live. Just wait until a hot day comes with a good rain afterwards; the people in that big house will have to move out. I am moving our temporary chicken lot for the young chickens further to the North. Mommie has an old hen in the pot for dinner today even though she was laying. But we want to eat all of them before the little chickens get big enough to shut up in the chicken house.

By the way, did you know that Little Sis is teaching the Beginners Class at the Methodist Sunday School now? She says it gives her practice for handling kids if she ever gets a job teaching. By going to College here through the summer, she can get through in three years. Then by taking a Masters degree at Butler she can be a dandy teacher in four years. Of course if the right man comes along she'll probably marry and settle down as a house wife but the education she can get won't hurt her, no matter what she does.

I am sending you a picture of Mommie and Little Sis and her new Easter hat that she made out of an old one for about a quarter. She is pretty proud of her hat and ability to make things for herself.

Annie [Cox] has moved back to the old house on the back of their lot and is renting out the two new houses. I suspect she gets $39 a month out of the two houses, and with only herself to care for she is sitting pretty. She still goes back and forth to Indianapolis and cooks for a restaurant.

All of our garden is planted now and if we get some warm weather it may come up. Some radishes are already up and the beans that Margaret Gobel sent us from London are coming along in good shape. We will write and tell her and would have sent some seed corn but I don't believe it gets warm enough over there to even sprout it.

Love,
Daddy

14

V-E DAY

Hotel Windsor, Paris
May 8, 1945

Dear Dad and Mother,

V-E Day is here at last! Last night the celebration started with the Arc of Triumphe lighted up and planes flying over dropping flares. Today the festivities really got under way.

We worked as usual, but at 3 PM the sirens started to blow the "Last All Clear of the War," and after that the Church Bells were rung all over Paris.

It gave me an odd feeling; there is something not quite real about it. Since, we have waited so long for it—now it is hard to believe. And of course, the Army's job is not finished and I am not referring to the Japs either. There is a great deal of mopping up to be done here yet.

All afternoon planes were buzzing Paris. I have never seen a four motor down so low. The buildings are not more than seven stories tall and the thunder of the motors as the planes just skimmed the chimney tops was unnerving. I was on the fourth floor of the Majestic Hotel and that is a lot of airplane seemingly just a few feet over your head. They shook the buildings. Some of the fighters flew under the bridges over the Seine.

On the way back to the billet after work, we could hardly get across the Champs-Elysées for the crowd just milling around and walking up and down. The French people simply have to be out and see for themselves.

How the crowds are tonight, I can't say because I am staying in. My roommates are out and I'll get all the news about it first hand.

We have had drill practice every evening for a couple of weeks now. We are to have a parade on the 14th (WAC anniversary), hence the practice. We should look quite sharp, swinging down the Avenue in our yellow gloves and scarves, but oh, those evening practices. After you have worked all day, it isn't so exciting to spend your evening "hutting" up and down.

Much love,
Frances

[That was a poignant moment for me, remembering the other "All Clears" here and in London. I never heard the sound of a church bell in England. The bells were reserved for a warning of invasion.]

Danville, Indiana
May 13, 1945

Dear Old Big Sis,

We just got back from Church and Sunday School. Took Mommie along as our passport for Mother's Day. Little Sis sings in the choir now besides teaching the Beginners Class at Sunday School. She is getting to be a pretty good sort of a kid.

I wondered if you had a big time on V-E Day. Here in Danville all the stores closed in the afternoon; the school band was out and they had a speech around the flag pole on the square. A big crowd was there. Neither Pug [Edward J. Weesner] nor I could see much to whoop it up about with still another war to be won. He said, "I'll feel like whopping it up when Joe Stalin declares war on Japan." And I told him that I wouldn't until I saw you step off the bus, and streak for home to get out of your uniform.

Little Sis and Lee Collins took their Girl Scout troop on a hike to the Twin Bridges yesterday. They went ahead through the fields and woods and laid a paper trail for the kids to follow. They cooked a one meal dish in the open over a camp fire and had a grand time generally.

I got a long letter from Chuck [Lowrie] and will answer it today. The more I hear from him the more I think that you are a darned good picker-outer.

Here it is Sunday night and Mommie and I just came back from Baccalaureate Service at the Christian Church. The Preacher kidded them by saying he very seldom spoke longer than an hour and a half and then he proceeded to talk almost that long. And after he was through he hadn't said very much.

On Tuesday afternoon I got my twenty-five chickens and the old hen took to them just like she had hatched everyone of them out of that one egg. It has been a little chilly and one of them died today but I think the others will make the grade all right now that the weather has started to warm up. We have even let the fire go out in the furnace. The cool weather hasn't been very good for the garden. The corn is peeping through and the tomatoes and cabbage plants are looking good.

I am glad that you WACs get to strut your stuff tomorrow and I hope that you get to show the French what a good old fashioned American girl looks like. I'd give a lot to be there and see you. You are getting to see a lot of events over there that will make history. It may not look so very important to you now; but fifty years from now you can look back on these days and be thankful you had a chance to watch the wheels go around in the big War.

Dinsmore moved those big wall boards covered with Service pictures up into his big show window [Dinsmore ran a store that was located next door to the *Danville Republican*] for the V-E Day celebration, and your picture looms up as big as life.

I'll be seeing you some of these days when the War with the Japs is over and I am hoping it won't be so very long. Thumbs up Big Sis.

Love,
Daddy

Hotel Windsor, Paris
Middle of May 1945

Dear Dad and Mother,

The letter came from Dad yesterday and a V-mail from Momma today. I also received an April 2nd TIME on the 9th. That is really up to the minute news! But whether they are a week or 3 months old, I read them just the same, from cover to cover. You gave me a fine present when you gave me a subscription. I always give an extra happy sigh when they are at Mail Call.

I had a typhoid "booster" shot last night and today my arm is really sore. I could stand the arm, but along with it I have an ache from head to toe. It seems my shot is taking effect! I should be all right by tomorrow, but right now I feel like digging a hole and crawling in it.

We have nice weather and then a few days of dreary weather. I suppose spring is just unsettled, but I have a suspicion that summer here will be very warm. However, the big stone buildings always seem to retain some of their chill and dampness, no matter how warm the sunshine is.

Last week, we switched to double summertime, which speeds up the day. Now it is only dusk at 9 o'clock and the sun streams in the west window of our Hotel room, while we are here. After dinner tonight, I parked myself and my typhoid shot, down in an easy chair right before the open window and soaked up the sun. After the damp cold winter we've had, the sun is wonderful.

Another milestone passed, we are to turn in our "Hobby Hats," after packing them across an ocean. I am certainly glad to get rid of it. That hat was a mistake the WAC will never live down.

In his letter, Dad said he'd like to send something to Chuck too. My suggestion is to write him a letter. He gets very little mail from California and you know how the Army feels about mail. I also realize I am taking my reputation in my hands—just leave me a little glamour for my future. He calls me a washed-out blond, already.

He is pretty sensitive about not being overseas and maintains that I was suppose to relieve him not visa versa. But, he has tried again and again—that I know. The Army puts you where they want to and that is all. I know he would enjoy a letter from you. He is a pretty wonderful guy.

Lots of love,
Frances

✖   ✖   ✖

PARADE ON MAY 14, 1945

We paraded on May 14, the anniversary of the founding of the Corps. We marched six abreast around the Arc de Triomphe, the Tomb of the Unknown Soldier, and down the Champs-Élysées. We were the Headquarters Company and at the head of the parade just behind the band.

Captain Wilton, our Company Commander, led, and Lucille Verzano, one of my roommates, was in the first row. Lee Noyes and I were shorter, so we were four rows back.

We wore our Class A uniforms with brass buttons, gleaming of course, yellow scarves, and yellow cotton gloves to match. We also wore our new overseas caps, which had been designed for us. Previously we had worn the men's caps that were constructed on a straight line. The new caps were designed on a curve, which fit our heads much better.

The Champs-Élysées was a perfect setting for a parade. The crowds along the sides, cobblestones under foot, and photographers, both military and civilian, dashing back and forth to get the best angles, as down the hill we went.

WACs marching down the Champs-Élysées, May 14, 1945.

Danville, Indiana
May 21, 1945

Dear Old Big Sis,

I didn't write to you Sunday when I had the time so I am doing it Monday night. I am enclosing a bill (advertising) we printed for V-E Day when we were suppose to celebrate our Victory in Europe. Well, we didn't celebrate much here; just took half a day off on Tuesday. Mommie and Little Sis went to Church that evening.

The other bill I am sending to you is a Royal Theatre bill which I print every Friday. You will notice that Tuesday and Wednesday nights are Bank Nights. Everybody registers and if you are there when your name is called you get at least $100. If the person wasn't there it goes up to $15 each week until someone is lucky. Dick Helton's Dad drew $300 one night and his sister drew over $200 about a year later. Mommie goes faithfully every Wednesday night but has never been lucky yet.

Pug just received a wire from LOOK magazine wanting to come here to Danville and go to a party for Durwood Vaughan who is coming home soon from a German Prison Camp. Maybe you've read some of their "Look Goes to a Party" stories; it devotes two pages each week to those special stories with two pages of pictures. It would be the biggest thing ever to come to Danville. But that darned fool Dad of Durwood's may throw a monkey wrench into the gears yet. So we don't know just what will happen. Durwood maybe all right but I wouldn't give two whoops for the rest of the family. His Dad tried to grab off a special Service for Durwood last Decoration Day because he was reported as a prisoner in Germany. It pretty nearly took the Sheriff to stop him pulling it off. And at the same time there were eighty boys in the County who would never come back again; The Ketters with their last two boys gone for good. People who knew about it were awfully sore at the Vaughans for that stunt.

Sunday will be Decoration Day in Danville; with the school band out and the firing squad firing salutes at the Cemeteries. I have your old camera loaded and if there is anything that might interest you I will try and get it.

I wrote to Chuck last week but I expect he is on furlough in California. That is where he said he was going in his last letter; said he had some business that needed attention. I wish he could drop by here so we could get a little better acquainted. You know, in his last letter he called me Dad just like you kids. Dog gone it sounded good. You know Mommie and I always wanted a boy in the family and now we've got one. You and Little Sis were such helpless little warts when we first met you that we just decided to keep you instead of trading you off for boys. Maybe it is just as well for boys are an awful bother to raise. Of course when you can get one like Chuck already raised, that makes it better, and from his letters I think Chuck did a mighty good job of raising himself.

Keep your chin up, Sarge. This War can't last forever and sooner or later you and Chuck will be on your way home. There is a great day coming bye and bye. Don't ever doubt that. Just soak up as much of Paris as you can while you are there.

The little chickens are coming home OK and will make the skillet smell in about three months. We still have 23, one died and the old hen stepped on one. Those with a back log of 8 old hens ought to keep us going. We had our first mess of radishes today out of the garden. Meat is almost out of the question, about once a week is all the meat we can get with our limited red points; but we are willing to do without a whole lot to shorten the War and bring you kids back home again.

Love,
Dad

Hotel Windsor, Paris
June 1, 1945

Dear Mother and Dad,

We all feel unsettled—the War is over and we know a good many changes will be made. I think we will move out of here and that feeling of not knowing where you will go, or what you will do is a little nerve wracking. But that is the Army and something I will never get use to. I guess I like to be my own boss instead of a number on a sheet of paper.

My furlough is still hanging fire. It will probably be July or August now. I wanted to go to Scotland or Switzerland, at least somewhere. By then a good many people will have had their furloughs and I shouldn't have any difficulty.

I went to the Opera last week, the first time in months. We heard Madame Butterfly and La Boheme at the Opera Comique. It was good. I will never get my fill of music. It is hard being without a radio.

A letter came from Peg [Allison Nightingale] and she wants to know if I am taking out French papers. Heaven forbid. I had two boxes from you a couple of days ago. Kleenex, cheese, crackers, coffee and soup, all appreciated I assure you. The dates are delicious, but do remember, I don't want you to use any of your points for things of this type. You keep those for yourselves.

Much love,
Frances

[FROM MARY UMHOLTZ.]
[Mary always wrote the whole letter and then went back and put in the punctuation.]

Philippines
June 2, 1945

Dear Frances,

I am nearly as bad as you are at answering mail. I made up my mind to spend this Saturday night home, although some of the invitations to dances were tempting.

We came up here about a week ago from New Guinea. Flew up and no airsickness. Hope I get to fly home, instead of the long boat ride, but according to the credit system, I have some time to think about that. I have nine more points to go. I sure hope you will be seeing the States soon, that is if you won't join the Army of Occupation.

We are living in barracks up here now. We have inspections and we are getting more GIs all the time. Sometimes I wish I was still with the girls in F.E.A.S.C. [Far Eastern Air Service Command]

If you could know all of the jobs I've had in the last month you would realize how smart the Dutch are—to give you an idea—tailor shop, mail clerk, A-2, PRO and at present AG filing. "Jack of all trades and master of none." I just hope my patience endures until the photo lab gets on the way. Never was so disgusted since I've been overseas.

Thursday was my day off, while I changed jobs, so a gang of us went into Manila. Not much there to see besides ruins and places to get rid of money darn fast. I made up my mind to save mine and have a good time when I come home. It was terribly hot and dirty, so we were glad to come back. We visited the Presidents Palace, which wasn't in very bad shape. The Chapel impressed us the most. On our way, we went to the Chinese Cemetery. That was worth seeing; words can't describe the architecture and monuments. In some places there are still the Japanese guns dug in right among the graves. After walking over the whole area in the dust and hot sun we really appreciated our little canvas cots with mosquito nets to tuck in every night.

Are you still single or do you still have the same intentions as when you left Florida. (I mean with the Beam staff.)

One advantage we have here is no KP. Filipino men do it and the girls do our laundry. They certainly do a good job on the rice starch and ironing. They do the cleaning in the barracks while the men do the work outside. They are always outside our gate selling bananas, pineapple, and other fruit. Seven bananas are sold for a peso—50¢ in American money.

I'll be looking for an answer if you find time before going home. That no doubt is a laugh. Don't do anything I wouldn't approve of. Checking the commas, now!

Love, Dutch

15

SUMMER

Hotel Windsor, Paris
June 6, 1945

Dear Dad and Mother,

Summer is just around the corner, again. This climate is a little like Chicago, cold and then hot—continually. We swelter in our ODs [olive drabs] and then freeze.

Another box arrived from you, the day before yesterday. I do appreciate the time and trouble you take to send me these things. It makes me feel that I still belong somewhere. I feel cut off from the familiar somehow.

Lee [Noyes] and I were off today so we shopped a little. I wanted to buy some extra watercolors and paper, and then if we are shipped out of here, I can go on sketching. They have fine materials here; the handmade rag watercolor paper is in a class by itself.

We have a holiday tomorrow. It is an observation of D-Day, coupled with my time off today, it will seem like a vacation.

The TIME magazine still comes through as usual and also the LIBERTY. It is a big help.

I am sleepy now, so Good Night. By the way, just what sort of pointers are you giving Chuck [Lowrie]?

Love,
Frances

Hotel Windsor, Paris
June 17, 1945

Dear Dad and Mother,

I seem to be slipping; I can't make myself write letters. It is because I don't do anything out of the ordinary, or at least that is what I think.

One of the sergeants at the office invited me to a piano recital a couple of days ago. It was a Polish pianist and very good. I enjoyed it.

Lee and I had the day off and planned to do a little shopping, but we came back empty handed. To tell the truth, there is very little here worth buying. The troops in on pass have about picked the shops clean, coupled with the high value of the franc, you find yourself paying enormous prices for fairly worthless goods.

I have mailed some more packages home, glassware, books and letters just pile it in the corner for me. Several sketch books are enclosed. Personal things, so please don't show them to everyone. I know you will think them interesting, but they are all mixed up together, the good and the bad and I am pretty sensitive about the bad ones.

We had our money converted again, brand new francs. It will be a relief to get back to U.S. currency. I am tired of these odd shaped bills and computing value in my head.

We still hear rumors of a move into Germany, possibly Frankfort. The Army has given me so many clothes, I'm not sure I'll fit them into the Duffle bag.

There is no special sign of our coming home. There is a lot of work to be done yet and G-3 is handling Redeployment of Troops, so we are expanding day by day.

Love,
Frances

P.S. When I think of the pictures you've sent to Chuck and all of the things you've probably told him, I shudder. By the way, he never complains about my handwriting.

Fran

✖   ✖   ✖

G-3

The middle of June, when our section was expanding, the G-2 (Intelligence) drafting room, with a staff of two or three was merged with the G-3 drafting room, which at that time consisted of me. Then in a matter of a few weeks the staff was increased to about ten, a dizzying number after working alone or with Sergeant Frank Martello.

The drafting room at that time was on the ground floor of the Majestic Hotel, next to the G-2 war room. These rooms looked out over the Rue de la Perouse. Two WACs were added to the section along with other draftsmen. All of the other departments were expanding, and a new section, the Water Embarkation Department, was created.

We were continually finding new faces around us. One morning I came to work, crossed the war room, and said "Good Morning" to several new GIs. One of them was Halton Brown, but he was back in a corner and I hardly noticed him. Afterwards, he always said I said good morning to everyone but him. In a few weeks, the drafting room was moved up to the fifth floor. He was assigned to water embarkations, and from then on he hung around the nearby drafting room.

BLACK MARKET AND MONEY EXCHANGE

We were always aware that the exchange rate for us was not favorable. Although it was probably necessary in view of the large numbers of American troops interacting with the civilian populations, we felt that we were being asked to bear an additional burden.

England was very strictly controlled, with no visible black market, but France was very different. The black market in Paris was an important component of the economy. The Parisians resorted to it for items not available elsewhere. Troops on leave spent the money that they had been unable to spend while in rural areas and this, coupled with poker winnings and the money from war souvenirs, was unloaded on the rear echelon, feeding the black market.

Cigarettes, desired by so many, were a standard item of exchange. Many of the items we were allowed to buy at the PX were also greatly in demand. The prices we paid at the PX were very normal, providing many opportunities for enterprising traders.

✖   ✖   ✖

Hotel Windsor, Paris
June 20, 1945

Dear Mother and Dad,

Here I am writing for something else! I need some more shirts. My GI shirts are as unsatisfactory as ever, and my own are wearing out. The shirt you bought at Strauss is fine. The label says (Regulation sanforized Military Shirts, Form fit styled by Yale). You sent a 13 ½" collar, and about a 28" sleeve. I would like 3 cotton shirts of that make, if possible and washable spun rayon. Please take the money from my bank account.

If I am to spend the rest of my life here, I may as well have some shirts that fit. Right now, the prospects for sailing home are remote.

The rolls of film, Dad sent me came. Thanks again, I am trying to save a roll for that still awaited furlough. I am always upset with the French developing and printing.

We are having a very hot spell now. Today it was 92 degrees. That is hot when you are in winter uniform! But along will come a cold snap and we will shiver again. What a climate. Give me Chicago, any time; at least the air is fresh.

> Love,
> Frances

✖   ✖   ✖

ISSUED SHIRTS

The issued shirts were styled with a convertible collar and without the standing collar band of the men's shirts. The shirts never did fit neatly around the neck with a necktie, which we always wore. The sleeve length could be anything, so early on I started shortening the sleeves by hand. Permanent press was a much later process, so the cotton shirts were washed by hand with a bar of soap, starched, dried, sprinkled, and ironed. The spun rayon could be only lightly pressed. It was a slow, labor-intensive process.

✖   ✖   ✖

Chicago, Illinois
June 24, 1945

Dear Fran,

Well my honey, you are a -----! You didn't write to me until two weeks after V-E Day or more and I had no idea where you were. I miss you. Bill [Nightingale] just doesn't appreciate Michigan Avenue at all.

We have had most peculiar weather here and for Chicago that is something. You think of peculiarization here as natural, anyway spring got lost somewhere. It was cold and rainy clear up to June 21, now it is as hot as blazes. I even wore my fur coat in May, Imagine!

I love my job. It is from 9 AM to 1:15 PM at the Board of Trade. I am a messenger, I work for a Company who has a phone on the floor, they phone in the order to buy or sell, put it on a paper and I take it to the broker who deals in it. It is interesting and excellent pay for the hours—keeps me busy.

How come you're in ODs yet? Didn't you get any summer issue, or a chance to buy those new dresses? Also where do you live now—still in the Hotel? Send some pictures, please. Need anything—Birthday is coming.

Love,
Peg [Allison Nightingale]

✘   ✘   ✘

HAMBURGER IN A CAN

In the summer of 1945, an advertisement from the Ladies Home Journal *came into our hands. It was a full page showing two beautifully browned, luscious hamburgers next to an open army ration can. The background was a soft red color, setting off the patties to perfection. The caption read:*

GRILLED HAMBURGERS IN A CAN
"Our fighters in the front lines were hungry
for hamburgers. So the US Army Quartermaster
Corps. Put millions of these precooked
Hamburgers into the combat rations of our men
All over the world."

We hung this beautiful picture on the wall of the drafting room and contemplated it with great pleasure. However, no man who had been in combat, visitors from other theaters of war, or personnel in our own headquarters had ever laid eyes on one of them, or heard of anyone who had consumed one of those beauties!

✗　　✗　　✗

Hotel Windsor, Paris
July 11, 1945

Dear Mother and Dad,

Janie [Baranowski] is a T/Sergeant, isn't it grand! It is about time, she certainly deserved it. We had a cracker jack of a storm last night, thunder, lightning and everything, just like Indiana. It was the first real rain storm I've seen on this side of the ocean. Usually they are only light showers, so I had decided they just didn't have them here. But sure enough, we did and I felt almost at home.

Lee and I saw the Mickey Rooney "Stage Show" at the Marigny Theater last Friday. It was good. Then tonight, I saw the play "French Without Tears" with Anna Neagle and Rex Harrison. It was excellent and very, very English.

Paris is about the same, thousands and thousands of soldiers in on leave and prices as high as ever.

We have personal inspection tomorrow evening. It means I rise and shine at 6 AM. I am also on CQ tonight, with Bed Check at 1 AM. Ho, hum a little while longer to go.

Chuck wrote and said he received some more cookies from you. I am on pins and needles expecting him to be shipped out of there and there is little chance that I'll get back before he is gone. Since if he goes to the Pacific that is what it will be. Added to the months behind, it is hard.

Much love,
Fran

P.S. Lee and Lucille [Verzano] said not to use a CHEZIT box for Ritz crackers, it is too great a disappointment. They love cheese crackers.

✗　　✗　　✗

GERTRUDE STEIN

On one of the long summer evenings, a lieutenant from G-3 and I were walking along the Left Bank near Notre Dame Cathedral. Standing at the railing overlooking the embankment, we looked below and saw some young French people dancing what appeared to be a folk dance. As we watched, a stocky gray-haired woman turned to us and my eyes bulged because she certainly resembled the pictures of Gertrude Stein. I tried not to stare, but "a rose is a rose is a rose" ran through my head.

My companion was straightforward and asked politely if she was Gertrude Stein. She smiled and said, "Yes, I am," and proceeded to tell us about the dancing below. It was a type of dance associated with the season. After a few moments we parted. It all seemed an integral part of Paris.

✖   ✖   ✖

Hotel Windsor, Paris
July 15, 1945

Dear Dad and Mother,

The hot weather we've had the last few days! Golly, can't remember when I have been so hot! It was suppose to be 90 degrees yesterday and I think that was underestimated. We wear woolen clothes, with jackets buttoned up and it is pretty bad. I have almost forgotten what it would be like to wear a short sleeved dress.

Yesterday was July 14th, Bastille Day and the French celebrated as usual. Because work was slack, they let me go to the Hotel in the afternoon, but it was so terribly hot I couldn't bear the idea of dressing in my uniform to go out, so about 11 o'clock we went up on the roof to watch the fireworks. It was very impressive. The Arc, Napoleon's Tomb, Sacred Heart and Notre Dame were all lighted with flood lights and the City was really beautiful, spread out before us. That sight, coupled with a breeze blowing made me hate to go back inside.

Today was my regular day off, so I was lazy until about 2 PM when I finally gathered enough energy to take myself off to the Louvre Museum. They now have a collection of about 80 masterpieces and I do mean masterpieces! Just about the cream of the collection. They have made an effort to get a number of the well known pictures, so the American Troops could take advantage of it. They were really wonderful.

Yesterday morning, asked Major [Florence] Clark for a 3 day pass to Brussels. She said

"Certainly." Lee and Lucille have permission also barring unforeseen circumstances, we should be in Brussels next Sunday I am thrilled. I have always wanted to see it and going with my roommates will be extra special.

There is also the inducement of ice cream, all flavors. How much do you think I can eat in three days?

We know we are scheduled to leave for Germany soon but don't know the date. I said Major Clark gave me the pass without question. She has been my direct boss ever since I've been in G-3 and I couldn't ask for a better one. Many WAC officers leave much to be desired but she is tops. I have enjoyed working under her.

Love,
Frances

✖   ✖   ✖

LOUVRE MUSEUM

When I first visited the Louvre Museum in the winter, there were no pictures on display, only pieces of sculpture in the cold, bleak galleries—Abyssinian, I believe. In the summer of 1945, however, the officials acclimatized the Grande Gallerie and hung a collection of masterpieces so the American troops could see a few of the museum's treasures.

The Mona Lisa*, in a standing frame, all to herself was in a prominent part of the middle section of the gallery. There were two Rembrandts—the famous* Slaughtered Ox*, a medium-size picture and a self-portrait of the artist wearing a turban that was painted in his later years. I stood and looked at it a long time; the eyes were filled with sad wisdom. It was a portrait that did literally speak to you.*

My favorite was The Lace Maker *by Jan Vermeer. I had seen many reproductions of the work, but the size of the painting was a surprise. It is difficult to judge the size of a painting from a print. I had always thought this one to be a life-size portrait. But no, it was very small (nine inches by eight inches), and was truly beautiful. How Vermeer could place all of those sparkling highlights without causing them to be a distraction in the picture I'll never know. That one I would have been tempted to carry home with me.*

The very large Liberty Leading the People *by Eugène Delacroix was striking, but the others are vague in my memory. At the head of the stairs were the* Victory of Samothrace *and the* Venus de Milo. *I assume they were the originals, but of course they could have been copies. I did not have the knowledge in sculpture to determine it.*

The entire Bayeaux Tapestry, from the Norman Conquest of England, was displayed in a long chest-high case hanging on the wall just before the entrance of the Grande Gallerie. I gazed at it, enthralled by the handwork and the echoes of history I fancied I could feel coming from it.

PICASSO

One of the draftsmen told me that he had been in a small Left Bank café and had met Pablo Picasso. At first I thought someone must have been having fun with him. Since the sighting was at the Café Deux Maggots, a favorite spot for Picasso, it evidently was true. I thought that I too would like to get a glimpse of the famous artist, but not to the extent of venturing into a strange bistro.

There was a great lack of knowledge about artists and paintings. One occasional visitor to the drafting room, who had become very friendly with a French family, insisted that they had given him a Vincent Van Gogh painting. I told him there were many copyists busily working, and it would be very unlikely that it was an original Van Gogh. He was firmly convinced, however, that he had been presented with a great treasure.

HALTON

I went out with Halton Brown for the first time on July 16, which I later found out was his birthday. We saw a stage show at the Marigny Theater. He had been with G-3 a month and was billeted in the Petit Palais that was just across from the Grand Palais.

✖   ✖   ✖

16

THREE-DAY PASS TO BRUSSELS

Hotel Windsor, Paris
July 28, 1945

Dear Mother and Dad,

I had that pass to Brussels and it was wonderful, everything that I hoped it would be. Lee [Noyes], Lucille [Verzano] and I left Paris on the train at 10 PM Saturday night. The European trains are not very comfortable and the journey of 10 hours was a little rugged. There were six in our compartment, three WACs and three civilian women. There were a good many English and American Troops on the train.

We arrived at 8 AM Sunday morning, 195 miles and 10 hours on the train. We were filthy from the soot coming in the open windows.

After we found our Hotel, which was the SIRU—Annex, a Belgium Leave Club, we ate breakfast and made for the bath tubs and bed. In the afternoon we went first to the Finance Office to convert our French francs into Belgian money, and then we looked over the town.

First—everything was so very clean, the whole place sparkles and the people are very nice. A high percentage of them speak English and we had no difficulty in the shops or on the trains. They are much friendlier than the English or the French. I think I went around with a grin from ear to ear, feeling like a starved dog who has been tossed a bone. After living in war time cities for this long, I am not accustomed to especially nice treatment.

The ice cream shops were all they were rumored to be. Such a sight, we could hardly believe our eyes. But that didn't stop us, in addition to the three huge meals we managed to eat, we also had a sundae between meals.

We walked and walked up and down the streets. It was fascinating. We saw St. Gudule Cathedral and the Market Place with the adjoining Town Hall and the Guild Houses.

We went to the Opera Monday night and visited shops galore. We saw them making the famous Brussels lace while they explained the different types of lace and the way they were made (Mother would have loved it). There were several galleries open at the Museum.

We enjoyed ourselves immensely, and spent all of the money we had. I borrowed a camera from one of the fellows and used up the 116 film you sent me.

We left at 10:30 PM and finally arrived in Paris about 9:30 Thursday morning feeling really grimy again. Since I didn't have to report back to work until Friday, I relaxed the rest of the day.

It was a marvelous time and I needed it. I've had only 48 hours at a time away from the Drafting Room since I've been overseas, and I had become snappish and on edge, I feel better now.

When I went to work this morning, they all asked me about the trip and said that everyone from privates to Colonels had been asking where I was, and "How long was a 3 day pass, anyway?"

It is all right being back and I will get to work as usual. We still hear rumors about going home, so I'll keep my fingers crossed. One day.

I'll let you know how the pictures come out. I am pretty proud of Emma and her College education.

That is all for now and I have Reville tomorrow—so goodnight.

Love, Frances

✖   ✖   ✖

THREE-DAY PASS TO BRUSSELS

We left from the Gare du Nord Station. It was a "Leave" train, carrying American and allied troops with a few civilians to Brussels. The car we were in was reserved for women. The army did try to see that the soldiers who had been on duty for many months were able to take furloughs and leaves in attractive surroundings. But it was a steam train, burning coal as fuel and producing clouds of soot that came in through the open windows. There was no air-conditioning so the windows had to be open. All in all it made for a grimy ride.

I made sketches for watercolors of the Grand Place, which had the ancient guild houses near by. The center was a market with colorful flower stalls under large umbrellas. The cobblestones under foot made for unsteady walking. When I sketched, one of my friends usually would stand near and glare at any curious people who wandered into a close proximity. It was very difficult for me to sketch in public; I felt too self-conscious. However, after a time, with the people on the street I could remember enough of their faces and appearance to make a drawing later in my room or at the drafting board.

Lee Noyes (left) and Lucille Verzano (right) in front of the Brussels opera house, July 1945.

Chicago, Illinois
August 9, 1945

Dear Fran,

Hi there me darlin'—really been thinking about you today. First of all went by to see Hilda [a commercial artist] for a bit and I am going to keep it up so you'll have a contact or so when you need 'em later. She is taking a leap into an illustration studio—no guarantee, just hopes to hit the jackpot—Says she's scared stiff too—cause she's just turned down an Art Director's job that they were willing to start her at $200 a week—yes—I'm not fooling—anyhow the man she's going in with used to be head of Art at J. W. Thompson. So I think she's wise—also she's good—has a bit of Ladies Home Journal cover in her kids—but Colliers said the kids were too fashion conscious—myself I thought they were darlings. Also our Hilda has turned into a "tres'chic" young lady. She looked quite stunning today—in navy and white crepe and quite snazzy shoes—she informed me she'd keep her eyes and ears open for you—I told her I thought you'd set your heart on "Spot Illustration"—she thinks there is plenty of future in them—that was part of the $200 deal—So my child—even tho you may not be released for quite awhile—why don't you start sketching again.

The #2—Mildred Bailey was on Kraft Music Hall and tho she didn't sing any "oldies"— It was still Bailey and wonderful—#3 Woody Herman was on the air after the President and so you see this letter just had to be forth coming.

There has been quite a long silence from you and I have several explanations—#1 You're in love and mooning—I suppose but you could send a postcard or V-Mail. #2 Howard [friend of Peg's] finally came to Paris and you are doing the town.

By the way Bill [Nightingale] has transferred to Illinois Institute of Technology at 33rd Street and Federal—better school—but will have 2½ more years.

So be good and sweet and hope to be seeing you next Feb—I think that is your dead line—according to the paper.

Peggy [Allison Nightingale] and Bill

✗   ✗   ✗

BICYCLES

In the summer of 1945 the street traffic increased somewhat. The normal traffic of wartime Paris consisted almost entirely of military vehicles and a few essential civilian ones. There were very few buses. I do remember seeing one small car that had a steam engine. The driver was pulled over to the side of the street and was feeding wood into the boiler, building up steam before he could continue driving. So civilians and most military personnel walked or rode the subway (Metro).

The Arc de Triomphe at the Place dé Étoile was on a hill and the Champs-Élysées ran down the hill to the Place de la Concorde. We crossed the avenue about three blocks below the Étoile. There was just enough space to give a bicyclist coming down the hill a good rate of speed. I was accustomed to crossing busy city streets and dodging cars, but I looked up and saw forty or so bicycles pedaling straight for me—I lost my nerve! A few cars is one matter but dozens of bicycles trying to hit you is another.

✖   ✖   ✖

Hotel Windsor, Paris
August 11, 1945

Dear Dad and Mother,

I was aroused from a comfortable bed to go on CQ (Charge of Quarters) at 3:30 AM. The third shift is from 3:30 to 7 AM and this is my turn. I hope I can keep my eyes open.

The office buzzed with all kinds of rumors yesterday. The Japs had quit or they were on the verge of it, at last! I think we are all a little afraid to believe it. The "Atomic Bomb" and the War's end seems too much of a miracle to be true.

How long it has been, all the way back to 1937 and the "Munich Crisis" when my ear was glued to the radio, knowing that WAR was spreading like a dark shadow. Now I can see my life coming out from under the shadow. I don't regret enlisting, but 2½ years is a good chunk of time and it will be wonderful to have a life of my own again.

We will have to wait and be happy that those boys we have been sending to the Pacific can turn around and go home instead of stopping on the far side. I know I will have to wait for the Army to take its own sweet time about letting me return to civilian life!

My roommates, Lee and Lucille, are leaving this week to move on into Germany with the Judge Advocate Section. Woodie [Marjory Woodring] has already gone and I feel like the last leaf on the tree.

I am also scheduled to go, but it could be next week or in three months. The three of us enjoyed living together and I will miss them. They have 54 and 47 points, so they should be turning homeward soon.

Otherwise—life in Paris is about the same. I said Good Bye to Paul Denson, nearly two weeks ago and he was homeward bound. Has he arrived there yet? He certainly was happy and I told him that with people "leaving for the States" on every side of me, I felt more optimistic.

The box with the wonderful chocolate candy arrived three days ago and was gone in a flash. The box of cheese assortment came yesterday. Lee likes the mild cheese and Lucille and I feasted on the Cheddar. Thanks for your trouble, I do appreciate it.

I have one eye propped open waiting for 7 o'clock.

Love,
Fran

✖   ✖   ✖

TALK ABOUT LIFE AFTER THE ARMY

We continually talked with each other about what we would do out of the army. At that time, in the newspapers General Lewis B. Hershey, director of the Selective Service, announced that it would be better to keep large numbers of army personnel in uniform, rather than to have great numbers of recently discharged men suddenly flooding the labor market.

This went over like a lead brick! From then on in the ETO (European Theater of Operations) the gold stripes worn on our sleeves, one for each six months of service overseas, were known as "Hershey Bars." In retrospect, there was a sound economic basis for his statement, but balanced against the overwhelming hunger to go home and be reunited with families, it seemed foolish and cruel.

POINT SYSTEM

The Point System was devised as a fair way to release service personnel. One point was received for each month of active duty, and additional points for every month of overseas duty. In addition there were extra points for decorations, such as medals and Purple Hearts. Families were taken into account with a certain number of points for each child. We did not receive credit for our WAAC service. I had 45 points.

LEE AND LUCILLE

When Lee and Lucille went to Germany, I was moved to another room on the third floor that had only one WAC. The room was much smaller and we saw each other only in passing. Everything was subject to various rumors that changed daily. All of my close friends except Caroline Chaffee had already left, so I saw Halton Brown nearly every night.

Lee and Lucille arrived in Frankfurt and in less than a week were returned to a camp in the Forest of Compeigne, which was a staging area for troops who had been in Germany. They were under canvas and anxiously awaiting to begin the trip home.

Nancy Carter, our first sergeant, and Peggy McFadden were both good friends of Lee and Lucille. Nancy found out where they were and had the resources to obtain a jeep, and the three of us drove from Paris to see them. It was my first ride in an army jeep; my usual transportation was in the back of an army truck. We found them without any trouble and spent a couple of hours catching up on the news and wishing them the very best on their homeward journey. I know Lee was apprehensive because we suffered from the same type of seasickness. Bad stuff!

✖   ✖   ✖

17

HALTON

HALTON

Halton Brown was wounded for the last time on March 23 and spent April, May, and two weeks of June at the army hospital in Nancy, France. He was assigned to G-3 in Paris the middle of June, working in the Water Embarkation Department, which had the responsibility for shipping the troops back to the States.

He was in and out of the drafting room for a month before he asked me to go out. When he called for me at the hotel, my height was a definite shock to him. I suppose he had seen me so often sitting on a tall drafting stool, that he misjudged my size. As we went outside, he observed that we would be a better match if I walked on the sidewalk and he down in the street—a matter of three or four inches.

I was accustomed to walking nearly everywhere, and it was a very nice evening, so I said, "Shall we walk down to the Marigny Theater?" He looked down at me and said simply, "It reminds me of the Infantry." So we took the Metro.

We were very compatible and he asked me to marry him. This was a great difficulty for me, because I really did love Chuck Lowrie—but we had been apart for a long time. Halton became more and more important to me.

On our days off and through the long evenings of double daylight savings time, we wandered over Paris. There was a service club with a dance floor on the second level of the Eiffel Tower. The elevator worked, and we were spared the long climb I made when I first arrived in Paris. The Rainbow Red Cross Club also had a dance floor and a band. There were always performances of various kinds at the Marigny Theater and movies at the garrison cinema.

Several times we visited Luna Parc, the amusement park with the tall, tall roller coaster. There were hamburgers at the American Legion Post Number 1, where we received puzzled looks from other army personnel that we knew. I explained to Halton that was because I had dated so very seldom they couldn't believe their eyes. We walked along the embankment near Notre Dame Cathedral and sat in the little park next to the walls.

The Parc Monceau, not far from the Windsor Hotel, was our favorite. A small park with classic statues and pseudo ruins near the lake, it was used chiefly by the French residents who lived nearby. If you sat on one of the fragile folding chairs, a French woman was immediately there to collect the small charge for use of the chair.

The wide boulevard had park benches, where we sat and talked about home and the events that were rapidly transpiring. One topic was the atomic bomb, what it was, and how it would affect the war and our future.

We had no advance warning of the bomb, and until it was dropped on Japan we were definitely facing an extended period of time in Germany. So this was a sudden major change in plans.

Halton spent six months studying at Johns Hopkins in Baltimore, and he said that whenever a fire alarm was turned in, every fire engine in the city of Baltimore responded. There was endless speculation about this until it was discovered that one of the labs was experimenting with heavy water. After the bomb was dropped we realized the connection. Not many people in the army at that time had any conception of what "splitting the atom" meant.

After the war's end, I found out that the first test of atomic reaction took place at the University of Chicago in December 1942. I was only a few miles from the spot at that time, and undoubtedly they conducted the first test with their hearts in their mouths.

One of the evenings, on impulse Halton bought me a small spray of red roses from a flower cart. We used the ETO Ribbon with three battle stars to pin the flowers to my lapel. Back in my room, I placed the jacket over the back of a chair and made a watercolor of it.

✖   ✖   ✖

Hotel Windsor, Paris
September 12, 1945

Dear Dad and Mother,

I have been waiting for a letter in answer to the bomb-shell I sent you about my decision to marry Halton instead of Chuck. If this change seemed sudden to you, it was earth shaking to me. My mind is usually made up in slow easy stages.

There is still hope that I will be on one of the October shipping lists, but whether it will be on the first or the last of October is anyone's guess. Lee [Noyes] and Lucille [Verzano] should have docked by now and be on their way West. I hope so. It gives me a lift to know that they are on their way out.

I am eager to tell you about Halton. I want you to like him almost as much as I do. For a description, 6' 3" (far too tall, to my way of thinking, but then he thinks I am too short) very light brown hair and blue eyes, quite presentable, and a very, very nice guy.

He is from a small town in Mississippi, attended a Teacher's College for three years, and then went into the ASTP (Army Specialized Training Program). They sent him to the Citadel, a military college in Charleston, South Carolina for 6 months, and then he was sent to Johns Hopkins, a medical school in Baltimore for 6 months.

Last summer he shipped to France as a rifleman and fought in the front lines with the 4th Division until last March. The front line last winter was Hell and he jokingly says he is really 60 years old, that he spent 40 years in the Line—except it isn't a joke. He was wounded, Purple Hearts and ribbons, then classified for limited service and sent to Headquarters in Paris and the G-3 Section. I knew him a month before we went out together. To me, he is quite wonderful and he certainly understands me. I really had no idea that I could be so happy. The important part is a love that keeps on growing. How I can love him more day by day is an eternal mystery.

He is quite a ways from the ground and is as big inside as out. I am still waiting to hear from Chuck. I can only wait. I am a happy, bewildered and homesick "chick." I'll be seeing you soon.

Big Sis

Halton Brown once proposed to Frances on the observation deck of the Eiffel Tower. He proposed many times.

✳   ✳   ✳

CITADEL

At the Citadel engineers were being trained. Halton achieved a very high score on a test for medical aptitude and was sent to Johns Hopkins to be trained as an assistant battlefield surgeon.

✖   ✖   ✖

Paris, France
September 14, 1945

Dear Mother and Father (2nd edition),

Gulp, my very characteristic beginning. I usually spend all of my time gulping when I write a letter, but somehow as a confirmed wolf, I never got around to writing this kind of letter before—and a girl from Yankee Land, too.

Still, I believe for your sakes a short life history is very much in order. I was born of early American stock in the little town of Camden, Arkansas. I spent most of my early youth in the oil fields of Smackover, Arkansas. My father decided that this was not the proper surroundings to bring up two children so we moved to Lake Village, Arkansas. I had all of the normal teenage crushes. My father is a wise man. He always insisted when I had a crush on a local belle that I date other girls. Mother didn't like the idea but Father said when the right girl came along that I would know it.

I graduated from Lake Village High School and my Father was transferred by his company, the International Harvester Company to Cleveland, Mississippi. I went to College there and worked for John Deere when I was not going to school or playing basketball.

In 1942 I decided that time was "a wasting'" and I went into the Army. The Army sent me to school at the "The Citadel" in Charleston, South Carolina and then to Medical School at Johns Hopkins in 1943. But I couldn't sit out the War in Baltimore so here I am on this side.

For five months I existed, seeing men die, losing buddy after buddy until I was afraid to look a new bunch of replacements in the eye because I knew they wouldn't last a week. I went out on patrol night after night alone—ever waiting. Then something inside began to change and I wasn't a kid anymore but a worn out man. I wanted to leave, I had done my share but something held me there. Two voices—One said, "Son, it isn't too bad—stick it out—I won't let you down if you believe in me," and I believe. The other voice said "You'll never find me if you don't stay, Tex." When the heavy stuff skidded to a stop near by those two voices led me on. Then on the 24th of March I was hit for the last time, and my fighting days were over.

I suppose that Frances has already described me. Can you see a 195 pound, six foot three guy walking down the street with a five foot three girl? Why did it happen to me? I am about to get used to the fact now. By the way, Frances tells me that my being a "Rebel" isn't a strike against me. It seems strange to be called a "Rebel," because in Mississippi, we are Americans—first, last and always.

Frances and Halton stroll along a Paris street on one of their many dates.

When I found Frances I knew she was the one—and I certainly must love her, because—me, a true Mississippi wolf, who never waited on any female more than ten minutes, waited three and half hours yesterday for her without a bitter word from my usually sharp tongue.

I asked Frances to be my wife and the "Brown Luck" held true blue. I promise you and her nothing except an undying love and an adventurous life. For "better or worse" is the way I ask and the way she accepted.

I am looking forward to meeting you, and I only trust that I can measure up to your hopes for your daughter. I hope someday I shall stand only one half as high in your eyes as you stand in hers.

Halton

✖   ✖   ✖

TEX

"Tex" was Halton's nickname in the army. The three and a half hours he refers to, I was working outside Paris for a couple of days on detached service and was late returning. He waited in the lobby of the Windsor Hotel until I returned.

✖   ✖   ✖

Marianna, Florida
September 15, 1945

Dear Dad,

By now, I suppose you have heard the news. I had a letter from Frances the other day, the first in over a month, so deep down inside I figured something had happened. We had an agreement before she left that if either of us found someone else we would let the other one know. I don't feel sorry for what happened and I respect her all the more for telling me.

Time has a way of changing things, as has a long separation and it has been a long while since I've seen her. I believe everything happens for the best and he must be a pretty swell guy or she never would have picked him.

As soon as I get out of the Army I am going back to something I never would have done if I had gotten married and that is flying. My friends have been deviling me to go in with them and buy an airplane. This entails the small item of teaching them to fly too. Republic has come out with a four place amphibian, which is the plane I have set my heart on and it sells for around $4,000. So now those inaccessible lakes will be duck soup to get to.

They just came back from a trip up to the Rogue River in Oregon and they had quite a time. They caught 300 fish, two were chased by a bear and a good time was had all around. As I read that letter I felt like "going over the hill."

The Army is a bunch of baloney now. All we do is detail after detail. Today we hoe weeds and mow grass, the inspections, and one right after another. I am actually ashamed to draw my pay.

Right now we are sweating out a hurricane. Yesterday, it seemed as the whole Navy landed here. From noon until 5 o'clock Navy Torpedo Bombers came in, refueled and took off. Today our planes went on a low-level strike practice mission to Chicago. They are going to fly under 200 feet all the way. I tried my darndest to get on that flight, but the darn grass detail was more important. I hope the Hurricane doesn't hit here. If it does I have a nice deep ditch picked out and it won't take but two hops and a skip to be in it.

Well, Dad, guess I'll sign off. It has really been swell writing to you and the family. I am sorry I never had the chance to meet you but the letters made it seem as though I had. Give Little Sis and Mom my love and the best of everything to all of you.

Yours,
Chuck

Paris, France
September 20, 1945

Dear Mother and Father, (2nd edition)

You would never know your daughter now. The same green troubled eyes, the same laugh but she is different—because she is in love.

Somehow, the other night it actually seemed that I was speaking to God with Frances by my side when we were on the Eiffel Tower. Paris spread out below us with the lights of the City scattered around like bits of bright glass. A cool wind blew over the rail and all was quiet and peaceful. I was thankful that I had been allowed to live through the last winter and to know someone as dear as Frances.

From the Eiffel Tower we wandered down town to the American Legion Post No. 1, where I established a record of hamburgers eaten at nine. Frances was right behind me with two hamburgers.

Today, we started wandering through the Parc Monceau and ended up in the Royal Gardens. It is a lazy day, with blue skies and a gentle wind rustling the leaves. Small children are running around the walks, laughing. It is the kind of day when home seems near and somehow so do you. I guess I am the luckiest fellow in the world. Keep your fingers crossed and maybe we will both be home soon.

Halton and Frances on the roof of the Hotel Majestic, Paris, 1945.

Halton

P.S. I received a letter from Lee a couple of days ago. She landed September 10th, so she and Lucille should be civilians now. Happy Day! I should be homeward bound sometime next month and believe me, I am ready for it. Enclosed are a few snapshots. Doesn't your daughter look happy?

Frances

✗   ✗   ✗

AMERICAN LEGION

The American Legion opened a club, the only place of its kind in Paris, where soldiers and WACs could buy hamburgers, coffee, and beer. They were small hamburgers and the very first we had had since leaving the States. I had never been there before. For months we had referred to ourselves as "Hamburger Tickets."

✖   ✖   ✖

Hotel Windsor, Paris
September 23, 1945

Dear Dad,

Here I am, wishing so much that I could cry on your shoulder. "Mixed up" is no word for it. I feel as though I am on a merry-go-round. The letter I had from you yesterday indicated that you had not received my letter telling you about Chuck and Halton. Your letter must have been held up, because I wrote to you at the same time I wrote to Chuck.

Dad, he is wonderful. I have a good idea what it cost him to write it, but there it is. He was a very important part of my life for nearly two years, and I thought the world of him. Then again, one and a half years is a very, very long time to be away.

Now there is Halton and I am all mixed up. I sometimes think it is the Army and being here for so long that has me befuddled. I'd give anything to be able to talk to you. But now I'll stop singing the blues—it is probably because I want to come home so much. I have been in the Army too long. I even think in shades of olive drab.

Now that I have had my cry, I'll go to bed and worry some more. Thanks for listening to me.

A special love,
Big Sis

Hotel Windsor, Paris
September 27, 1945

Dear Mother,

I just received a letter from you, the first since I wrote telling you about Halton. To tell the truth, I am not absolutely sure which way is up. After reading your letter, I can see what a shock it was for you. I have been here alone, thinking by myself for so long that I can't properly imagine how you do feel. It has been such a long time, I am so tired and so very sick of the Army that I can't quite explain it. My patience is short and everyone seems far, far away.

But Mother, don't believe I didn't care, I did. Chuck meant a great deal to me and we

have always been honest with each other. But, now Halton means much more to me. I need to be a civilian again and feel like myself. But please, never believe that I did not care—you should see how my skirts hang on me. I am even more sorry that any letter of mine should cause you unhappiness.

I can tell you now that the shipping list for the 10th of October was posted yesterday and my name is on it. True, it is hard to believe. That means, we leave here for a staging area on the 10th. It should take at the most a month between that date and when I should be home. You can probably expect me about November 10th.

To tell the truth, it is almost too much for me to imagine.

Very much love,
Frances

*Frances and Caroline
Chaffee, Le Havre, France,
1945.*

Hotel Windsor, Paris
October 3, 1945

Dear Mother and Dad,

If you could know how very slowly, the days are moving toward the 10th. Then I suppose time will stop altogether when I hit camp. I should like to skip that month and land at home, but it will have to be done the hard way. This last bit of time in the Army seems three times as hard as that before.

There are letters from Peg [Allison Nightingale], Janie [Baranowski], and Lee—Lee seems to be better adjusted now. It was hard for her at first. Janie thinks she may have to wait for the WAC to be disbanded in February, but she loves her work so much, she doesn't mind.

I am glad you are still receiving packages from me. I am trying to get everything possible in the mail, to save the bother of carrying it. We will be spot checked all the way across.

Caroline [Chaffee] (Signal Corp) will be leaving on the 20th. I would have liked to be with her crossing, but it is no go. I can't think of much to say except—I am homesick and I want to see you all very much.

Love,
Frances

18

LE HAVRE

Paris, France
October 10, 1945

My very dear Frances,

It has been only 12 hours since you left, but it feels like ages and ages. It seems so very silly to be writing a letter that you may not get for 3 weeks—but three little words are running over and over in my mind—I love you. My ears are burning; I hope it is because you are thinking of me, too.

Hank [Craven] was over a few minutes ago and said that Major Mial was asking for you this morning. He did not know that you were gone.

It is a beautiful day with a very blue sky. You picked a good time to go home. How does it feel to be a Miss now? Keep your fingers crossed for me.

I love you,
Halton

Le Havre, France
October 11, 1945

Dear Dad and Mother,

I may arrive before this letter does, but just in case I don't we left Paris, October 10th at 11 PM and spent 20 hours on the train. We wandered all over Northern France, arriving after dark. How long we will be here is hard to tell, but the huts are fairly comfortable and I can wait.

In a way I am excited and then again I simply can't believe it. As far as I know now, I will receive my discharge at Fort Dix, New Jersey. So I'll see Janie [Baranowski] for a few hours at least. The exact date is uncertain, but I should be home November 1st, at the latest. It will be a grand and glorious day! Is the red carpet out?

Much love,
Frances

✖   ✖   ✖

LEAVING PARIS FOR THE PORT OF LE HAVRE

We assembled in the lobby of the Hotel Windsor, and Halton Brown was there to see me off. We boarded the buses with all of our equipment, handbags slung across the body, the musette bag filled with personal items—hose, pajamas, underwear, extra shirts, toilet articles—the pistol belt with canteen, and mess kit. We wore our utility coats and the battle jacket with wool slacks and field boots. I also had the map case that we liberated in Valognes, containing sketchbooks, watercolor box, brushes, and my French camera.

The bus took us to the train station where we boarded a French train with the usual compartments and proceeded to wander all over northern France. We were frequently pulled over on sidings to wait for any other traffic to go through. We carried K rations for our meals. The next day at one of the long stops, one of the adventurous WACs got off the train, walked up a hill, and purchased several sandwiches. They were made with the wonderful French bread and filled with goose pate. They were delicious, it was almost the only really French food I had the whole year.

The staging area was divided into five camps that were named for cigarette brands. We were in Camp Philip Morris, which immediately ran out of hot water. Whenever the WACs arrived, they started to wash hair, clothes, and almost anything in sight.

The semipermanent huts had wooden floors, wood sides up about four feet and the rest was canvas. There were round potbellied stoves for heat.

Basic supplies in our musette bags were a small roll of toilet paper, two roofing nails, and about six feet of heavy cord. With the heel of a shoe used as a hammer, we had a temporary clothesline installed. I carried one of the metal keys used to open ration cans on my dog tag chain.

In camp we wore our WAC coveralls and field boots, ate from mess kits, and were served by field kitchens. I never did get the hang of managing my mess kit easily. Every possible combination was tried, but somehow my arrangement was never satisfactory.

Our hair was washed frequently, there was nothing else to do, and we used the issue tan scarves to wind into a turban that concealed our bobby pins during the day. There were no hair rollers.

We were warned emphatically when we arrived in camp, NEVER to walk where we did not know someone else had been. The paths were well laid out, but the areas between were not free of mines. The day before we came, a soldier, who had survived months of combat, stepped off the path and lost a leg!

There was a Quonset hut with wooden benches where we watched movies at night. One night the power went out during the film. We waited awhile sitting in the darkness, and then we started to sing as we usually did. It was "Home on the Range," never one of my favorites, but that night in the crowded hut there was a depth and power to it. I remembered the grassy plains and hills of South Dakota and the gently rolling fields of central Indiana.

✺ ✺ ✺

Frances and an uniden-
tified WAC, Camp Philip
Morris, Le Havre, France.

Paris, France
October 12, 1945

My darlin' Frances,

It has been another wonderful day and things are looking up but I can hardly believe that I may be able to get home by Christmas. When I look at the Calendar I see that it is only three days—yet you seem to have been gone for months. I don't know just how I am going to sweat out the rest of the time over here.

I have heard at the Office a rumor to the effect that the "Queens" might not be carrying soldiers anymore. If that is true then you are hurting. I do hope that you get home OK and in one big Hell "of a hurry."

Gee, in trying to write a newsy letter all that I can think of is I love you. Don't forget me while you are a civilian.

Halton

✺ ✺ ✺

THE QUEENS

I went over on the HMS Queen Mary. *It carried a full army division of fifteen thousand men. Returning I know some of the soldiers shared bunks, changing every twelve hours. So the loss of the "Queens" would require many other smaller boats. Halton eventually returned on the* Vulcania *(an Italian ocean liner), which I believe was a very much newer ship.*

✖   ✖   ✖

Paris, France
October 14, 1945

My dearest,

"An Hour Never Passes" but I think of you. Gee but I have missed you. It seems so very odd to go to the barracks and go to bed at 9 o'clock. I went back to see "Murder, He says." Some of the fellows hadn't seen it so I went again. You should have heard the remarks during the spooky parts of the show.

The French have an exposition at the Grande Palais and part of it is on the bank of the Seine near the spot where we went so very often. Nothing new is happening to the rest of the town but there is a very nice snap in the air.

Gee, Honey—it seems like such a long time to wait until I see you. I am realizing just how much you mean to me.

Love,
Halton

✖   ✖   ✖

AN HOUR NEVER PASSES

The words were from a song "An Hour Never Passes" that someone played on the piano in the lobby of the Windsor Hotel. Halton called for me and left me there—and it was the place where he waited three and half hours for me.

It was the back hall of the hotel where he kissed me good-bye before I boarded the bus that took us to the train station. Although the back hall of the Windsor was a busy place with employees going back and forth, it was slightly more private than the front lobby and sidewalk, where a large shipment of WACs with their friends and well-wishers were congregated.

✖   ✖   ✖

Port of Le Havre, France
October 15, 1945

Dear Mother and Dad,

A very uneventful day, our processing is nearly finished, so we sit here waiting. As far as we know, the sailing date is still the same but with the port strikes and all of the re-shuffling of boats back and forth, it is hard to tell. I am keeping my fingers crossed and hope to be back by Thanksgiving at least. The Port of New York was closed by strikes.

We had our anti-influenza shot yesterday and it made my arm as sore as usual. These last weeks in the Army seem as long as several months. Walking up the gangplank, which I have thought about for so long, doesn't seem real, just a figment of my imagination. It's difficult to believe, that Lee [Noyes] and Lucille [Verzano] have been civilians for nearly a month. Lee is squared away now, but I used to worry about her. She wasn't at all well and sinus trouble is extra bad in Paris.

We have had gray gloomy days recently. I'd like for the sun to shine, but as long as it doesn't rain I can't complain. In a good rain, this camp would literally be a "sea of mud," and sloshing through it would be very unpleasant.

We went to the PX for ice cream this afternoon. We stood in line about 45 minutes, which wasn't bad—anything under an hour is considered a breeze. There is nothing else to do so I thought I'd rather be in line than on my cot.

The ice cream is very good, when we do get it. I am assuming that there is no shortage at home. When I arrive, I've decided to take a foolish dollar that I have saved, hand it over to someone at the soda fountain and say "Move over, I'd like to mix my own!"

Ditto with fried eggs, I wonder just how many I could eat. Here we alternate between French toast and powdered egg omelet. Preserve me from powdered eggs ever again. I have consumed my patriotic share!

The German PWs do the cooking and most of the work details. In fact they seem to be all over the place. It surprises me to see them so completely without guards, but that seems to be the way it is handled here.

This is the first time I have been in direct contact with German PWs. We have one, quite young, who works here in our hut. He fires the stove, sweeps and does other chores. He says in broken English, that he is 19 years old, has been in the Army 3 years and away from home all that time. Aside from this, it is the expression on his face that causes shudders to go up and down my spine. He is so completely beaten down.

Lee said the Red Cross met them at the dock with fresh milk instead of coffee and doughnuts. It was fortunate that I have never been a milk lover, because we have had none at all for 18 months. I'll be happy to see "Potato Chips" again.

It is time for lights out, so I'll crawl between my blankets. Now that the soreness has left my arm, I should be able to sleep.

I wonder if I'll have mail waiting when I do get home. The mail was very slow for a couple of weeks before I left Paris and now I can't expect any at all from you until I am a civilian. It is not so bad, when I am moving in the right direction. Home will seem mighty wonderful.

Love,
Frances

P.S. Believe me, sealing my own letters is still a treat.

✗   ✗   ✗

FLU SHOT

I was sick about a day and half from the flu shot. I lay on my cot remembering how seasick I had been on the voyage over, and that coupled with the way the shot made me feel was almost too much. For about twelve hours I said to myself, "I just won't go back! I'll stay on this side to keep from being seasick again." When my arm felt better I changed my mind.

✗   ✗   ✗

WAITING

It was a long empty time. We were in limbo, nothing to do except go to mess, sleep, and wait. There was hardly any mail, very little to read, and no work detail—we were in a suspended state.

Frances, wearing her "zoot suit," empties her mess kit into a trash can, Le Havre.

The camp at Le Havre was on a flat plain just above the harbor. The light in the western sky was like nothing I had ever seen before, a golden glow. It puzzled me for several days because in some way, it was familiar. Then I realized it was the same golden light I had so often seen in the old Dutch landscapes. It was beautiful, and I have never seen it anywhere else in the world.

There were tents and necessary facilities. The rain came and went and the camp became a sea of mud. The rain on the tin roofs and the wind over the mudflats made me feel cut off from the past and even the future. Everything was unreal; my ordinary life had slipped into the mist.

Soon the smell of fresh dirt, rain, and wind gave me a kind of contentment. A tall, tall wind blew one night, and the sky over the waste of mud was an ever-changing wonder. I could stand and see the full sweep of the horizon. And the wind, a part of me will always rise to meet a wind.

✖ ✖ ✖

Paris, France
October 17, 1945

Dear Mother and Father (2nd Edition)

Something very important to me has happened in the past week. During my life I have left friends, relatives and family numerous times, but never before, a week later, has there been the empty void that seems to have swallowed me up when Frances left.

I know that you are happy that she is on the way or maybe already at home. I am glad, too, for she needed to be out of the Army. But never the less I miss her so much. It has been said that it is tougher on those left behind, and I believe it now. I hope when you feel like picking up another member of the family you will write to me.

Halton

T/5Halton Brown
HDQRS TSFET
G-3 OP CON DIV
APO# 887 C/O PM NY NY

Le Havre, France
October 20, 1945

Dear Dad and Mother,

I am still here. We were scheduled to load on trucks for the ride down to the boat yesterday at 5 PM. We were all dressed in our best, slacks and wool shirts, with bags packed and ready to go.

At 2 PM, they told us there had been a change in the shipping list. Only the girls going to Fort Sheridan and Camp Beale were shipping—a mere 130. That left about 600 of us "waiting at the Church."

It was a disappointment, I had a huge lump in my throat, and it was a sad crowd of gloomy faced WACs. You can't describe the feeling. You have waited months thinking about going home and then when you are finally on the way, being left from a shipping list at the last moment is hard to take.

We are given all sorts of explanations but the strikes on the sea coast are adding fuel to the flame. We are not in such a bad spot because we've only been here 10 days, but some of the poor guys have been here weeks and weeks.

It is just a "SNAFU" [Situation Normal, All Fouled Up] all over. We hear that now the sailing date will be the 25th. I hope those Separation Centers are going full blast because this Port waiting is mighty wearing on the nerves.

Immediately after the news yesterday, we were told to move to another area because 500 WACs were expected in that night. We moved! Across the road into an area used for staging nurses. The quarters are much nicer. Huts again, but honest to goodness hospital beds with springs and sheets and pillows! It really is more comfortable but we still have little water and the electricity goes off at odd intervals.

The hardest part is nothing to do. If we do have the biggest Navy and Merchant marine in the world, why aren't we using them?

Much love,
Frances

✳   ✳   ✳

LEAVING LE HAVRE

We were dressed in Eisenhower jackets, wool slacks, wool shirts and tie, utility coat with lining, and field boots. We had our musette bags, and I had the map case. We were minus several pieces of equipment that we carried going over, such as gas masks and "Hobby Hats."

ARMY REGULATION

Another army regulation—we were given transportation to the point of our enlistment, but you never traveled back. Fort Sheridan in Chicago was much nearer Indianapolis, but it was a few miles farther west. So I was discharged at Fort Dix, New Jersey, and given a travel allowance to go by train to Indiana.

✖   ✖   ✖

Frances and her gear ready to board a ship for home.

Paris, France
October 29, 1945

My dearest darling,

So you were kicked off the "Parker." One thing though, sweet. You said that you were in the Fort Dix shipment and then you turn around and say that only the Fort Dix and Camp Beale girls went home. Let's check up, maybe you got left behind.

I am sweating out this afternoon in the War Room. General Ike [Dwight D. Eisenhower] is around so Lt. O'Brien ducked his job and it was dropped in my lap. It is not bad, except for the principle of the thing.

Things look both good and bad. It has been rumored that all of the men in TSFET after Jan 1st are stuck, but maybe I will leave as planned and maybe it will be from Paris. I will not be sorry to see the last of Paris, France or Europe.

One question, sweetheart, are you painting anything now-a-days? All of the drafting room, except John, are painting pictures. Not too bad either.

I love you and miss you,
Halton

P.S. Here is a snapshot for you of the street cleaner if you have time to draw it.

H

✖ ✖ ✖

ZOOT SUIT

We had already turned in many items of clothing and equipment when we were scheduled to leave on October 20. That included our WAC coveralls that we had worn in camp exclusively. It was necessary to be issued other fatigue clothing. I was issued a pair of men's fatigue pants with the flap pockets. This would have been all right except they were at least a size forty. Fortunately, I borrowed a leather strap to use as a belt. We had no belts as regular issue. With the fatigue pants I wore one of my army shirts, and to complete the costume I used my dog tags as a watch chain and fob. I had a "zoot suit."

✖ ✖ ✖

Le Havre, France
October 28, 1945

Dear Mother and Dad,

We are still waiting—after the shipping strike; we would have the worst Channel storm in 20 years. Now we are waiting for our boat to come into the Harbor.

We are suppose to board the boat tomorrow morning about 6 AM. But I wouldn't be surprised to find myself here writing to you a couple of days from now. We have been here nearly three weeks and in my opinion winter has set in. We have had rain and wind continually. There is very little to do except slosh through the mud and kill time as best we can.

We are comfortable, but wouldn't we like to be started home. Woodie [Marjory Woodring] was in the WAC area across the way. She left this morning to cross the Channel to England. They will leave on the Queen Mary about November 4th. Her boat will be much faster than ours, so I may see her at Fort Dix when we are discharged.

Such lovely words, we sit around talking about being discharged and it is still something I can hardly believe. Then again, it is pretty serious. We have joked a lot about being civilians again and I always said—it would take about five minutes for us to become re-adjusted to civilian life. But now that I am face to face with the fact that it maybe less than a month, it seems different.

It is hard to explain, but clothes are an example. After wearing skirts, shirts with long sleeves and neckties for 2½ years, I can't imagine how I will feel in normal clothes again. The much publicized WAC Off Duty dress, I wore twice. I felt much too uncomfortable in it and I only wanted to get back into my old ODs [olive drabs], in which I felt at home. After awhile I know I will feel all right, but when I get down to brass tacks and start thinking about being a civilian, I get a little panic stricken.

Janie can show me around New York City for a couple of days. She has been stationed there nearly 2 years. She is a good friend and I will be glad to see her.

Please don't mind my griping and complaining. It isn't too bad; we just want to get on home now that we are started on the way. Unless more of this bad luck dodges us, I'll be there for Thanksgiving.

Love you very much,
Frances

Chingford, London
27.10.45

Dear Frances,

Was so very pleased to hear from you again. I expect by the time you get this you will be home—or at least in your own Country. I am glad for you, for my part I am sorry you have to go. I would have liked to have seen you again. Still, who knows, perhaps one day I'll be able to visit you.

All the family sends their love and hope you will be back with your folks soon. Eileen [Wyatt] also sends her love and if "Long George" knew I were writing, I'm sure he'd want me to send his best wishes.

Do you remember Norma (Canadian)? She has been home for a couple of months. Both she and her husband are discharged now. My friend Jean will eventually be going to the States as an American bride.

Betty [Gobel] has had her hair cut and now looks quite grown up. She is still very interested in her dancing and was in a concert on Thursday. She is quite good! Bill [Gobel] is in Baghdad now and likely to be out there another couple of years. Eileen's George is not likely to be home for another year either.

You wouldn't know our front room now that we have the shelter down. We have a new billiard table in there, which is also a dining table and we can even use it for table tennis—so we are living in style, sleeping in bed every night and not waking up in the middle of the night. It is wonderful! Remember how we all used to pile in the bunks?

Do write and let me know how you get on. I expect you will be spending Christmas with your family. Will you be going back to your job in Chicago or will you stay in Indiana, or even California.

How are your Mother, Father and Emma? Very well I hope. Did the beans ever come up? We had some marvelous ones, this year.

This must be all for now, write soon. Cheerio and happy landings in the USA.

> With love from us all,
> Margaret Gobel

Paris, France
October 29, 1945

My very dearest,

There is a pretty big lump somewhere between my heart and my throat. I have spent the day remembering—I started off early with a trip to the Parc Monceau and then just kept on walking until I was tired. After dinner I went down to the Latin Quarter and bought some presents. Then I went down to the "Hamburger Joint" and I ate six hamburgers—five for me and one for you. As I sat there it struck me just how much I missed you, that's why I didn't eat more than six. Then I joined the American Legion Paris Post No. 1, bought some stationary and came back to the office.

We are going to Frankfort somewhere between the 10 and the 15th. I sort of hate to go, but maybe I can find Daddy some field glasses. That's all I want out of the ETO besides a discharge.

I love you,
Halton

✖ ✖ ✖

After Frances left for the States, Halton filled his time revisiting some of the couple's favorite sites in Paris.

ON THE OCEAN

Before dawn on October 30, 1945, we loaded into trucks for the ride down to the docks, a very quiet group of WACs. Halfway to the harbor, we heard church bells ringing for early Mass. In the dark I remembered other times—the first bomb-gutted buildings in England, the sound of enemy planes overhead, and the sirens of Paris sounding the "Last All Clear of the War."

There was a glow in the east and the dark hulls of ships lined the piers next to the bombed remnants of the original docks. There was no visible excitement, we were just unbelieving. Down past the buildings labeled "Port of Embarkation" and along the water's edge were the signs Americans always leave behind us.

"We've had it—now you can have it"
"Go West Young Man, Go West"
"The Lady with the torch is waiting for you"
and
"USA—Here we come"

We sailed from Le Havre on the SS Alexander. Boarding the boat we were assigned bunks and then told to eat breakfast. To our surprise we were ushered into the ship's dining room. There were small tables, seating five or six, tablecloths, and the usual china and serving pieces. The mess steward handed us menus—MENUS with breakfast choices! We were stunned! We had spent thirteen months in Paris eating only in our army mess. We looked at each other, thinking that there surely was some mistake. After one WAC said timidly, "We can have fried eggs?" The steward assured us that we could, so everyone at the table ordered them. It was true, we had the usual first-class shipboard food and the evening meal was wonderful. Apparently I could stand only about twenty-four hours of the movement of a ship. That first day was the only time I made it to the dining room, from then on, I was flat on my back as much as possible, but I did have fresh fruit.

AT SEA

One night, we went up on deck and listened to the girls and GIs singing. The songs they choose—"Lili Marlene," "Sentimental Journey," "Let Me Call You Sweetheart," and as always "Home on the Range." The songs sounded poignant and deeper in tone. You could sense the emotions and thought around you. Not all of the light was gone from the sky, and that last blue in the dusk was as bright as the promise of the future.

SEASICK

And I was seasick, a repeat of the trip on the Queen Mary. *Caroline Chaffee, who caught up with me in Le Havre, was my salvation. After a few days, she simply put a strong arm around me and hauled me from place to place. Anything I could eat, she brought me from the dining room. And once again I did manage to walk down the gangplank.*

MONEY CHANGING

Midway in the voyage, our currency was changed—we turned in our French francs for American bills. To reduce the profit from the black market "dabbled in by numerous GIs," there was a limit to the amount of money that could be exchanged. One enterprising GI used his French francs to buy perfume. He had a canvas carryall filled with assorted bottles of perfume when he boarded the boat. After the GIs had received their converted U.S. money, he reminded them that they needed presents to take back to wives and sweethearts. Then he proceeded to receive the U.S. currency in which they had just been paid, in return for bottles of "French Parfum"! I am sure he "cleaned up."

I had about seventy dollars in francs to be changed. The money we received had the U.S. Treasury seal stamped in yellow ink. This denoted U.S. currency used to pay troops outside the continental limits of the United States.

ABOARD THE SS ALEXANDER

We are only two days out of Boston, tonight we begin to say over and over softly, "We are going home, we are going home." I have been a serial number in a list on a desk, subject to deployment by anyone—and always conscious of an ocean between me and everything I have known before.

And the ocean was a great deal wider then than it is now. Fast ships took at least five days to cross it, and the only planes flying over it regularly were military aircraft.

Day by day, month by month, home had slipped a little farther away. It was only an address on the envelope and words on a sheet of paper.

BOSTON, MASSACHUSETTS, FORT MILES STANDISH

After arriving in port on November 6, 1945, we were trucked to Fort Miles Standish and again nurses' quarters were hastily made ready for us. With delight we discovered our first army PX in the States. The ice cream was wonderful, and I purchased a can of cashew nuts that I proceeded to eat in quantity! Did I have a stomach ache! The past year and a half I had eaten a very healthy diet, and suddenly my stomach was overindulged.

Some of the first advice we received after arriving referred to contacting our families. We were strongly urged if there was any heart trouble in the family, to send a telegram first and then telephone. There had been several cases of parents dropping dead from the shock of an unexpected phone call.

From Fort Miles Standish we were moved by train to Fort Dix, New Jersey. There we went through the rest of our processing before discharge.

SEPARATION CENTER
FORT DIX, NEW JERSEY

I was handed my honorable discharge at 11 o'clock on November 11—ARMISTICE DAY. A coincidence! The insignia of an eagle inside a circle was sewn on my battle jacket. This signified to the public that I was a recently discharged veteran. We also had a similar gold lapel pin to wear with our civilian clothes. Very shortly we were calling this a "ruptured duck."

We were allowed to keep one uniform—the battle jacket, matching skirt, and slacks. We gave up our old faithful utility coat because we kept our warm overcoats. Personal items such as shirts, ties, underwear, pajamas, one pair of service oxfords, the pair of field boots, and our musette bag were to be ours. Literally the clothes we stood in. I also had the map case, my cap, scarf, and gloves. That was all.

I took the bus from Fort Dix to New York City, then the subway to the ferry for Staten Island. My friend Janie Baranowski was the head pharmacist at the general hospital there. She was barely five feet tall but had eleven men pharmacists under her direction. I stayed that night in the WAC quarters, and then we went into the city to a hotel.

I enjoyed the food at several fine restaurants, and we talked about all the things that had been left out of our letters. The visit to the Metropolitan Museum was a wonder to me. Especially a portrait by Frans Hals, another unforgettable painting lodged in my memory.

TRAIN FOR HOME

Then I caught the train for Indiana. I sat up and slept in my seat all night covered by my overcoat and arrived in Indianapolis the next morning. I had phoned from New York, giving the day, but of course I had no idea of the exact time of arrival.

After all of the past lonely arrivals and departures, I didn't expect to be met at the train, but Emma was there waiting for me. Later she told me she came to the Indianapolis train station early in the morning and met every train from New York until I arrived. It meant a great deal to me. We took the bus to Danville, and at last I was at home—November 16, 1945.

In spite of the buzz bombs, England was nearly normal, but France was quite different. I remember the first time I saw people searching the trash cans for food. In those autumn months that were all gloom and rain, I started to sketch the people, impressions from those on the street and riding on the Metro. When someone found me drawing, they invariably said, "That's good, but why such unpleasant people?" I wanted to say "I don't know but I can't rest until I have tried to put them on paper"—instead I answered, "They fascinate me," and then changed the subject.

After months and months, I sometimes thought, I could feel the misery, like heat waves, rising from the old streets. There had been so much of cold, bone-chilling, gray, gray days and people a long time at war. These visual impressions filled my mind and memories and couldn't be erased in a few weeks or even months. I had a deep sense of unhappiness and sorrow. It was like always living in the darkness away from the sun. Inside I felt pale and wan. And I brought it back with me. Those poverty-ridden faces were still in my mind. It was impossible for me to walk into a grocery store, stocked with hoards of food on the shelves, without an actual physical shock at the plenty. I wouldn't change it, I wanted America to be this way, but I couldn't forget. I struggled to fit in with people around me.

One of my friends replied in response to my exclamation of "I remember that dress." "Well, after all, we civilians have had to wear the same clothes!" I had only been delighted at something familiar out of the life that had gone on without me. Her irritation was such a contrast to my English friend, who looked forward cheerfully to years more of severe clothing rationing.

Frances poses in her all-weather coat outside her house in Danville, Indiana.

I swallowed a lump in my throat and walked away, not seeming to belong. Perhaps after a time of living among contented well-fed people I would lose that haunted feeling, but at the time I was a "lost soul." While I replied to "Good Morning" and chatted about pleasant meaningless things, I wanted to tell someone the pictures that stayed in my head.

The Belgian woman, who sat in our train compartment on the way to Brussels, had been a prisoner in Berlin, had been returned to Paris, and now was on her way home. She was middle aged, dressed in black, remarkable in no visible way—but she had been arrested for spying and kept in a German prison for three years. A quiet schoolmistress on her way home to a family who believed her dead.

A young Belgian girl, who spoke English, had been talking to her and told me about it. The girl dressed in a not so smart uniform of UNRRA (United Nations Relief and Rehabilitation Administration), and I think we looked down our noses at her a little when she came into the compartment. But as she spoke of the other woman I felt ashamed down to the ends of my toes. Her voice said quietly, "Some were very brave." The memory of the eyes of that schoolteacher was with me for a long while. I felt that I didn't fit in, that a part of me had been left somewhere.

Friends would say, "Glad to be back, I suppose?" How could I tell of all the hours and days spent dreaming of coming home? How to me, "the States" always had quotes around it—and I knew what one of the WACs meant when I heard a smattering of conversation drift down to me as I lay on my bunk on the boat. The voice said, a little brokenly, "Yes, the Promised Land." And I replied, "It is good to be Home."

✖   ✖   ✖

19

FRANCES'S WATERCOLOR DRAWINGS

While in Paris Frances began using watercolor paints and rag paper. The drawings show an Armistice day celebration, street scenes, people, a uniform corsage, and a hut at the Le Havre camp.

Armistice Day 1944

a Favorite
Venice

Ink wash – Paris

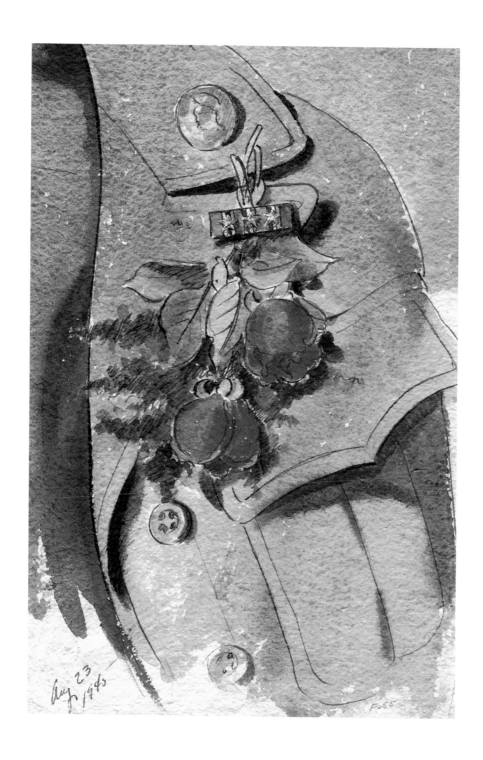

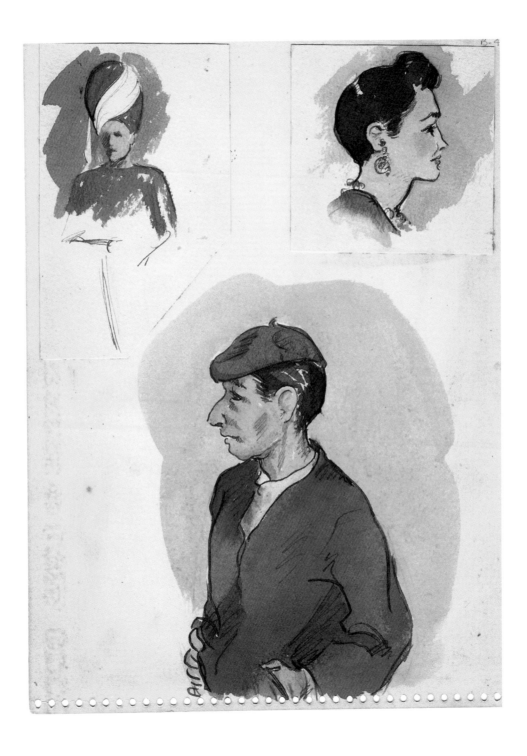

INDEX